GOLDEN
GUIDE

D0260419

CORNWALL

William Fricker

LOCATOR MAP

■ THE SOUTH EAST

■ THE EAST

■ THE NORTH COAST

■ THE SOUTH COAST

■ THE SOUTH WEST

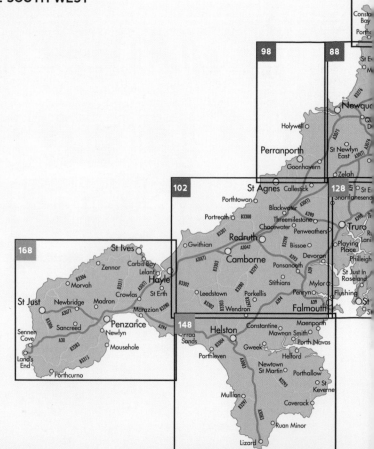

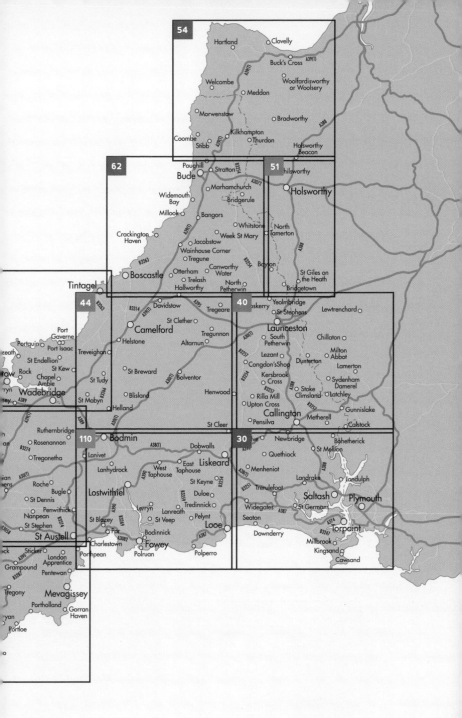

To my darling daughter Alice, bedridden with ME. I hope, will soon be fit enough to explore, and enjoy Cornwall, with the rest of us.

Research & Text: William Fricker
Photography: William Fricker (unless credited with an initial — see Acknowledgements)

Fifth Edition, 2016
First published in the United Kingdom, in 2006, by Goldeneye, Penryn, Cornwall TR10 8JL
www.goldeneyeguides.co.uk

Text copyright © 2016, William Fricker
Photographs copyright © 2016, William Fricker
Maps copyright © Goldeneye, 2016
Maps taken from Goldeneye's Digital Database
5th Edition
Original layout: Camonka. This Revised Edition: Flora Fricker
Editorial Assistant: Isabella Fricker

Abbreviations in Text

C14	14th Century
Mar-Oct	1 March to 31 October (inc.)
NT	National Trust property
EH	English Heritage property
BHs	Bank Holidays
W/Es	Weekends
East	Easter
E/C	Early Closing
TIC	Tourist Information Centre
M	Monday
Tu	Tuesday
W	Wednesday
Th	Thursday
F	Friday
Sa	Saturday
Su	Sunday
ss	Supplied by Subject (reference illustrations)

Beach & Surfing Abbreviations

HT	High Tide
HZ	Hazardous/Dangerous
Ls	Lefts (left turns)
LG	Lifeguard
LT	Low Tide
N	North
P	Parking
Rs	Rights (right turns)
S	South
S-B	Surfboard
SW	Southwest
WC	Toilets

Correct Information
The contents of this publication were believed to be correct and accurate at the time of printing. However, Goldeneye accepts no responsibility for any errors, omissions or changes in the details given, and/or the consequences arising thereto, from the use of this book. However, the publishers would greatly appreciate your time in notifying us of any changes or new attractions (or places to eat, drink and stay) that you consider merit inclusion in the next edition. Your comments are most welcome, for we value the views and suggestions of our readers. Please write to: The Editor, Goldeneye, Broad Street, Penryn, Cornwall TR10 8JL, United Kingdom, or email goldeneyeguides@frickeruk.com

Printed in the EEC

The Smuggler's Song

On, through the ground-sea, shove!
Light on the larboard bow!
There's a nine-knot breeze above,
And a sucking tide below.

Hush! for the beacon fails,
The skulking gauger's by;
Down with your studding-sails,
Let jib and fore-sail fly! —

Hurrah! for the light once more!
Point her for Shark's-nose Head;
Our friends can keep the shore;
Or the skulking gauger's dead!

On! through the ground-sea, shove!
Light on the Larboard bow!
There's a nine-knot breeze above
And a sucking tide below!

RS Hawker

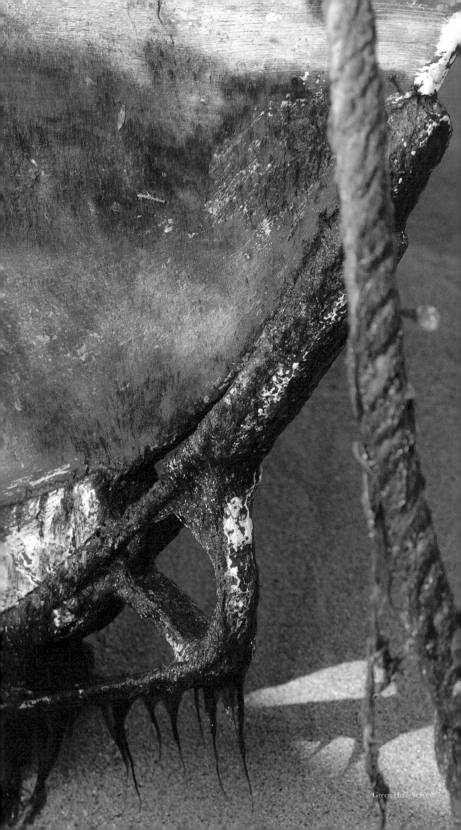

Green Hull, St Ives

While working on the fifth edition of this guidebook, I considered including a section on eco-tourism. As I looked at the range of environmentally conscious hotels, B&Bs and restaurants, not to mention the traditional artisans who work with natures' produce to create beautiful pieces of art, it occurred to me that many of the places I have already selected to feature have strong and positive environmental practices. Most of the eateries from pubs to country house hotels use locally produced food, with low food miles, thereby supporting local producers, and a lot of the places to stay focus their business on protecting their beautiful surroundings for generations to come.

It is surely no surprise that the inhabitants of such a beautiful county as Cornwall would want to use its resources but use them in a way that prolongs them rather than depletes them. With nearly 300 miles of coastland virtually wrapping around the whole county, it is little wonder that so much of the area has turned to the sea for its influences. Here the skills of the fisherman and the chef, come to the fore. Given the natural austerity of the farmland in the area, Cornish farmers have worked with nature to farm the livestock and crops that work with the natural vagaries of the area.

So, in short, you can assume that most of the places featured in this book use local food producers even though I may not say so. And, although not all hotels can be considered eco-friendly, many of the smaller guest houses and B&Bs in this book are just that (as well as being super places to stay).

I have also been greatly impressed by the energy, creativity and entrepreneurial vigour of those who are creating new art galleries, boutique hotels, cafés and restaurants, and who, against all odds, are determined to make these businesses a success.

As always, the places included in this book are chosen on merit, and merit alone, and do not pay any kind of advertising fee. This allows me the freedom to choose only those places that I think are special enough to be part of this Guidebook.

New for this Edition:
More variance in budget options – As times are tight and visitors don't always want a five-star meal, or an expensive bed for the night, I have included more options such as Light Bites (cafés, fish'nchips, burger bars, juice bars and fish mongers for self-caterers), and alternative places to stay, from a holistic spa (The Scarlet) to a rustic barn (Retorrick Mill), to a Shepherd's Hut (Tregothnan).

More beaches, more watersports – What would Cornwall be without its' beaches, surf schools, coasteeering and sailing clubs - with beach cafés, festivals, and family fun? More space is built into this edition to cover the delights of beach living and I have included my guide to the top ten beaches and harbours.

Navigation & Clarity – For ease of use, the county is split into five regions. At the start of each is an area map followed by the respective guide text and illustrations. Each section is colour-coded and the area maps either overlap, or juxtapose, to allow easy navigation. We have also re-designed the pages with new typography and many new images to provide a cleaner, clearer presentation.

Film and TV locations – Given the universal popularity of Doc Martin, Poldark and Rosumund Pilcher's books, it seems only apposite to include where these series were filmed. Not always 100% in Cornwall. We can look forward to more years of Poldark interest and memorabilia!

I believe Cornwall to be a truly magical holiday destination, whether you have a weekend, a fortnight, are alone, with friends, or family. Whether, you have a particular interest in beachcombing, gardens and historic churches, or simple, hedonism. There are no shortages of options available to you. Take a deep breath of sea air, shrug off your working persona, and live the life, fantastic.

William Fricker, Penryn, March 2016.

Box of Mackerel, St Ives

1   Title Page
2   Locator Map
4   Credits
5   Richard Stephen Hawker's Poem,
    The Smuggler's Song
7   Preface
9   Contents
11 Introduction
13 Recommendations
14 Which Beach to Visit
16 Which Harbour to Visit
18 Where to Stay
22 And So To Bed Images
24 Where to Eat
26 Where to Surf Where to Coasteer

● 28 THE SOUTH EAST
30 Saltash, The Rame Peninsula Map
32 Saltash, The Rame Peninsula
    Guide

● 38 THE EAST
40 Calstock, Launceston Map
42 Calstock, Launceston Guide
44 Altarnun, Blisland, Bodmin Moor,
    Camelford Map
46 Altarnun, Blisland, Bodmin Moor,
    Camelford Guide
50 Altarnun Church Image
51 Upper Tamar Map

● 52 THE NORTH COAST
54 Morwenstow, The Hartland
    Peninsula Map
56 Morwenstow Guide
59 Bude Shipwreck Images
60 Mike Dobie Painting
62 Boscastle, Bude Map
64 Boscastle, Bude Guide
70 Padstow, Port Isaac, Tintagel,
    Wadebridge Map
72 Padstow, Port Isaac, Tintagel,
    Wadebridge Guide
80 The Camel Trail Images
82 The Camel Trail Cycling Route
    Map

84 Padstow, Port Isaac, Tintagel,
    Wadebridge Guide
88 Newquay, St Austell, St Columb
    Major Map
90 Newquay, St Austell, St Columb
    Major Guide
96 Coastal Fishing Boats
98 Perranporth, St Agnes Map
99 Perranporth, St Agnes Guide
102 Camborne, Redruth Map
104 Camborne, Redruth Guide

● 108 THE SOUTH COAST
110 Bodmin, Fowey, Liskeard, Looe,
    Lostwithiel Map
114 Bodmin, Fowey, Liskeard, Looe,
    Lostwithiel Guide
123 Spring Time In A Cornish
    Garden
130 Falmouth-Penryn, Mevagissey, St
    Mawes, Truro Map
132 Falmouth-Penryn, Mevagissey, St
    Mawes, Truro Guide

● 146 THE SOUTH WEST
148 The Lizard Peninsula Map
150 The Lizard Peninsula Guide
164 Geological Shapes Images
166 Beach Images
168 The Penwith Peninsula Map
170 The Penwith Peninsula Guide
174 Land's End & Porthcurno Images
180 Saxton's 1576 Map of Cornwall
186 Deep Sea Trawlers Images
200 Contemporary Art
202 The Modernist Artists of St Ives
205 The Newlyn School of Painters
206 Celebrities
214 Tourist Information Centres
215 Calendar of Events
217 Acknowledgements
218 Index to towns, villages, places of
    interest described in the book
223 Map Symbols Explained
224 About The Author/Photographer

The Pinuccia, Hotel Tresanton, St Mawes

Cornwall is a county of great diversity, of strange customs and superstitions, of romantic legends and Arthurian myths. A county with its own language, culture and outlook. Remote, and cut off from the rest of Britain by the River Tamar, the Cornish have developed a proud individuality and resilient independence. The close proximity to the Gulf Stream provides a warm and equable climate. The magnificent coastline, relentlessly shaped by the elements, with its contorted rocks, precipitous cliffs, deep estuaries, smugglers' coves, golden beaches and picturesque harbours, is unmatched elsewhere in England.

For generations, Cornwall has been the playground for family holidays thanks to its multitude of varying beaches, its warm climate and the gulf stream raising the sea temperature (to above freezing!). The variety and number of beaches is remarkable and there is something for all tastes – from rocky beaches and from steep, ominous cliffs that demonstrate the force that nature has exerted on this coastline, to wide sandy beaches which rival the best in the world.

The landscape is haunted by countless landmarks of early man (and relics from the industrial past); Long Barrows (burial chambers), Quoits/Dolmens (stones from Megalithic-Neolithic tombs), Fogues (underground storage chambers), Hill Forts and Promontory Forts (strategic settlements or animal enclosures) and Stone Circles (ancient boundary/grave marks, or places of ritual). Only a small selection is described in this book - but many others are indicated on the maps. To put them into an historic context, the Neolithic Period gave place to the Bronze Age around 2000 BC, the Iron Age lasted from about 500 BC up to Roman times, the first 4 centuries AD.

The Cornish skyline has been shaped by the remains of chimneys and engine houses, and by ramshackle desolate buildings beside the road - the remains of a once prosperous tin and copper mining industry. Many examples are to be found in the Camborne - Redruth area, and on the Penwith Peninsula. A number of engine houses have been restored by the National Trust and other organisations. They often stand in spectacular positions and are worthy of a visit. The better known are of Wheal Coates Mine, nr St Agnes and Wheal Prosper Copper Mine, nr Porthleven. In areas of past mining activity it is vitally important to keep to the evident pathways. Walkers and their dogs have been known to disappear down hidden shafts!

With few exceptions, Cornwall has been noted for the setting of architecture rather than architecture itself. However, there are fine examples of medieval fortresses created by Henry VIII, and elegant country houses surrounded by spacious gardens, as well as an increasing number of more modern buildings: The Eden Project, Truro College or the RNLI Lifeboat Station at Trevose Head. And, the new University of Falmouth & Exeter buildings at Tremough Campus, Penryn.

This new academic endeavour has perhaps come full circle. For is it not ironic that Glasney College (of Penryn), the Collegiate Church founded in 1275 by Bishop Bronescombe of Exeter was to be the leading ecclesiastical powerhouse in Cornwall? Glasney College upheld and promoted the Christian faith, and secondly, the Cornish language, which was left to languish along with its ruins following Henry VIII's Dissolution of the Monasteries, 1536-1545. Today, scholars from Exeter, and beyond, have returned to Penryn to study the Cornish language, and its cultural affinities.

Fiona Millais, Cornwall Contemporary, Penzance

- Walk the Causeway at low tide and explore St Michael's Mount.
- Cycle the Camel Trail starting from Wadebridge.
- Treat yourself to a surf lesson.
- Evensong Truro Cathedral.
- Port Eliot Literary Festival.
- Make a pilgrimage across the dunes to Sir John Betjeman's grave at St Enodoc.
- Visit Botallack tin mines.
- Admire the magnificent stained glass at St Neots.
- Take a boat trip up the Fowey River to Lostwithiel.
- Lunch in one of the stupendously sited cafés overlooking a golden beach.
- Listen to the Polperro fisherman's choir practice.
- Walk a section of the coastal footpath. For drama, try the North Coast or Penwith Peninsula, for a flattish surface, the South Coast.
- Bag five ancient monuments. Either from Bodmin Moor or Penwith.
- Shop for a piece of Cornish art.
- Play 'Count the Windmill' on your journey through Cornwall. What percentage are actually working?
- Fish and chips in Padstow. At Stein's of course. Where else?
- Visit the home of a former genius; Richard Trevithick or Barbara Hepworth.
- Book a ticket at the Minack Theatre. Just being there is enough. It's the view, Darling.
- Buy fresh fish from one of the Newlyn fish merchants for a beach barbeque.
- Day out at the Royal Cornwall Show, Wadebridge.
- Experience the contrast of colour and light. First wander the back streets of St Ives, then emerge into the open spaces and bathe in the brilliant, Mediterranean light.
- Rame Head – for the views on either side. Imagine the ships who have passed this way, some for the last time, and for the sailors whose last glimpse of England this has been.
- Join a sing-song with the Cadgwith Singers in the Cadgwith Cove Inn on a Friday night.

Porthmeor

Cornwall is perhaps best known for its coastline and the multitude of beaches that pepper it. Nowhere in England is there such a quantity and variety of beaches – from wide, flat and open windswept beaches akin to many in the Southern Hemisphere, to tiny rocky coves with caves and imposing cliffs. Whether you want a safe place to visit with your family, somewhere to paddle in the shallows and eat ice cream, or if you want the rawness of nature to take your breath away, there are plenty of choices. The following is a taster of what is out there …

1. BEDRUTHAN STEPS

One of Cornwall's most dramatic beaches with a series of rock stacks which legend says were built by the giant Bedruthan, who used them as stepping stones. If you can negotiate the access which is via a steep staircase, you reach firm golden sands with massive rocks and caves.

2. PORTHLEVEN SANDS

The steep shelving beach has a strong undertow and swimming is not encouraged, making it less suitable for families. Ideal for a brisk walk across the four miles of sands – blowing away the cobwebs and enjoying the fantastic views across to Mounts Bay.

3. KYNANCE COVE

At low tide, there are white sands and good bathing (in summer) as well as serpentine rocks shaped over centuries by the rushing tides. At high tide it is too dangerous to swim but you can listen to the roaring noise of blow holes. Get there early at low tide in summer and you could believe you were on a desert island.

4. FISTRAL

The most popular surf beach in Cornwall and the clarity of the turquoise water is unparalleled. There are wide sands even at high tide and cafés for snacks to sustain you while you people watch.

5. DAYMER BAY

Popular family beach – ideal for young children due to its firm golden sands and sheltered position.

6. SANDY MOUTH

Expansive beach with swift currents and strong rip tides making it popular with surfers. Fabulous rock formations that glow at dusk. Firm sands and rock pools at low tide.

7. PORTHCURNO

This is a white shell sand beach washed by turquoise sea and surrounded by high granite cliffs - a place of real beauty.

8. PORTHMEOR

Just one of St Ives' fabulous town beaches which is well served by local eateries and overlooked by the Tate St Ives. Wide flat sands at low tide and popular with all.

9. TREBARWITH STRAND

Extraordinary rock formations at the head of the beach. Very attractive at dusk when the setting sun hits the surrounding cliffs.

10. WATERGATE BAY

One of the few beaches in Cornwall that you can see from the road. It affords fantastic vistas even when you're driving by. Very popular for extreme sports and, therefore, good for people watching.

Mevagissey

Second to the number of beaches and coves in Cornwall is the number of harbours which range from quiet, sleepy and sheltered spots whose days of activity have long since passed, to busy harbours that still form the centre of local communities and provide successful businesses. These harbours hold interest for all ages and even on a miserable day there is always something going on. Importantly, due to the deliveries of fresh seafood, there is excellent food to be had in the environs.

1. CHARLESTOWN
Originally built for the export of coal, tin and china clay, with its old buildings and nostalgic atmosphere seems to remain locked in the C18 or C19, hence its frequent use as a setting in historical TV films and a home to Tall Ships.

2. ST IVES
Surrounded by a large sea wall this is a wide and open natural harbour with protection from winds. Home to many small craft and fishing boats.

3. FALMOUTH
This is one of the most superb natural harbours in the world. Follow in the footsteps of the Phoenicians and Romans and come to admire the fleets of fishing and sailing crafts.

4. BOSCASTLE
One of the few safe havens on the treacherous North Coast – although its tight entrance makes it quite tricky to dock especially on a stormy night. Still home to a small number of fishing boats.

5. MEVAGISSEY
Quite a unique spot with a fine inner and more recent outer harbour. Despite the fact that it has been a working harbour for centuries, the locale remains picturesque and unspoilt.

6. MOUSEHOLE
Probably my own personal favourite, this is a quintessential Cornish fishing village with the harbour at its hub. A visit here will make you feel like time has stood still.

7. NEWLYN
Home to Cornwall's largest fishing fleet and busiest fish market, there is never any shortage of things to see here.

8. POLPERRO
Cute, sweet, idyllic – and any other similar adjective you can think of. Along with Mousehole, this village and harbour draws the crowds.

9. PORTHLEVEN
Quite an unusual harbour, Porthleven was protected by massive stone walls made from slabs of granite after the gales of 1824 and 1855. Still frequently lashed by gales, the force of nature is apparent here.

10. PADSTOW
Due to the effect of the most famous resident of Padstow this is a thriving harbour with a decent amount of fishing boats to supply Mr Stein's needs. This makes it an interesting spot to soak up the atmosphere.

Panoramic Terrace View, The Idle Rocks, St Mawes ss

The Beach, Bude ss   St Petroc's Bistro, Padstow ss   Turn-a-Penny cottage, Wild Escapes ss

This is a selection to make choosing your B&B or hotel an easy and quick process. We suggest you view their websites to find one that suits your tastes, expectations and budget. It is often the unexpected that will surprise you with a luxurious bathroom, an exquisite view or a quirky temperament that will draw you back again and again.

COUNTRY HOUSE HOTELS
Hotel Endsleigh, Tamar Valley.
01822 870000 www.hotelendsleigh.com
Hotel Tresanton, St Mawes.
01326 270055 www.tresanton.com

COUNTRY HOUSE B & B
Collon Barton, Lerryn.
01208 872908
Coswarth House, Padstow.
07907 626084 www.coswarthhouse.com
Hornacott, South Petherwin.
01566 782461 www.hornacott.co.uk
Lambriggan Court B&B.
01872 571636 www.lambriggancourt.com
Merthen Manor, Constantine.
01326 340664 www.merthenmanor.co.uk
Molesworth Manor, Little Petherick.
01841 540292 www.molesworthmanor.co.uk
The Old Parsonage, Forrabury.
01840 250339 www.old-parsonage.com
The Old Rectory, St Juliot.
01840 250225 www.stjuliot.com

The Old Vicarage, Morwenstow.
01288 331369 www.rshawker.co.uk
Tregoose, Grampound.
01726 882460 www.tregoose.co.uk
Trereife Park, Penzance.
01736 362750 www.trereifepark.co.uk
Trevigue B&B.
01840 230492 www.trevigue.com
Trevilla House, Feock.
01872 862369 www.trevilla.com

BOUTIQUE HOTELS
Artist Residence, Penzance.
01736 365664 www.artistresidencecornwall.co.uk
Boscundle Manor, St Austell.
01726 813557 www.boscundlemanor.co.uk
Chapel House, Penzance.
01736 362024 www.chapelhousepz.co.uk
Driftwood Hotel, Portscatho.
01872 580644 www.driftwoodhotel.co.uk
Elements, Marine Drive.
01288 352386 www.elements-life.co.uk
Lugger Hotel, Portloe.

The Gurnard's Head

01872 501322 www.luggerhotel.co.uk
Old Coastguard Hotel, Mousehole.
01736 731222 www.oldcoastguardhotel.co.uk
Primrose Valley Hotel, St Ives.
01736 794939 www.primroseonline.co.uk
The Idle Rocks, St Mawes.
01326 270270 www.idlerocks.com
Trevalsa Court Hotel, Mevagissey.
01726 842468 www.trevalsa-hotel.co.uk

FARM HOUSE B & B
Ardensawah Farm B&B, St Levan.
01736 871520 www.porthcurnofarmholidays.com
Buttervilla Farm, Polbathic.
01503 230315 www.buttervilla.com
Hartswell Farm, Lostwithiel.
01208 873419
Hay Barton, Tregony.
01872 530288 www.haybarton.com
Lantallack Farm, Landrake.
01752 851281 www.lantallackgetaways.co.uk
Park Farmhouse, Washaway.
01208 841 277
www.parkfarmhousewadebridge.co.uk
Rame Barton B&B & Pottery.
01752 822789 www.ramebarton.co.uk
Reddivallen, Trevalga.
01840 250854 www.redboscastle.com
Sheviock Barton, Sheviock.
01503 230793 www.sheviockbarton.co.uk
Treglisson, Hayle.
01736 753141 www.treglisson.co.uk
Trevadlock Manor.
01566 782227 www.trevadlockmanor.co.uk

FAMILY HOTELS (CHILD FRIENDLY)
Bedruthan Steps Hotel.
01637 860860 www.bedruthan.com

Fowey Hall Hotel.
01726 833866 www.foweyhallhotel.co.uk
Polurrian Hotel.
01326 240421 www.polurrianhotel.com
Rosevine Hotel, Portscatho.
01872 580206 www.rosevine.co.uk
Sands Resort Hotel & Spa, Newquay.
01637 872864 www.sandsresort.co.uk
St Enodoc Hotel.
01208 863394 www.enodoc-hotel.co.uk
The Hotel, Watergate Bay.
01637 860543 www.watergatebay.co.uk

FAMILY-RUN HOTELS
Boskerris Hotel, Carbis Bay.
01736 795295 www.boskerrishotel.co.uk
Mount Haven Hotel, Marazion.
01736 710249 www.mounthaven.co.uk
Talland Bay Hotel.
01503 272667 www.tallandbayhotel.co.uk

GUEST ACCOMMODATION
Bedknobs at Polgwyn, Bodmin.
01208 77553 www.bedknobs.co.uk
Dwelling House, Fowey.
01726 833662 www.thedwellinghouse.co.uk
Treleaugue B & B, St Keverne.
01326 281500 www.treleaugue.co.uk
Westcroft Guesthouse (Gallery), Market St., Kingsand.
01752 823216 www.westcraftguesthouse.co.uk
Zennor Chapel Café & Guest House.
01736 798307 www.zennorchapelguesthouse.com

Driftwood Hotel , Portscatho ss

HOUSE PARTIES & HOLIDAY COTTAGES

The Abbey, Penzance.
07930 347911 www.theabbeyonline.co.uk
Beachmodern, No. 28, Bude.
01288 275006 www.beachmodern.com/no28
Caerhays Estate, Portholland.
0800 032 6229 www.nicheretreats.co.uk
Clipper House, West Looe.
01503 265607 www.clipperhouse.co.uk
Ennys, St Hilary.
01736 740262 www.ennys.co.uk
Halzephron House, Gunwalloe.
07899 925816 www.halzephronhouse.co.uk
Mesmear, St Minver.
01208 869731 www.mesmear.co.uk
Mother Ivey Cottage, Trevose Head
01841 520329 www.trevosehead.co.uk
Pencalenick House, Lanteglos-By-Fowey
020 7243 1460 www.pencalenickhouse.com
Lamorna Cove Hotel,
01736 732866 www.thelamornacovehotel.com
The Tide House, St Ives.
01736 791803 www.thetidehouse.co.uk
Tregirls Cottages, Padstow.
01841 532648 www.tregirlscottages.co.uk

INNS WITH ROOMS

Bush Inn, Morwenstow
01288 331242 www.bushinnmorwenstow.com
Driftwood Spars Hotel,
Trevaunance Cove 01872 552428 www.
driftwoodspars.co.uk
Gurnard's Head.
01736 796928 www.gurnardshead.co.uk
Halzephron Inn, Gunwalloe.
01326 240406 www.halzephron-inn.co.uk
The Port William Inn, Trebarwith Strand.
01840 770230 www.theportwilliam.co.uk
The King of Prussia, Fowey
01726 833694 www.kingofprussiafowey.co.uk
Old Success Inn, Sennen Cove.
01736 871232 www.oldsuccess.co.uk
Trengilly Wartha Inn, Constantine.
01326 340332 www.trengilly.co.uk

LUXURIOUS B & B

Ednovean Farm, Perranuthnoe.
01736 711883 www.ednoveanfarm.co.uk
Hen House,Tregarne.
01326 280236
Little Roseland, Treworga.
01872 501243 www.littleroseland.co.uk
Park Farmhouse, Washaway.
01208 841 277 www.park-farmhouse.com
Rick Steins, Padstow.
01841 532700 www.rickstein.com

The Scarlett, Mawgan Porth 88

Hotel Tresanton, St Mawes 88

Henry's Campsite, The Lizard

The Old Rectory, St Juliot.
01840 250225 www.stjuliot.com
Trevose Harbour House, St Ives.
01736 793267 www.trevosehouse.

RESTAURANT WITH ROOMS
Kota, Porthleven.
01326 562407 www.kotarestaurant.co.uk
St Petroc's Hotel, Padstow
01841 532700 www.rickstein.com
27 The Terrace, St Ives.
01736 797450 www.27theterrace.co.uk

ROOM WITH A VIEW
Beacon Crag, Porthleven.
01326 573690 www.beaconcrag.com
Blue Hayes Hotel, St Ives.
01736 797129 www.bluehayes.co.uk
Cormorant Hotel, Golant
01726 833426 www.cormoranthotel.co.uk
Lewinnick Lodge, Pentire Headland.
01637 878117 www.lewinnicklodge.co.uk
The Old Quay House Hotel, Fowey.
01726 833302 www.theoldquayhouse.com
Shamrock Cabin, Tregonhawke,
Whitsand Bay.
07719 332287 www.shamrockcabin.co.uk

SPA STYLE - THE WORKS
(GYM, SAUNAS, MASSAGE,
SHEER UNADULTERATED HEDONISM)
St Michael's Hotel & Spa, Falmouth.
01326 312707 www.stmichaelshotel.co.uk
St Moritz, Trebetherick
01208 862242 www.stmoritzhotel.co.uk
The Scarlet, Tredragon Rd,
Mawgan Porth.
01637 861800 www.scarlethotel.co.uk

CAMPING
Ayr Holiday Park, St Ives.
01736 795855 www.ayrholidaypark.co.uk
Camptivity, Nr Penzance.
01736 332648 www.camptivity.co.uk
Henry's Campsite, The Lizard.
01326 290596 www.henryscampsite.co.uk
South Penquite Farm.
01208 850491 www.southpenquite.co.uk
Cornish Tipi Holidays, Tregeare.
01208 880781 www.cornishtipiholidays.co.uk
Ruthern Valley Holidays. Nr Wadebridge.
01208 831395 www.ruthernvalley.com
Treen Farm, St Levan.
07598 469322 www.treenfarmcampsite.co.uk
Trelowarren Chateau Camping.
01326 221224 www.trelowarren.com

Driftwood Hotel, Portscatho 58

Hotel Tresanton, St Mawes 55

Artist Residence, Penzance 58

The Scarlet, Mawgan Porth 88

Hotel Endsleigh, Tamar Valley 88

The Idle Rocks, St Mawes 88

Bike Night, Strong Adolfos Café, Hawksfield ss

Rod & Line, Tideford   Driftwood Hotel, Portscatho ss   Pandora Inn, Restronguet

Cornwall has some of the most amazingly located places to eat and drink in the UK. Either by overlooking a golden beach, a rugged headland or boat infested harbour. It also has a fast-growing café culture where you can buy some amazing bread and cakes. But, just watch your waistline. Better still, get out onto the Coast Path.

Many will choose a pub, or café, at the beginning, or end of a circular, or cliff top walk. I hope our selection below will make your life a little easier to plan. All entries are described in the following pages.

SEAVIEW CAFÉS/BARS

Bodhi's Café, Fistral Beach.
01637 850793 www.bodhisfistral.co.uk
Beach Hut, Watergate Bay.
01637 860877 www.watergatebay.co.uk
Ben Tunnicliffe, Sennen Cove.
01736 871191 www.benatsennen.com
Blue Bar, Porthtowan.
01209 890329 www.blue-bar.co.uk
Cabin Beach Café, Perranuthnoe.
01736 711733 www.thecabinbeachcafe.co.uk
Fistral Beach Complex, Newquay.
www.fistralbeach.co.uk/fistral-complex

Godrevy Beach Café, Godrevy Towans.
01736 757999 www.godrevycafe.co.uk
Hole Foods Deli, Mousehole.
www.holefooodsdeli.co.uk
Life's A Beach, Summerleaze Beach, Bude.
www.lifesabeach.info
Porthminster Café, St Ives.
01736 795352 www.porthminstercafé.co.uk
Sunset Surf, Gwithian Towans.
01736 752575 www.sunsetsurf.com
Schooners Bistro, Trevaunance Cove.
01872 553149

Waterfront, Beach Rd, Polzeath
01208 869655 www.waterfrontpolzeath.co.uk
Watering Hole, Perranporth Beach.
01872 572888 www.thewateringhole.co.uk

CAFÉ CULTURE
Hewitt's, Wadebridge.
01208 368191 www.picturesandcoffee.com
Hidden Hut, Porthcurnick Beach.
www.hiddenhut.co.uk
Mowhay Café & Restaurant, Trebetherick.
01208 863660
Mount Zion Coffee. St Ives.
01736 888419 www.mountzioncoffee.co.uk
Nauti But Ice, Porthleven.
01326 573747
Pinky Murphy's Café, Fowey.
www.pinkymurphys.com
Potager Garden & Glasshouse.
01326 341258 www.potagergarden.org
Provedore, Falmouth.
01326 314888 www.provedore.co.uk
Stones Bakery, Falmouth.
07791 003183 www.stonesbakery.co.uk
Strong Adolfos, Atlantic Highway.
01208 816949 www.strongadolfos.com

FARM CAFÉ/RESTAURANTS
Boscastle's Farm Shop & Café.
01840 250827 www.boscastlefarmshop.co.uk
Rectory Tea Rooms, Morwenstow.
01288 331251 www.rectory-tearooms.co.uk
Roskilly's.
01326 280479 www.roskillys.co.uk
Trevathan Farm, St Endellion.
01208 880248 www.trevathanfarm.com

FOODIE PUBS
Bush Inn, Morwenstow.
01288 331242 www.bushinnmorwenstow.com
Gurnard's Head.
01736 796928 www.gurnardshead.co.uk
St Tudy Inn, St Tudy.
01208 850656 wwww.sttudyinn.com
Rod and Line, Tideford.
01752 851323
Roseland Inn.
01872 580254 www.roselandinn.co.uk
Tinners Arms, Zennor.
01736 796927 www.tinnersarms.com
Trengilly Wartha Inn.
01326 340332 www.trengilly.co.uk

CAFÉS/RESTAURANTS/PUBS WITH A VIEW
Alba, Wharf Rd., St Ives.
01736 797222 www.thealbarestaurant.com
Bay View Inn, Marine Drive.
Widemouth Bay.
01288 361273 www.bayviewinn.co.uk
Devonport Inn, Kingsand.
01752 822869 www.devonportinn.com
Driftwood Hotel, Portscatho.

01872 580644 www.driftwoodhotel.co.uk
Nathan Outlaw, 6 New Rd, Port Isaac.
01208 880896 www.nathan-outlaw.com
Fifteen Cornwall, Watergate Bay.
01637 861000 www.fifteencornwall.co.uk
Muddy Beach Café, Jubilee Wharf, Penryn.
01326 374424 www.muddybeach.co.uk
Restaurant Nathan Outlaw, Port Isaac.
01208 862737 www.nathan-outlaw.com.co.uk
The Cove, Lamorna.
01736 732866 www.thelamornacovehotel.com
The Port William Inn, Trebarwith Strand.
01840 770230 www.theportwilliam.co.uk
Old Coastguard Hotel & Restaurant,
Mousehole.
01736 731222 www.oldcoastguardhotel.co.uk
Old Quay House Hotel, 28 Fore St., Fowey.
01726 833302 www.theoldquayhouse.com
View Restaurant, Rame Head.
01752 822345 www.theview-restaurant.co.uk

SEAFOOD RESTAURANTS
Blue Plate, Downderry.
01503 250308 www.blueplatecornwall.com
Kota, Porthleven.
01326 562407 www.kotarestaurant.co.uk
Lugger Hotel, Portloe.
01872 501322 www.luggerhotel.co.uk
Prawn On The Lawn, 11 Duke St., Padstow
01841 532223 www.prawnonthelawn.com
Seafood Café, 45 Fore St, St Ives.
01736 794004 www.seafoodcafé.co.uk
Seafood Restaurant.
01841 532700 www.rickstein.com
2 Fore St, Mousehole.
01736 731164 www.2forestreet.co.uk
The Cove, Maenporth Beach.
01326 251136 www.thecovemaenporth.co.uk
Wheelhouse Crab & Oyster Bar, Falmouth.
01326 318050

TOWN RESTAURANTS
Boathouse, The, Newquay.
01637 874062 www.finns2go.com
Gravy Boesti, 8 Edward St. Truro. 01872
222237 **www.gravy-boesti.co.uk**
Harris's, 46 New St. Penzance.
01736 364408 www.harrisrestaurant.co.uk
Hunkdory, 46 Arwenack St., Falmouth.
01326 212997 www.hunkydoryfalmouth.co.uk
No 6 Restaurant & Rooms, Padstow. 01841
532093 www.number6inpadstow.com
Olivers, Falmouth.
01326 218138 www.oliversfalmouth.com
Trewithen Restaurant, Fore St, Lostwithiel.
01208 872373 www.trewithenrestaurant.com

SURF SCHOOLS NORTH COAST:

St Ives - St Ives Surf School
01736 793938
stivessurfschool.co.uk

Newquay - Fistral Beach
01637 850584
fistralbeach.co.uk

Newquay Activity Centre
01637 877722
newquayactivitycentre.co.uk

Extreme Academy, - Watergate Bay
01637 860840
extremeacademy.co.uk

O'Neill Surf Academy, Watergate Bay
01841 520052
oneillsurfacademy.co.uk

Discovery Surf School, Whitsand Bay
07813 639622
discoverysurf.com

Cornwall Surf Academy, Holywell Bay
0870 2406693
cornwallsurfacademy.co.uk

Holywell Bay School of Surf
01872 510233
holywellbayschoolofsurf.com

Crantock Bay Surf School
07536117966
crantockbaysurfschool.com

Quiksilver Surf School
01637 851800
quiksilversurfschoolnewquay.com

Hibiscus Surf School
01637 879374
hibiscussurfschool.co.uk

Ticket to Ride
01637 222 565
tickettoridesurfschool.co.uk

Mawgan Porth - King Surf School
01637 860091
kingsurf.co.uk

Padstow - Harlyn Surf School
01841 533076
harlynsurfschool.co.uk

Constantine Bay Surf School
07837488083
constantinebaysurfschool.co.uk

Waves Surf School
01841 521 230
wavessurfschool.co.uk

Polzeath - Surfs Up Surf School
01208 862003
surfsupsurfschool.com

Perranporth - Perranporth Surf School
07974 550823
perranporthsurfschool.co.uk

Nr Hayle - Gwithian Academy of Surfing

01736 757579
surfacademy.co.uk

St Agnes - Breakers Surf School
01872 55381
surf-lessons.co.uk

Bude - Big Blue Surf School
01288 331764
bigbluesurfschool.co.uk

Raven Surf School
01288 353693
ravensurf.co.uk

SURF SCHOOLS SOUTH COAST:

Falmouth - Falmouth Surf School
01326 212144
falmouthsurfschool.co.uk

Praa Sands
07980 432313
globalboarders.com

Sennen Cove - Sennen Surfing Centre
01736 871227
sennensurfingcentre.com

Sennen Surf School
01736 871817
sennensurfschool.com

Lizard Peninsula - Barefoot Surf School,
Church Cove 07790 350133
barefootsurfschool.weebly.com

Dan Joel Surf, Poldu
danjoelsurf.com

Young Surfer

Walking the Dog

Gunwalloe lif

WATERSPORTS CORNWALL NORTH COAST:

Bodmin - Lakeview Wake Park
07895 325724
lakeviewwakepark.com

Siblyback Lake Country Park -
Watersports, Liskeard
01579 342366
swlakestrust.org.uk

Bude - Bude Surfing Experience
07779117746
budesurfingexperience.co.uk

Outdoor Adventure
01288 362900
outdooradventure.co.uk

The Bude Canoe Experience
07595 922248
southcombe.net

Newquay - Newquay Sea Safaris
01637 850930

Newquay Activity Centre
01637 879571
newquayactivitycentre.co.uk

Kingsurf, Newquay
01637 860091
kingsurf.co.uk

Padstow - Harlyn Watersports
01841 533076
harlynsurfschool.co.uk

Perranporth - Mobius Adventures
01637 831383
mobiusonline.co.uk

Perran Sands Surf School
01872 573551
haven.com

St Agnes - Koru Kayaking
07794321827
enquiries@korukayaking.co.uk

Polzeath - Cornish Rock Tors
07791 534884
cornishrocktors.com

Portreath - Walk on Water Ocean
Adventure
07732 350078
wowlife.org.uk

Porthtowan Surf School
01326 212144
porthtowansurfschool.co.uk

WATERSPORTS CORNWALL SOUTH COAST:

Falmouth - Sailaday Falmouth
07786 232270
sailaday.co.uk

Sea Kayaking
01326 37826
seakayakingcornwall.com

Gylly Adventures
0734189049 5
gyllyadventures.co.uk

Maenporth Beach Hire
0799051526
arvorseakayakingcornwall.co.uk

Swanpool Beach
01326 314740
swanpoolbeach.co.uk

Elemental UK, Swanpool
01326 318771
elementaluk.com

Fowey - Encounter Cornwall Canoe
trips and Kayak Hire
07976 466123/01726832104
encountercornwall.com

Fowey River Hire
01726 83362
foweyriverhire.co.uk

Helford - Koru Kayaking
07794321827
enquiries@korukayaking.co.uk

Helston - Kennack Diving
07816 903260

Looe - Looe Beach Water Sports Centre
looebeach.co.uk

Mylor - Mylor Sailing School
01326 377633
mylorsailingschool.co.uk

Mylor Yacht Cruising
07581 625089
mylorcruising.com

Windsport International
01326 376191 windsport.co.uk

Newlyn - Global boarders
07980 432313
globalboarders.com

Par - Polaris Beach Watersports
01726 813306
polkerrisbeach.com

Penryn - BF Adventure
01326 340912
bfadventure.org

Penryn - Sail Agnes
07790 638084
workingsail.co.uk

Kernow Wake Park
07817 662962
kernowwakepark.com

Redruth - Stithies Lake, Country Park
and Watersports
01566 771930
swlakestrust.org.uk

St Mawes - Bohella Sailing Club
01326 270389
thebohellabar.co.uk

St Mawes Kayaks
07971 846786
stmaweskayaks.co.uk

Paddleboarding Tuition
07766168788
getaboardsup.co.uk

Pinuccia, Hotel Tresanton skipper
tresanton.com

Tregony - Greenleisure
greenleisure.co.uk

Old Pilchards Works, Kingsand

For Peace & Tranquility, Smugglers' Haunts, the Cry of the Curlew and Sub-Tropical Gardens.

As you enter Cornwall over the River Tamar on the A38, stop and admire Isambard Kingdom Brunel's last great masterpiece of engineering, the Prince Albert Bridge. Looking south down the river, you may be able to spy the Rame Peninsula, the 'Forgotten Corner.' Here you will discover the former smugglers' villages of Kingsand and Cawsand. Their narrow streets snake between colour washed cottages, inns and art galleries. There are fine views over Plymouth Sound, and if feeling energetic you may wish to tackle the coastal path through Mount Edgcumbe, or walk south to Rame Head, where you will counter more stunning views. All around you is peace and calm, an oasis of tranquillity, the antidote to a stressful life.

Travelling west you must make a special journey to St Germanus Church to admire the stained glass window designed by Edward Burne-Jones, and made up by the William Morris Co. Next door, Port Eliot, home to the arts and music festival. The St Germans or Lynher River passes by, to rise up and down with the tides. You will hear the baleful cry of the curlew and the screech of the oyster-catcher, both reminders of the calming effects of estuary life.

However, if you choose to cross the Tamar further upstream via the A390 you must tackle the densely wooded lanes through St Dominick to Cotehele Quay with fine views over the Tamar. This is an area rich in industrial heritage. You may wish to think back an age and imagine the bargees working the riverbank between Cotehele and Morwellham, as they shipped the iron ore down to Plymouth.

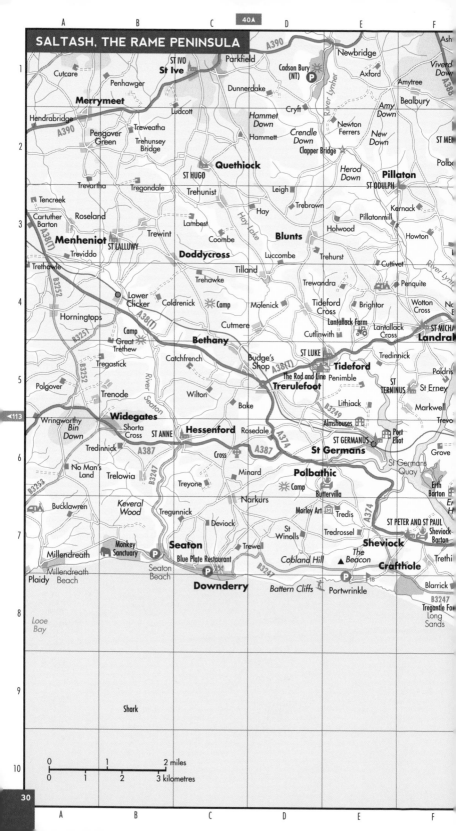

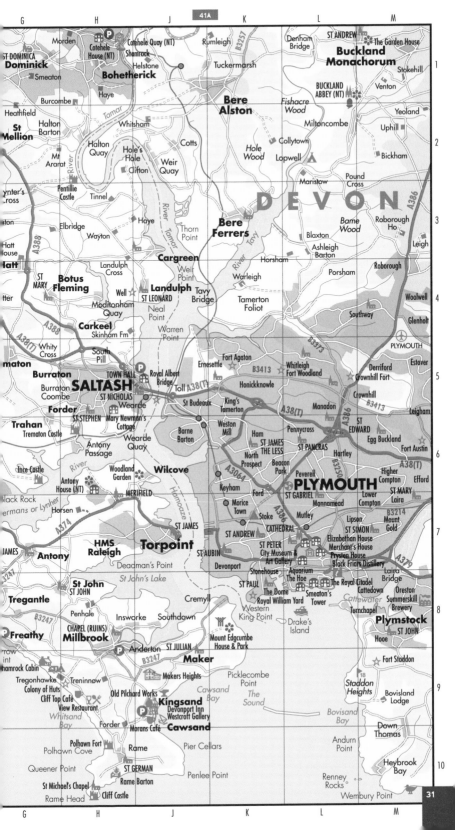

G · H · J · K · L · M

DEVON

Morden
Cotehele House (NT)
Cotehele Quay (NT)
Shamrock
Rumleigh
Denham Bridge
ST ANDREW
The Garden House
Buckland Monachorum
Stokehill

ST DOMINICA
Dominick
Smeaton
Bohetherick
Helstone
Tuckermarsh
BUCKLAND ABBEY (NT)
Venton

Burcombe
Haye
Bere Alston
Fishacre Wood
Yeoland

Heathfield
St Mellion
Halton Barton
Whitsham
Miltoncombe
Uphill

Halton Quay
Hole's Hole
Cotts
Hole Wood
Collytown
Bickham

Mt Ararat
Weir Quay
Clifton
Lopwell

Pentillie Castle
Tinnel
Maristow
Pound Cross
Bame Wood
Roborough Ho

ynter's cross
Elbridge
Wayton
Haye
Thorn Point
Bere Ferrers
Blaxton
Leigh

Hatt house
Cargreen
Weir Point
Warleigh
Horsham
Ashleigh Barton
Roborough

latt
ST MARY
Botus Fleming
Landulph Cross
Well
Landulph
ST LEONARD
Tavy Bridge
Tamerton Foliot
Porsham

tter
Carkeel
Moditonham Quay
Neal Point
Woolwell

Skinham Fm
Warren Point
Southway
Glenholt

maton
Whitly Cross
South Pill
Fort Agaton
Ernesettle
B3413
Whitleigh Fort Woodland
Derriford
Crownhill Fort
PLYMOUTH
Estaver

Burraton
TOWN HALL
Royal Albert Bridge
Toll A38(T)
Honickknowle
Crownhill
B3413

Burraton Coombe
SALTASH
ST NICHOLAS
Wearde
St Budeaux
King's Tamerton
Manadon
Leigham

Forder
ST STEPHEN
Mary Newman's Cottage
Weston Mill
Ham
Pennycross
ST EDWARD
Egg Buckland
Fort Austin

Trahan
Tremation Castle
Wearde Quay
Barne Barton
ST JAMES THE LESS
North Prospect
ST PANCRAS
Hartley
A38(T)

Antony Passage
Beacon Park
Peverell
Higher Compton
Efford

ince Castle
Woodland Garden
Wilcove
A3064
Ford
PLYMOUTH
ST GABRIEL
Mannamead
Lower Compton
ST MARY
Laira

lack Rock
ermans or Lynher
Horsen
MERIFIELD
Keyham
Morice Town
Stoke
Mutley
Lipson
ST SIMON
Mount Gold
B3214

A374
ST JAMES
ST ANDREW
CATHEDRAL
ST PETER
Elizabethan House
Merchant's House
Prysten House

JAMES
Antony
HMS Raleigh
Torpoint
ST AUBIN
City Museum & Art Gallery
Black Friars Distillery
A379

B3247
Deadman's Point
Devonport
Stonehouse
Aquarium
The Hoe
Laira Bridge

Tregantle
St John
ST JOHN
St John's Lake
Cremyll
ST PAUL
The Dome
Royal William Yard
Smeaton's Tower
The Royal Citadel
Cattedown
Oreston
Summerskill Brewery

Penhale
Insworke
Southdown
Western King Point
Drake's Island
Turnchapel
Plymstock
ST JOHN

Freathy
CHAPEL (RUINS)
Millbrook
Anderton
ST JULIAN
Mount Edgcumbe House & Park
Fort Staddon
Hooe

row int
hamrock Cabin
B3247
Maker
Makers Heights
Picklecombe Point
Staddon Heights
Bovisland Lodge

Tregonhawke
Colony of Huts
Cliff Top Café
View Restaurant
Treninnow
Old Pilchard Works
Kingsand
Devonport Inn
Westcroft Gallery
Cawsand Bay
The Sound
Bovisand Bay
Down Thomas

Whitsand Bay
Forder
Morans Cafe
Cawsand
Andurn Point
Heybrook Bay

Polhawn Fort
Polhawn Cove
Rame
Pier Cellars
Renney Rocks
Wembury Point

Queener Point
ST GERMAN
Penlee Point
Rame Barton

St Michael's Chapel
Rame Head
Cliff Castle

CAWSAND & KINGSAND

Twin villages, and former C18 smuggling centres with narrow streets and colourful houses, and an historic anchorage for Plymouth. Park in Kingsand (location for recent film, Mr Turner) and walk through to Cawsand, the prettier of the two. A stroll across the bay to the ancient pilchard works is worthwhile. If pub crawls are your hobby you will have found a true home. Fine walks along the coast to Cremyll Ferry. Light Bites in the Old Boatstore Café, and Morans. (J9)

WHERE TO STAY...

Buttervilla Farm, Polbathic.
Eco-friendly, organic farm of 15 acres. The dècor is contemporary and comfortable, the showers are solar heated. Dinner is by arrangement. Most vegetables are home grown. Wi-Fi access. (E6) 01503 220229 www.buttervilla.com

Cliff House, Kingsand.
Grade II listed house with three bedrooms and bath. First floor Living Room overlooking Plymouth Sound and coastal path. Wholefood cuisine from local suppliers. Self-catering cottages. (J9) 01752 823110

The Library, Antony House ab/nt

Lantallack Farm, Landrake.
Grade II Georgian farmhouse provides large, comfy bedrooms and organic breakfasts. Your hostess Nicky is an artist and will teach you printmaking, painting and sculpture. (E4)
01752 851281
www.lantallackgwetaways.co.uk

Rame Barton B&B & Pottery. A delightful C18 farmhouse close to the coast path, and equiped with crisp linen sheets and comfy beds. Self-catering, weddings and cream teas, as well as Paul Cardew's ceramic pots and teapots. (H10) 01752 822789 www.ramebarton.co.uk

Shamrock Cabin, Tregonhawke, Whitsand Bay. Kick off your shoes and play at being shipwrecked in this perfectly formed log cabin atop the cliffs at Whitsand Bay. Nothing ahead of you but an endless sea view. All you need is the cabin, and the Clifftop Café and View Restaurant within walking distance. Leave the car keys in the suitcase and let your cares drift away. Sleeps 2. (H9)
07719 332287
www.shamrockcabin.co.uk

Sheviock Barton. Spacious old farmhouse epitomises the good life symbolised by the oak beams and flagstone floors of the kitchen. You can relax in your bedroom, the sitting room, games room or large gardens. (F7) 01503 230793
www.sheviockbarton.co.uk

SPECIAL PLACES OF INTEREST TO VISIT...

Antony House & Garden (NT). Built for Sir William Carew from 1711-1721 and considered the most distinguished example of early C18 architecture in Cornwall. Colonades, panelled rooms and family portraits. House open East to Oct Tu, W, Th, Su & BH Ms 12-5. Garden Mar to

Oct Sa-Th except M, 11-5. (H6)
01752 812191
www.nationaltrust.org.uk

Antony Woodland Garden.
Privately owned by the Carew Pole Garden Trust. 100 acres of woodland, 300 types of camellias bordering the River Lynher. Open daily except M & F Mar-Oct 11-5. (H6) 01752 812191. www. antonywoodlandgarden.com

Freathy Colony of Huts.
To avoid the Plymouth Blitz during World War II many set up camp on the cliffs of Freathy. Their tents and shelters grew into cabins and a community was born. The site is dramatic and properties sell for large sums. The Cliff Top Café is open throughout the year. (H9)
01752 822069

Landulph Church. Woodland setting beside the River Tamar. Rood screen. Bench Ends. Fine wagon roof in north aisle. (J4)

Maker Heights. Home to the Rame Conservation Trust as well as artists and artisans. The woodland is being tended and the site is used as a venue for live music and theatrical events. From 1926-1985, thousands of inner-city children holidayed here, inspired by Nancy Astor in 1925, the first female MP (Sutton, Plymouth). (J9)
01752 822152
www.makerheights.org.uk

Monkey Sanctuary (Trust).
The first protected breeding colony of Amazon Woolly Monkeys in the world. It's also a rescue centre for ex-pet capuchin monkeys. Refreshments. Open Feb & Oct 1/2 terms, then East., or (Apr)-Sept Su-Th 11-4.30. (B7)
01503 262532
www.monkeysanctuary.org

Mount Edgcumbe House & Park. Sensitively restored Tudor mansion in beautiful

Monkey Sanctuary ss

Devonport Inn ss

landscaped parkland. Formal English, French and Italian Gardens. National Camellia Collection. Park and gardens open daily all year. House and Earl's Garden open East., or (Apr)-Sept Sa-Th 11-4.30. (K8) 01752 822236 www.mountedgcumbe.gov.uk

Rame Church. C11-15. Rough stone with spire. No electricity; hand-pumped organ. Nearby, simple chapel on Rame Head built by monks who directed ships with fire beacons into Plymouth Sound. A place for contemplation and solitude; the last sighting of an English shore for many sailors buried at sea, and beyond. (H10)

Tregantle Fort. In imposing position overlooking Whitesands Bay. Built to guard the sea approaches to Devonport Dockyard. During World War I various Worcestershire Battalions were stationed here, and injured soldiers were sent here to convalesce from their wounds. In use today by the MOD. For the rare 'Open Days' see local advertising. (F8)

Westcroft Guesthouse (Gallery), Market Street, Kingsand. Newly renovated boutique B&B, formerly a Georgian coaching inn houses an art gallery, and is perfect for coastal walks, beaching it, café culture and relaxing in some style. (J9) 01752 823216 www.westcroft-gallery.co.uk

PLACES TO EAT, DRINK & BE MERRY...

Blue Plate, Main Road, Downderry. An award-winning eatery that will reward your pit stop with scrummy delights from their restaurant, deli, cafe and bar. Open W-Su from 10. (C8) 01503 250308 www.blueplatecornwall.com

Clifftop Café, Treninnow Cliff Road. Friendly café affords stunning views, and a welcome pit stop if walking or cycling the steep paths. Kids menu, and dogs welcome. Open daily 10-4. (H9) 017523 822069

Morans Café & Deli, Cawsand. The home of freshly baked goodies and full-English breakfast, lunches, cream teas

and cakes. B&B. Open daily from 9. (J9) 01752 656215

Devonport Inn, Kingsand. This is a simply decorated (a little eclectic) and traditional inn with charm that provides unpretentious, good fare, in a special place. Al fresco dining with harbour views. Dog friendly. Open daily for lunch, tea and dinner (closed Tu in winter) (J9) 01752 822869

Rod and Line, Tideford. If you yearn for a small, traditonal pub, untainted by contemporary trends, but with the ambience of times gone by, and wish to sup from local fayre; crab, king prawns and scallops, and to listen to musicians as varied as the late John Martyn or Chris Jaggger, none better. (E5) 01752 851323

View Restaurant, Trenninow Cliff Road. Fabulous position. Food is classic French with English ingredients. Can't better that. Child and Veggie friendly, and a cool place to relax and admire the view. (H9) 01752 822345

Port Eliot.

This, the ancient seat of the Eliot family, has been described as the oldest house in Cornwall, and believed to have been the oldest, continually, inhabited house in the UK. The home of Lord and Lady St Germans who hold an annual Literary and Music Festival in the grounds beside the River Lynher. There is historic evidence of some 1,500 year old tiles, to the C18 remodelling of the Priory by Sir John Soane, to works by Reynolds, Van Dyck and Robert Lenkiewicz. Teas. Guided tours. Gardens open 1 Mar to late June 2-6 except Sa. (E6) 01503 230211
www.porteliot.co.uk
www.porteliotlitfest.com

Brunel's Royal Albert Bridge, Saltash

SALTASH
An attractive river port with steep streets running down to the Tamar Estuary. C18 Guildhall. Royal Albert Bridge. May Fair - 1st week. Regatta - June 3rd week. (H5)
www.saltash.gov.uk
www.thisissaltash.co.uk

Mary Newman's Cottage, 48 Culver Rd. C15 Cottage of Mary Newman, first wife of Sir Francis Drake. Furniture supplied by the Victoria and Albert Museum. Open East-Oct W, Th, Sa, Su 12-4 and BH M's 11-4. (H5)

Royal Albert Bridge. This 'Bowstring Suspension Bridge' is an iron, single-track railway bridge, built by I.K. Brunel in 1859, his last great feat of engineering. The design comprises a wrought iron tubular arch or bow, in the form of a parabola, in a combination with sets of suspension chains hanging on each side of the tube in a catenary curve. (J5)
www.royalalbertbridge.co.uk

ST GERMANS
Cornwall's great Cathedral City until 1043. An attractive village with almshouses (six houses with six gables and miniature ground and upper floors), and the magnificent church - see below.

St Germanus Church. Founded as an Augustinian priory, and later a Cathedral in the Anglo-Saxon period. Only the south aisle and nave remain. Magnificent Norman doorway and East Window stained glass by E. Burne-Jones executed by William Morris (E6).

St Germanus Church, St Germans

Freathy Colony of Huts

| 600 BC | Iron Age settlement at Trevelgue Head | 325 BC | The Greek traveller Pytheas records seeing the people of Land's End preparing metal by beating it on leather, and then trading it at St Michael's Mount. |

Cotehele House ab/nt

The White Room, Cotehele House nt

The Hall, Cotehele House nt

Cotehele Quay

Cotehele House (NT).
A medieval house of grey granite, built from 1485-1627, and set in a romantic position overlooking the River Tamar and Devon, beyond. For centuries, the Edgcumbe family home containing their original furniture, C17 tapestries, armour and needlework. The gardens lie on several levels. Medieval dovecote. Ancient clock in chapel. Refreshments and shop. House open daily mid-Mar to 31 Oct 11-4. Gardens open all year, dawn to dusk (H1) 01579 351346 www.nationaltrust.org.uk

Cotehele Quay (NT).
A set of quite charming and picturesque C18 and C19 buildings overlook the River Tamar. A small outstation of the National Maritime Museum, and berth for the restored Tamar sailing barge, 'Shamrock' Museum, Edgcumbe tea- room. Open daily 11-4. The C19 Cotehele Mill holds corn grinding shows on Th & Su. (H1)

Cotehele Gallery (NT).
Showcasing professional artists and craftmakers from the South-West in seven annual exhibitions. Open daily mid-Feb to Christmas - Summer 11-5, Winter 11-4. (H1) www.nationaltrust.org.uk

COASTAL FOOTPATH...

Looe to Cremyll Point:
Approx 26 miles. The path
crosses National Trust land
and soon descends into Seaton
to be followed by a stiff climb
up to Battern Cliffs (450ft), the
highest cliffs in South Cornwall,
and a reminder of the gruelling
ascents and descents of the
North Coast, all now a distant
memory. A quick descent to the
little harbour of Portwrinkle.
The path now hugs the cliff
edge and you can walk through
the M.O.D. ranges at Tregantle,
except during firing when
you will be re-routed inland.
Around the great sweep of
Whitsand Bay to Rame Head
with splendid views of Plymouth
Sound, and beyond. Along to
the twin villages of Kingsand
and Cawsand, passing Mount
Edgcumbe, and to Cremyll
Ferry which has carried
passengers across the Tamar
since the C13. (K8)

BEACHES AND SURFING...

Millendreath Beach. Sands
with patches of rock, bathing
pool for children. P/WC/Café.
(A7)

Seaton. Fine bathing, safe
beach with pebbles and
grey sand. P/WC. Surfing -
Sheltered position. (B7)

Downderry. Grey sands, rocks,
palm trees. P/WC/Inn. (C7)

Kingsand

Portwrinkle. Surfing - Good
following big swells. At HT
rocks are invisible so take care
with your fins. P. (E8)

Whitsand Bay. 4 miles of sand.
Glorious on a sunny day. But
BEWARE, this bay has a history
of fatal bathing accidents, and
is also a graveyard of many
ships. The strong currents make
bathing very HZ and is not
recommended for the casual
swimmer. Difficult access.
Surfing - Warm up with the 10
minute walk to (H9)

Tregantle. Good breaks at
HT. Rips are powerful. Popular
location for Plymouth surfers.
(F8)

Tregantle Longsands. Access
near M.O.D. range. Prohibited
when red flag flies. P/WC. (F8)

Freathy / Tregonhawke.
Smooth white sands, strong
currents, surfing. P/LG. (G9)

Cawsand / Kingsand. Easy
access to shelving, pebbled
beach - sand at LT. Good
bathing, well protected from
Sou'westerlies. Glorious views
of ships sailing up to Plymouth
Sound. P/WC/Café. (J9)

Kingsand   Salmon fishing, Cotehele Quay

The Cheesewring, Bodmin Moor

For Ancient Sites, Castles, Country Lanes, Stone Circles, Steam Railways and Wilderness.

Between the County Town of Bodmin and the walled town of Launceston lies the mysterious Bodmin Moor. A compact area of open moorland, a mere ten miles by ten, in size. And, yet, it appears far more expansive given its wildness and isolation. But, beware of sudden mists and descending clouds for they foster disorientation amidst bog, and Tor.

All about you is ancient history. Early Man settled here to escape the wild beasts of forest and plain. Stone Age Man left Stone Circles and burial chambers. The Moor's appearance of bareness was hastened by the clearance of granite boulders for building stonewalls, farms and villages. In the centre, isolated and bruised by the elements, stands Jamaica Inn, the legendary smugglers' haunt, widely known through Daphne du Maurier's novel. Imagine arriving on foot, or cart, lonely, tired and drenched, to be greeted by rough-tongued smugglers and highwaymen.

Not to be overlooked is the fertile countryside on the eastern side of the Moor drained by the rivers Tamar and Lynher. A blissful, pastoral landscape reminiscent of old England. Small farmsteads and hamlets with beautiful churches such as Linkinhorne, South Hill and Lezant, and often to be found, surprisingly good inns, for example the Springer Spaniel at Treburley. These villages are linked by narrow lanes and steep banks.

Launceston is dominated by its Norman castle and is the only walled town in Cornwall. It is a town of hills that calls for exploration. The exterior walls of the church of St Mary Magdalene are exceptional with images of foliage and shields carved out of the granite.

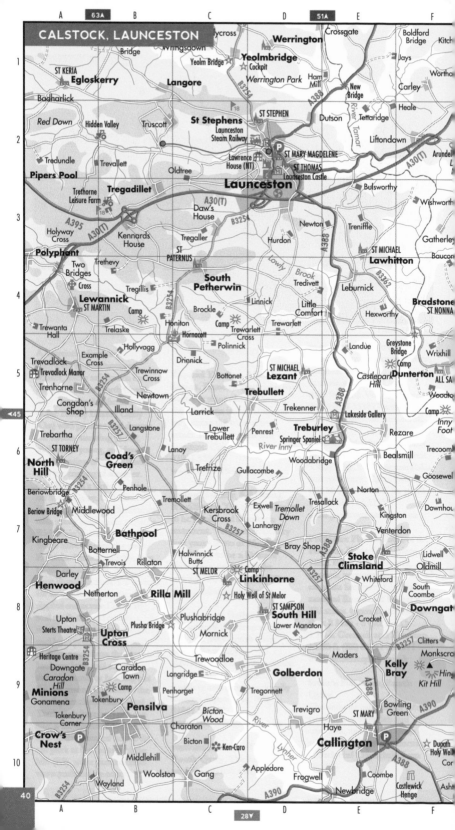

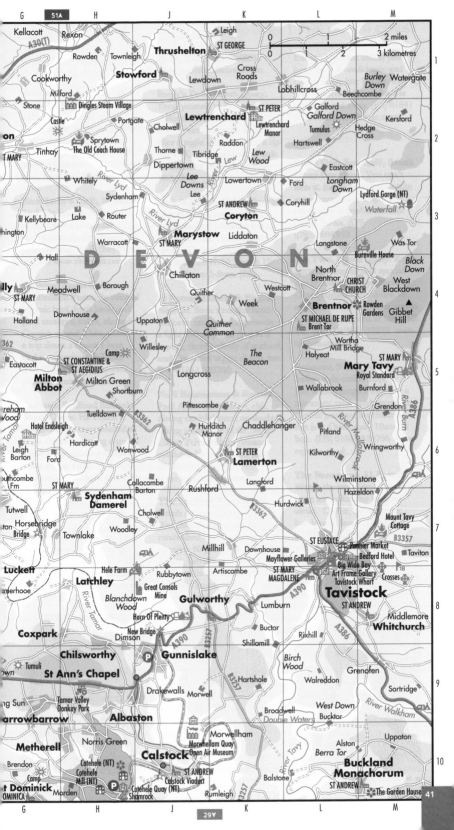

Launceston Castle

LAUNCESTON

A town of hills dominated by the commanding position of the Castle, and the only walled town in Cornwall. There is a splendid collection of Georgian houses in Castle St. C16 packhorse bridge. Agricultural show - July. E/C Th. (D2)

SPECIAL PLACES TO VISIT...

Church of St Mary Magdalene. Noted for the famous exterior; panels of foliage and shields carved in granite cover most of the walls. C14 tower and a rare painted pulpit. (D2)

Launceston Steam Railway. Two-foot gauge steam railway using Victorian Locomotives along a beautiful country line. After 2 1/2 miles, Newmills Station, with access to farm park. Transport and Industrial Museum with working exhibits. Café, shop and bookshop. Open East week, Spring BH & Oct 1/2 term, July-Sept Su-F, June Su-Tu, 10.30-4.30. (D2) 01566 775665 www.launcestonsr.co.uk

Launceston Castle (EH). Norman castle built in c.1070 in timber. It was the main seat of Robert de Mortain, brother of William the Conqueror. Rebuilt C12-13. Good example of a motte and bailey structure. Open East., or Apr to Oct 10-5 (-4 Oct). (D2) 0370 333181 www.english-heritage.org.uk

Lawrence House Museum (NT). Property used as a local history museum. Many objects of interest including the Feudal dues. Open Apr-Oct M-F 10.30-4.30. (D2) 01566 773277 www.nationaltrust.org.uk

SPECIAL PLACES TO VISIT OUTSIDE LAUNCESTON...

Hidden Valley. Adventure park and mini railway. Treasure hunts based around a shipwreck. Play area. Farm animals. Café. Open Apr-Oct 10-5. (B2) 01566 86463

Ken-Caro Garden. Five acre connoisseur's garden full of unusual plants and shrubs, making it a garden of interest all year. Panoramic views. Open daily late Feb–end Sept 10-5.30. (C10) 01579 362446

Lakeside Gallery, Nr Treburley. Permanent Tolkien Collection. Original paintings, drawings and prints by Linda, Seth and Roger Garland. Open daily 10-5. (E5) 01579 370760 www.lakeside-gallery.com

Sterts Theatre. Lively programme of music, amphitheatre (canopied) and dance. Open daily Café/Bar (10-4), (theatre June-Sept) except Su. (A8) 01579 362382 www.sterts.co.uk

Trethorne Leisure Farm. All-weather undercover family entertainment; milk a cow, bottle feed lambs, see chicks hatch. Ten pin bowling (open 10am-11pm), gladiator duels, dropslide, astraslide, restaurant, bar and shop. Open daily Jan-Oct 10-6.(B3) 01566 86324

WHERE TO EAT, SLEEP AND BE MERRY...

Hornacott, South Petherwin. Treat yourself to B&B in a traditional C18 Cornish farmhouse tucked away in a poppet of a valley close to Bodmin Moor, and conveniently near the A30, and thus, accessible to much of Cornwall. Or, you can just relax in their beautiful garden. (C5) 01566 782461 www.hornacott.co.uk

Hotel Endsleigh. One runs out of adjectives for Olga Polizzi's stunning fusion of country house style with contemporary boutique. This former fishing lodge overlooks beautiful, ornamental gardens, a Dairy Dell, an arboretum and the Tamar Valley. Is this Shangrila? The staff are friendly and discreet, and its the ideal, practical stop-over after a long journey before you enter Cornwall. (G6) 01822 870000 www.hotelendsleigh.com

Springer Spaniel, Treburley. A rustic pub with a focus on excellent food. Comfortable interiors with log fires, a light and welcoming dining room, as well as a sheltered garden outside. Now owned by Masterchef winner Anton Piotrowski. (E6) 01579 370424 www.thespringerspaniel.co.uk

CHURCHES OF INTEREST...

Calstock Church. Grand position above Tamar Valley. Two C17 monuments to the Edgcumbe family. (J10)

Linkinhorne Church. Tall C16 granite tower - the second highest in county at 120ft with wagon roof, stained glass, wall paintings in remote village. (C8)

North Hill Church. Large, ambitious church with C15 granite tower, elaborate and endearing C17 monuments. Set in unspoilt village. A pilgrimage to be undertaken by all church enthusiasts. (A6)

CALSTOCK
Attractive old river port on the Tamar. Steep wooded riverbank and the abundance of fruit trees provide a splendour in spring. 12-arch viaduct. Numerous disused mining chimneys and engine houses haunt the landscape. (J10)

Calstock Viaduct. 12-arch viaduct built to carry railway wagons from local mines to Calstock Quay. Whence the wagons were raised and lowered in a lift. (J10)

Atlantic Salmon, River Tamar

Hotel Endsleigh ss

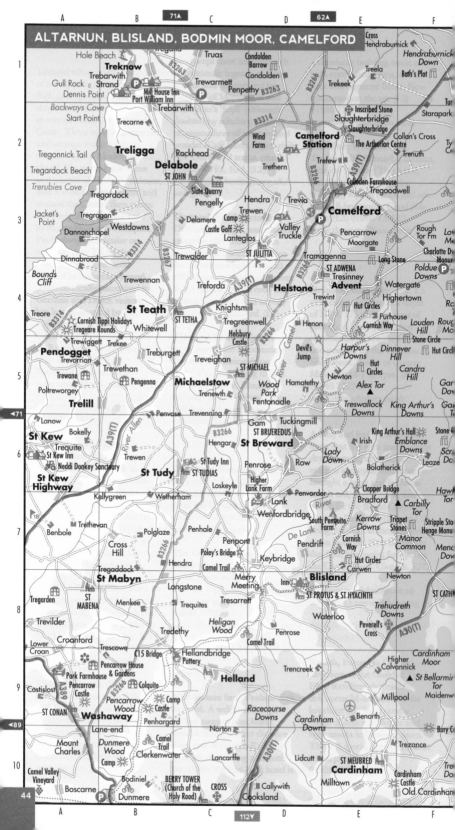

A B 71A C D 62A E F

1

Cross
Hendrabumick
Hendrabumick
Down
Bath's Plot
Hole Beach
Trekow
Tregardo
Truas
Condolden
Barrow
Condolden
Penpethy B3263
Treela
Trekeek
Tur
Starapark
Ty
Tregonnick
Trebarwith
Strand
Gull Rock o
Dennis Point
Mill House Inn
Port William Inn
Trebarwith
Trewarmett
B3314
Inscribed Stone
Slaughterbridge
Slaughterbridge
The Arthurian Centre
Collan's Cross
Trenuth

2

Backways Cove
Start Point
Trecarne
Trebarwith
Camelford
Station
Tregoodwell
Trefew
Tregonnick Tail
Treligga
Rockhead
Wind
Farm
Trethern
B3266
Culloden Farmhouse
Tregoodwell
Tregardock Beach
Delabole
ST JOHN
Trevia
Camelford
Trerubies Cove
Slate Quarry
Pengelly
Hendra
Trewen
Camelford
Rough
Tor Fm

3

Jacket's
Point
Tregardock
Tregragon
Westdowns
Delamere
Camp
Castle Goff
Lanteglos
Valley
Truckle
Pencarrow
Moorgate
Charlotte Dv
Monu
Poldue
Downs
Dannonchapel
ST JULITTA
Tramagenna
Long Stone
Dinnabroad
A39(T)
Treforda
ST ADWENA
Tresinney
Advent
Watergate
Bounds
Cliff
Trewennan
Helstone
Highertown
Ra

4

Treore
B3314
St Teath
Knightsmill
Trewint
Hut Circles
Louden
Hill
Roug
Mo
Cornish Tippi Holidays
Tregeare Rounds
Whitewell
ST TETHA
Tregreenwell
Helsbury
Castle
Henon
Furhouse
Cornish Way
Stone Circle
Pendogget
Trevorrian
Treburgett
Treveighan
ST MICHAEL
Devil's
Jump
Harpur's
Downs
Dinnever
Hill
Hut Circl

5

Trewiggett
Trewethan
Pengenna
Michaelstow
Wood
Park
Fentonadle
Hamatethy
Newton
Hut
Circles
Candra
Hill
Gar
Dov
Trewane
Poltreworgey
Trelill
Trenewth
Trevenning
Gam
Tuckingmill
Alex Tor
Treswallock
Downs
King Arthur's
Downs
Gar
Te

6

Lanow
Bokelly
St Kew
Trequite
St Kew Inn
Neddi Donkey Sanctuary
St Kew
Highway
Trewen
River Allen
B3266
Hengar
ST BRUEREDUS
St Breward
Irish
Lady
Down
Bolatherick
King Arthur's Hall
Emblance
Downs
Leaze
Stone
Scra
Do

7

18
Trethevan
Benbole
Kellygreen
Wetherham
St Tudy
St Tudy Inn
ST TUDIAS
Penrose
Higher
Lank Farm
Loskeyle
Row
Penvorder
De Lank
River
Bradford
Clapper Bridge
Carbilly
Tor
Kerrow
Downs
Trippet
Stones
Stripple Sto
Henge Monu
Cross
Hill
Polglaze
B3266
Penhale
Penpont
Poley's Bridge
Keybridge
Lank
Wenfordbridge
South Penquite
Farm
Pendrift
Cornish
Way
Hut Circles
Carwen
Manor
Common
Menc
Dov
Hawk
Tor

8

Tregarden
Hendra
Camel Trail
Tregaddock
St Mabyn
ST
MABENA
Longstone
Trequites
Tresarrett
Merry
Meeting
Inn
Blisland
ST PROTUS & ST HYACINTH
Newton
ST CATH
Trevilder
Menkee
Heligan
Wood
Penrose
Waterloo
Trehudreth
Downs
Peverell's
Cross
Tredethy

9

Lower
Croan
Croanford
Trescowe
C15 Bridge
Hellandbridge
Pottery
Camel Trail
Trencreek
Higher
Colvannick
Cardinham
Moor
Costislost
Park Farmhouse
Pencarrow House
& Gardens
Pencarrow
Castle
Pencarrow
Wood
Colquite
Camp
Castle
Helland
Racecourse
Downs
St Bellarmin
Tor
Maidenw
ST CONAN
Washaway
Penhargard
Benorth
Millpool
Bury C

10

89
Mount
Charles
Lane-end
Dunmere
Wood
Camp
Camel
Trail
Clerkenwater
Norton
Lancarffe
Cardinham
Downs
A30(T)
Lidcutt
ST MEUBRED
Cardinham
Trezance
Tre
Do
Camel Valley
Vineyard
Boscarne
Bodiniel
Dunmere
BERRY TOWER
(Church of the
Holy Rood)
CROSS
Cooksland
Callywith
Milltown
Cardinham
Castle
Old Cardinham

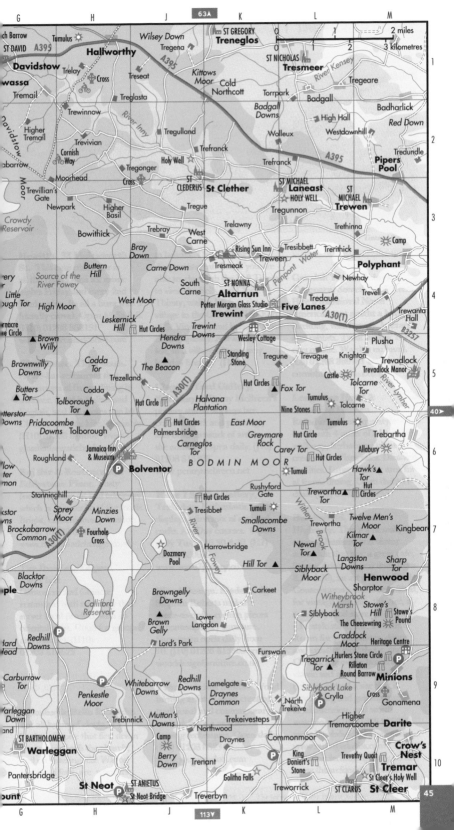

Minions, Bodmin Moor

The Cheesewring, Bodmin Moor

BLISLAND

A quiet, charming village on the edge of sparse, Bodmin Moor. Yet, it is surrounded by woodland and undulating roads leading to it. It has a Village Green, a fine pub and a co-operative village shop. Many of the smart, granite built houses are holiday lets. (D8)

BODMIN MOOR

A wild and remote landscape of sudden mists and mysterious legend. A vegetation of boggy moorland, open heathland, granite tors and hidden valleys. The highest point is Brown Willy (1377ft). This remote wilderness, far from the dangerous beasts of the forest and plain, attracted prehistoric man. Hut circles, burial grounds and stone circles litter the landscape. An exhilarating place for pony trekking and walking, but beware of sudden mists. (K6) www.bodminmoor.co.uk

St Nonna, Altarnun

SPECIAL PLACES OF INTEREST...

King Doniert's Stone. Possible remains of Durngarth's grave d.875, King of Cornwall. Interlaced with Hibernia-Saxon inscription. (L10)

Dozmary Pool. A remote, uninspiring pool where 'Excalibur was thrown into these waters.' (J7)

Fernacre Stone Circle. 64 stones, 150ft in diameter. Numerous hut circles. (G4)

Hurlers Stone Circle. Three stone circles 110ft, 135ft and 105ft in diameter. According to legend, men turned to stone for playing the old Cornish game of hurling on a Sunday. Similar game to Australian Rules. Access via 1/4-mile path from road. (M9)

King Arthur's Hall. Neolithic enclosure 159ft x 60ft with large facing stones. (F6)

Rillaton Round Barrow. A bronze dagger, and the Rillaton Cup were unearthed here in 1818. A gold cup, of ribbed and handled design (in British Museum) suggests it may have originated in Mycenae, Greece. (M9)

The Cheesewring. Extraordinary formation of granite slabs weathered by wind and rain. Bronze Age cup (now residing in the British Museum) found in grave on Stowe's Hill. It's a good fifteen minute walk from the car park. Follow the old quarry track. (M8)

Trevethy Quoit. Impressive Neolithic dolmen; 6 uprights support a massive capstone pierced by a circular hole. Park opposite. (M10)

ALTARNUN

A charming linear village with a superb C16 church, 'Cathedral of the Moors.' Packhorse bridge. (K4)

Rising Sun Inn. Popular C16 pub on the edge of Bodmin Moor providing a full range of ales. Delabole slate flagstone floors. Coal fires. Uncomplicated food. Camping. (K4) 01566 86636 www.therisingsuninn.co.uk

Potter Morgan Glass Studio. Traditional, stunning, handmade glass blown on the premises, in purpose-built studio. Open Tu-Sa 10-5. (K4) 01566 880122 www.pottermorganglass.com

St Nonna. Superb C16 church; tall perpendicular tower rises to 109 ft. Norman font with bearded faces at corner. C16 carved bench ends including man with bagpipes. Rood Screen. Known locally as 'The Cathedral of the Moors'. (K4)

787   Vikings invade and make a pact with the Cornish to repel the Saxons

814   The Saxon king Ecgberht of Wessex conquers Cornwall destroying all in his path.

Trevethy Quoit

Paul Jackson, Helland Bridge Pottery ss

Camelford Tower

Wesley Cottage.
John Wesley, the founder of Methodism, preached and rested here during his preaching tours of Cornwall. Furnished in C18 style with collection of Wesleyana. Open May-Oct Tu-Sa 10.30-3.30. (K4) 01566 782251 www.wesleycottage.org.uk

CAMELFORD
Attractive main square with some fine buildings; note the splendid clock. Worth stopping here if you've been held up on the A39. Free parking. Leisure Centre. (E3) www.camelford.org

WHERE TO STAY...

Culloden Farmhouse, 16 Victoria Rd. Charming old farmhouse offers vegetarian and vegan B&B, and three self-catering units within 100 metres distance of the town centre. (E3) 01840 211128 www.cullodenfarmhouse.co.uk

CHURCHES OF INTEREST...

Advent Church. Rare 8 pinnacle tower in lonely moorland setting. (E4)

St Protus & St Hyacinth, Blisland. Wonderfully restored church (a favourite of John Betjeman) in village with attractive village green and fine inn. C15 granite tower and Norman font. C15 brasses. (D8)

Cardinham Church. C15 buttressed and pinnacle tower with Celtic cross. (E10)

Lanteglos-By-Camelford Church. In picturesque valley, much restored, C10 Saxon pillars and 4 Celtic crosses. Evidence of Norman construction. Attractive C19 monument. (D3)

Laneast Church. Originally a C13 Norman church with fine C16 pulpit, granite south porch

and wagon roofing. Notable restored benches, the bench ends are interlaced knots, coats of arms and stars. Remarkable 9ft high Rood Screen. C15 stained glass. (L3)

Michaelstow Church. Original wagon roof. Font, bench ends and interesting C17 monument. (C5)

SPECIAL PLACES TO VISIT IN THE PROXIMITY...

Arthurian Centre. Site of Arthurian legend and folk lore. Exhibition centre, woodland and river walks, tea room and gift/ bookshop. Play area. Camping. Open daily. (E2) 01840 213947 www.arthur-online.co.uk

Helland Bridge Pottery. Riverside home and studio of Paul and Rosie Jackson. A wide range of stunningly decorated hand-made pottery and garden sculpture. Fabulous water

Wesley Cottage ss

South Penquite Farm ss

825   The Cornish rise against Ecgberht but are defeated at Galford

838   The Cornish-Viking alliance is defeated at Hingston Down near Callington

gardens. Open any time, but advised to call first. (C9) 01208 75240 www.paul-jackson.co.uk

Jamaica Inn. Former old coaching inn under new ownership, and inspiration for Daphne du Maurier's fictitious novel. Bars, restaurants, accommodation & gift shops. Attractions include the Daphne du Maurier Room, 'The Smugglers at Jamaica Inn.' Ghost Hunt. Inn open all year. (H6) 01566 86250 www.jamaicainn.co.uk A Start-Off point for circular walk to Brown Willy.

Minions Heritage Centre, South Phoenix Mine. Explores the history of the local landscape, from the Stone Age to the Present Day. Open daily from 10-dusk. (M9) 01579 341463 www.caradon.gov.uk

Pencarrow House. Busy Georgian home of the Molesworth-St Aubyn's set in extensive grounds. A fine collection of pictures, furniture and porcelain. Café, craft centre, plant shop and children's play area. House open daily 11-5 Apr-Oct except F & Sa. Gardens daily from 10. (A9) 01208 841369 www.pencarrow.co.uk

Slaughter Bridge. Possible burial place of King Arthur. A granite slab marks the grave. (E2)

WHERE TO STAY IN THE PROXIMITY...

Higher Lank Farm, Wenfordbridge. This is unique. No question about it. A working farm specialising in the needs of parents, and pre-school children (toddlers). Self-catering and guest house accommodation available. (D7) 01208 850716 www.higherlankfarm.co.uk

Park Farmhouse, Washaway. A luxurious B&B situated on the beautiful Pencarrow Estate. Here you can take part in a well organised hunt for local game, learn to cook game at the hands-on Cookery School under the stewardship of Mark Devonshire (formally of Rick Stein's Restaurant and Cookery School), or just enjoy feeling like a Lord of the Manor. (A9) 01208 841 277 www. parkfarmhousewadebridge.co.uk

Trevadlock Manor, Lewannick. Overlooks the upper reaches of the beautiful Lynher Valley. A substantial L-shaped manor built in 1530. You have the choice of farmhouse style B&B or self-catering cottages on the Estate. (M5) 01566 782227 www.trevadlockmanor.co.uk

South Penquite Farm. If you fancy a superb view from your own canvas shelter or from inside a Mongolian Yurt try camping in this 200-acre working farm high on Bodmin Moor, and close to the fine village of Blisland. (E7) 01208 850491 www.southpenquite.co.uk

Pencarrow House & Gardens ss

Carved Bench End, St Nonna, Altarnun

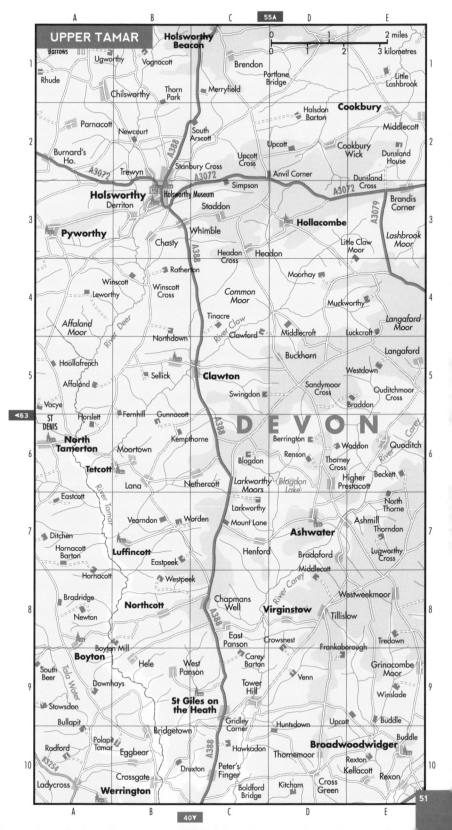

Towanroath Shaft, Wheal Coates Mine

For Dramatic Scenery, Family Holidays, Gastronomic Delights, Safe Beaches and Surfing.

The coastal footpath that runs along the North Coast must be one of the natural wonders of Britain. At times, wild and remote, and hard going in places, it affords spectacular views and rewards you with sheltered harbours where you can sample local fayre and fine ales. When the Equinoxes arrive you can, in places, walk the golden sands and admire the Atlantic waves that have rolled in untouched for 3,000 miles.

The North Coast is a fabulous playground for family holidays. Accommodation is available in many forms: campsites, holiday cottages, farmhouses, gastronomic B&Bs and hotels. The style of your holiday may lean to the surfing camaraderie of Bude or the quieter villages of the far north, the gastronomic pleasures and indulgences of Padstow, or the frenetic pace of Newquay to the more soulful, arty atmosphere of St Agnes. Cornwall now has a wealth of sophisticated hostelries offering superb food and luxury accommodation. It still has surf hostels although their numbers are dwindling for many on the road leading to Fistral Beach have been torn down and are being replaced by luxurious apartments.

Inland are small farms and hamlets, with the villages increasing in size as you move south nearer to the towns of Bodmin, Truro and Falmouth. In the Camborne-Redruth area there is much to interest the industrial archaeologist, and perhaps the most spectacularly located engine house is to be found at Wheal Coates, north of Chapel Porth.

This stretch of Cornwall has long held a special hold on many families who return year after year for their annual holiday. It is not uncommon to see three generations of the same family enjoying the calm waters of Daymer Bay or Trevone, that is, until their offspring progress to the surf schools of Polzeath, and the rips of Booby and Constantine Bays.

In recent years extreme sports such as coasteering and kite-boarding have exploded onto the scene. Surfing is no longer a niche activity. It is now an everyday sport available to all through the many surf and life-saving schools, and because of the access to protective wet suits and learner boards. This guide will direct you to the best beaches. The locals have a saying in Newquay: "Arrive with a bucket and spade... and leave with a surfboard!" So go and search for the Perfect Wave.

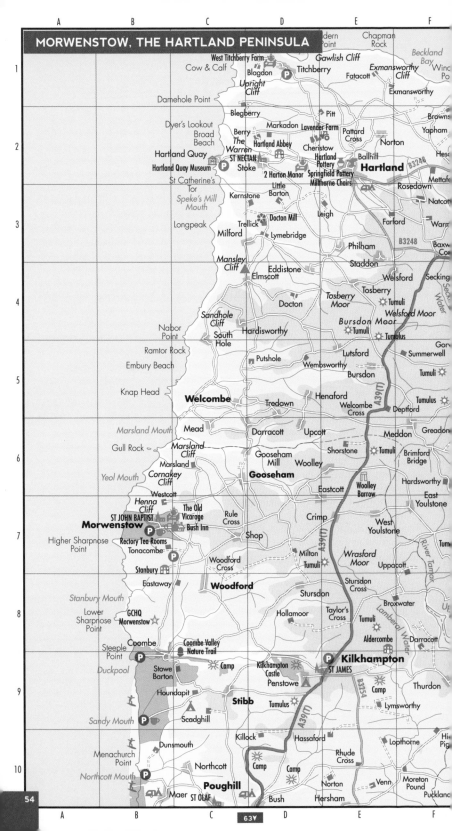

A B C D E F

1

Chapman Rock
Beckland Bay
dern
Gawlish Cliff
West Titchberry Farm
Cow & Calf
Blagdon
Titchberry
Exmansworthy Cliff
Wind
Po
Fatacott
Exmansworthy
Upright Cliff
Damehole Point
Blegberry
Pitt
Browns
Yapham
Dyer's Lookout
Broad Beach
Markadon
Lavender Farm
Pattard Cross
Norton
Hesc
Berry
The Warren
Hartland Abbey
Cheriston
Hartland Pottery
Ballhill
Hartland Quay
ST NECTAN
Stoke
Springfield Pottery
Hartland
B3248
Hartland Quay Museum
2 Harton Manor
Milkhorne Chairs
Mettafe
St Catherine's Tor
Little Barton
Rosedown
Natcott
Speke's Mill Mouth
Kernstone
Leigh
Warr

2

3

Longpeak
Trellick
Docton Mill
Farford
Milford
Lymebridge
Philham
B3248
Mansley Cliff
Eddistone
Staddon
Baxw
Cor
Elmscott
Welsford
Secking
Docton
Tosberry
Tosberry Moor
Tumuli
Welsford Moor
Secki
Water

4

Sandhole Cliff
Bursdon Moor
Tumuli
Tumulus
Nabor Point
South Hole
Hardisworthy
Gor
Ramtor Rock
Putshole
Lutsford
Summerwell
Embury Beach
Wembsworthy
Bursdon
Tumuli
Knap Head
Henaford
Tumulus
Welcombe
Tredown
Welcombe Cross
Deptford

5

Marsland Mouth
Mead
Darracott
Upcott
Meddon
Greadon
Gull Rock
Marsland Cliff
Gooseham Mill
Shorstone
Tumuli
Brimford Bridge
Yeol Mouth
Marsland
Woolley
Hardsworthy
Cornakey Cliff
Gooseham
Eastcott
Woolley Barrow
East Youlstone
Westcott
Henna Cliff
The Old Vicarage
Crimp
ST JOHN BAPTIST
Rule Cross
West Youlstone
Morwenstow
Bush Inn
Shop
River Tam
Higher Sharpnose Point
Rectory Tea Rooms
Tonacombe
Woodford Cross
Milton
Wrasford Moor
Tum
Stanbury
Tumuli
Uppacott
Eastaway
Woodford
Stursdon Cross
Stanbury Mouth
Hollamoor
Stursdon
Broxwater
Lower Sharpnose Point
GCHQ Morwenstow
Taylor's Cross
Aldercombe
Darracott
Steeple Point
Coombe
Coombe Valley Nature Trail
Camp
Kilkhampton
Kilkhampton Castle
ST JAMES
Camp
Thurdon
Duckpool
Stowe Barton
Penstowe
B3254
Lymsworthy
Houndapit
Stibb
Tumulus
Sandy Mouth
Scadghill
Killock
Hassaford
Lopthorne
Hi
Pig
Menachurch Point
Dunsmouth
Rhude Cross
Moreton Pound
Pucklan
Northcott Mouth
Northcott
Camp
Camp
Norton
Venn
Poughill
Maer
ST OLAF
Bush
Hersham

A B C D E F

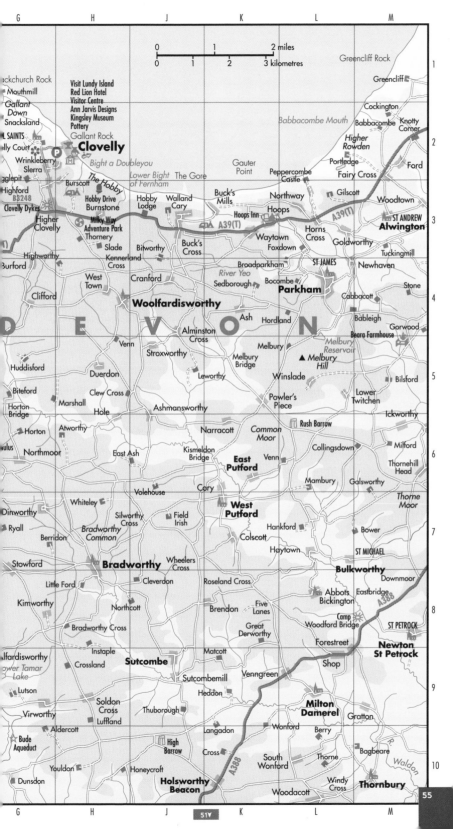

0   1   2 miles
0   1   2   3 kilometres

Greencliff Rock
Greencliff

ackchurch Rock
Mouthmill
Cockington
Gallant Down
Snacksland
Babbacombe Mouth
Babbacombe
Knotty Corner
L SAINTS
Higher Rowden
Visit Lundy Island
Red Lion Hotel
Visitor Centre
Ann Jarvis Designs
Kingsley Museum
Pottery
Gallant Rock
Portledge
Ford
lly Court
Wrinkleberry
Slerra
Clovelly
Bight a Doubleyou
Fairy Cross
gglepit
Highford
The Gore
Gauter Point
Peppercombe Castle
Gilscott
Woodtown
Clovelly Dykes
Burscott
Lower Bight of Fernham
Buck's Mills
Northway
A39(T)
St ANDREW
Alwington
B3248
Hobby Drive
Burnstone
Hobby Lodge
Walland Cary
Hoops Inn
Hoops
Horns Cross
Goldworthy
Tuckingmill
Higher Clovelly
Milky Way Adventure Park
Thornery
Bitworthy
Buck's Cross
Waytown
Foxdown
Newhaven
Highworthy
Slade
Kennerland Cross
Cranford
Broadparkham
St JAMES
Cabbacott
Stone
Burford
West Town
River Yeo
Bocombe
Parkham
Clifford
Sedborough
Bableigh
Gorwood
Woolfardisworthy
Ash
Hordland
Beara Farmhouse
D E V O N
Alminston Cross
Melbury Reservoir
Venn
Stroxworthy
Melbury
▲ *Melbury Hill*
Duerdon
Melbury Bridge
Bilsford
Huddisford
Leworthy
Winslade
Lower Twitchen
Biteford
Clew Cross
Powler's Piece
Ickworthy
Marshall
Hole
Ashmansworthy
Horton Bridge
Narracott
Rush Barrow
Horton
Atworthy
Common Moor
Collingsdown
Milford
ulus
East Ash
Kismeldon Bridge
Venn
Thornehill Head
Northmoor
East Putford
Mambury
Galsworthy
Volehouse
Cory
Thorne Moor
Dinworthy
Whiteley
West Putford
Ryall
Silworthy Cross
Field Irish
Hankford
Bower
Berridon
Bradworthy Common
Colscott
St MICHAEL
Stowford
Haytown
Bulkworthy
Downmoor
Bradworthy
Wheelers Cross
Roseland Cross
Abbots Bickington
Eastbridge
Little Ford
Cleverdon
Kimworthy
Brendon
Five Lanes
Camp
Woodford Bridge
St PETROCK
Northcott
Great Derworthy
Bradworthy Cross
Forestreet
Instaple
Matcott
Newton St Petrock
lfardisworthy
Crossland
Sutcombe
Shop
ower Tamar Lake
Sutcombemill
Venngreen
Lutson
Heddon
Milton Damerel
Gratton
Virworthy
Soldon Cross
Thuborough
Luffland
Wonford
Berry
Bude Aqueduct
Aldercott
Langadon
South Wonford
Thorne
Bagbeare
Waldon
Youldon
High Barrow
Cross
A388
Dunsdon
Honeycroft
Holsworthy Beacon
Woodacott
Windy Cross
Thornbury

Sir Christopher Wallpainting, Poughill

The Grenville Window, Kilkhampton Church

MORWENSTOW

Famous for Richard Stephen Hawker (1803-75), the eccentric and original vicar-poet, and originator of harvest festivals. A compassionate man, he would stalk the wild coast in beaver hat, fishermen's long boots and yellow cloak in search of shipwrecked sailors. Many are buried in his churchyard. And to stir his congregation he would dress as a mermaid. Hawker's Hut, made up of driftwood, stands on the edge of the cliffs. The Rectory Tea Rooms are opposite the church entrance. (B7)

WHERE TO STAY, EAT, DRINK & BE MERRY...

Bush Inn. Historic C13 Freehouse with log fires and flag stone floors offers fine ales and is developing a growing reputation as a fine, dining pub with its new, bright restaurant. Country B & B and self-catering accommodation. (C7) 01288 331242 www.bushinnmorwenstow.com

Rectory Tea Rooms. Savour old England at its very best: Cornish cream teas and farmhouse hospitality. Overlooks RS Hawker's famous church, and in the dip below the parking area, the Old Vicarage. Open daily Apr-Oct 11-5. (B7) 01288 331251 www.rectory-tearooms.co.uk

The Old Vicarage. To gauge the RS Hawker Experience you must stay here in his former home. Your hosts are a mine of information. Comfortable B & B with mounds of home cooking. Carrow's Stable to let. (B7) 01288 331369 www.rshawker.co.uk

WHAT TO SEE & VISIT...

Church of St John The Baptist. Impressive Norman doorway with vulgar heads of men and beast on the porch, original wagon roof and wall painting remains. C16 Rood Screen. Bench ends. Overlooking the Atlantic. (B7)

Combe Valley Nature Trail. The route starts at Combe Cottages and takes you through a green and peaceful wooded valley, rich in oak woods, honeysuckle and birdlife - buzzards, woodpeckers, dippers... Nearby Stowe Barton (National Trust property), home of Sir Richard Grenville (see Celebrities), County Sheriff of Cornwall in 1577 who was immortalised in Tennyson's poem 'The Revenge.' (C8)

Kilkhampton Church (St James). Norman South doorway. Perpendicular church of late C15 with superb collection of carved bench ends. Grenville family tombs. Fine East window. Jacobean pulpit. (E9)

Poughill Church. Carved bench ends with large wall painting of St Christopher repainted by Frank Salisbury RA in pretty village. (C10)

Tamar Lake Country Lakes. Fisherman's paradise, trout and coarse; boats for hire for sailing/windsurfing. (F8)

927   King Athelstan decrees the Tamar to be the boundary between Anglo-Saxon Wessex and Celtic Cornwall

981   Padstow Monastery destroyed by a "host of Danes"

The Beach, Hartland Quay

COASTAL FOOTPATH...

**Marsland Mouth to
Northcott Mouth**

Approx. 14 miles. A remote
and wild coastline; the rocks,
razor sharp and contorted,
the pathway hard going, yet
exhilarating and rewarding.
Rest at Morwenstow and visit
the church and tearoom or Inn.
Onwards to pass beside RS
Hawker's Hut. Two miles on,
the white dish aerials of GCHQ,
then into Duckpool where a
path leads up to the Coombe
Valley Nature Trail. At low
tide one can follow the sands to
Bude, or take the cliff top path.

BEACHES AND SURFING...

Welcombe Mouth. Haunt
of cruel Coppinger, an C18
smuggler. Pebbles, rocks and
sandy beaches at LT. (C5)

Stanbury Mouth. 15 minute
walk from P to isolated beach,
sand, swift currents, HZ at LT.
(B8)

Duckpool. Rocky with strong
currents. Footpath leads to
Coombe Valley Nature Trail.
P. Surfing - LT R breaks off the
rocks. (B9)

Sandy Mouth. Expansive
beach, rocky at HT, swift
currents, superb rock formations
at top of beach. HZ at LT. Bass
fishing, P/café. Surfing - Clean
with good beach breaks. Fine,
small swell, off banks. Beware
rip tides. (B9)

Northcott Mouth. Extensive
sand, pebbles and some
fascinating rock formations.
Bathing HZ two hours either
side of LT. P. Surfing - Banks at
LT create heavy hollow waves
backing off at HT except on
big swells. Good R hander at N
side. Beware rip tides. (B10)

Crooklets Beach, Bude

GCHQ, Morwenstow

1059   **Bishop's Seat of Devon and Cornwall appointed to Exeter (until 1876)**   1066   **Battle of Hastings starts Norman rule**

These images were discovered in the Archives of The Castle (Museum), Bude

Mike Dobie, Fannie & Fox, Penryn

0   1   2 miles
0   1   2   3 kilometres

Wide
Sa
Wanson M
Foxhole Point
Millook Haven
Outdoor Adventure
Cancleave Strand
M
Millook
Common
Dizzard Point
Trebarfoot
Chipman Strand
Cornish
Way
Dizzard
Tresmorn
Trengayor
St Gennys
Camp
Trewint
Pencannow
Point
ST GENESIUS
Treworgie
Bray's Point
Tren
Crackington
Haven
Cambeak
Coxford
Rosecare
Little Strand
Hallagather
Wainhouse
Corner
Be
The Strangles
Trevigue
Crackington
Voter Run
Baypark
Rosecu
Villa
Trevigue Wildlife Conservation
Rusey Beach
High
Cliff
Pengold
Pencuke
Camp
Buckator
Round
Hayes
Tumuli
Newton
Tresparrett
Posts
B3263
Trengur
Gull Rock
Camp
Collamoor
Beeny Sisters
Ringford
Head
Fire Deacon Point
Tresparrett
Downs
Cansford
Trevillian
Pentargon
Beeny
Trebyla
B3263
Cocksport
Marshgate
Cornish
Way
Penally Point (NT)
Farm Shop & Cafe
Cardew
Wilapark (NT)
Museum of Witchcraft
ST JULIOT'S
Hennett
Mill
Short
Island
The Old Parsonage
Valency
Valley (NT)
Trevilla
Long
Island
Boscastle
Napoleon Inn
Bottreaux
Castle
The Old Rectory
ST DENIS
Otterham
Trevalga
ST SYMPHORIAN'S
Treworld
R. Valency
Lesnewth
Trevilla
Down
Otterham
Down
Roose
Cross
B3263
ST PETROCK
MINSTER
Trelash
Polrunny
ST MICHAEL
Helset
Hallgarden
Trethevey
Tredorne
Tregrylls
St Nectan's Glen
Copplestone
Otterham
Station
Halgabron
Reddivallen
Tregray
Waterfall & Chapel
Vendown
Hallwell
Tumuli
Tumuli
St Nectan's
Kieve
Waterpit
Down
Hendra
Trenale
Cross
Hendraburnick
Tich Barrow
Tumulus
Hallwor

44▼

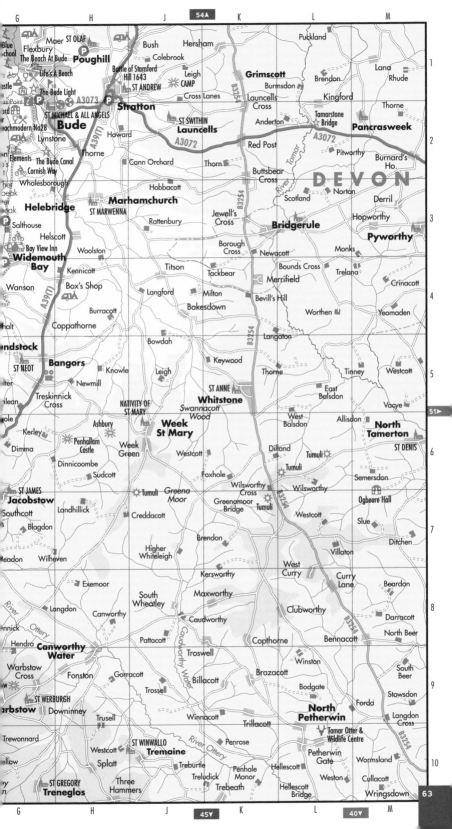

BUDE

A seaside resort first developed by the Victorians that has witnessed, of late, much resurgence, in no small part due to the popularity of surfing and beach activities. The long, extensive beaches, just a short walk from the town centre, and those to the south and north of the town, are breathtaking. The coastline has been the sad scene of many shipwrecks - 80 ships were foundered or wrecked between 1824-74. The town abounds with surf shops, hostels, countless coffee shops, and when the Low Pressure is in force the beaches are populated with black shadows, in summer and winter. It is the most accessible of Cornish surf resorts, and is host to 5 surf schools. Canal, carnival and fete - August (third week). 'Blessing of the Sea' - Aug. E/C Th. (H2) www.bude.co.uk www.visitbude.info

WHAT TO SEE & VISIT...

Atlantic Highway. The route into Cornwall from the Clovelly Roundabout, North Devon. A fast road with open views and flowing bends popular with motorcyclists. So, beware of bikers and the speed cams that pursue them. (G3)

Old Canal. Built in 1819-26 at a length of 43 miles (61km). For 60 years used to transport coal and lime inland, and to export grain and slate. Killed off by the railways. Best sections are at Marhamchurch, Hobbacott Down and Werrington. (G1) www.bude-canal.co.uk

The Castle Bude. Museum celebrates the heritage of Bude and Stratton with a tableaux of interactive displays and exhibits: Canal, shipwrecks, lifeboats and railways. New "Gurney" exhibition of Bude's Forgotten Genius, Sir Goldsworth Gurney. Café. Open daily, all year from 10. (G1) 01288 357300

WHERE TO EAT, DRINK & BE MERRY...

The Bay View Inn, Marine Drive. Surfers' hangout overlooking the roaring Atlantic. With chic, modern bedrooms. Encompassing three Driftwood Surf & Beach Hut restaurants; wholesome fayre from local farms for hungry surfers. (G3) 01288 361273

Life's A Beach, Summerleaze Beach. Bistro restaurant offers all types of food from locally caught sea bass, to burgers, and pizzas. A great place to watch the sunset, and to relax after a day in the surf. Open daily in season. (G1) 01285 355222 www.lifesabeach.info

LIGHT BITES...

Wander around the streets of Bude and be amazed at the number of Eateries. Herewith a selection for Starters: **Scrummies Café** for fresh fish direct from Cliff's own pots, lobster his speciality. For a burger, try **Revolution**, a coffee, multiple choices: **Arabica, Cornish Ice Cream** and **Bellinis**...wander down to the Canal, you have the **Olive Tree**. On the other side of town overlooking Crooklets Beach is **Roses Kitchen** - its quirky, arty and wholesome. If in need of a pint and some live music, **Bar 35** on Queen Street.

WHERE TO STAY...

Beachmodern. There are five locations to choose from, each is in the Bude area and you get 5-star luxury, stylish self-catering. Ideal for large families, extended house parties and those seeking space. (G1) 01288 275006 www.beachmodern.com

Elements, Marine Drive. A well equipped boutique hotel in a pretty coastal setting. Bar-bistro, terrace, gymnasium and leisure facilities. Offers 'Learn to Surf' breaks with the Raven Surf School. (G2) 01288 352386 www.elements-life.co.uk

North Shore Bude, 57 Killerton Rd. A specialist surf hostel with 12 rooms to choose from; ideal for family parties, couples and groups on a budget. (G1) 01288 354256 www.northshorebude.com

The Beach, Summerleaze Crescent. A little slice of New England-Boutique style has arrived in North Cornwall. With great sea views, fresh, airy rooms and precision cooked cuisine. (G1) 01288 389000 www.thebeachatbude.co.uk

STRATTON

A pretty village with a long and fascinating history. Now very much a suburb of Bude. C15 church. Battle of Stamford Hill, 1643. (H2)

CHURCHES TO VISIT...

Crackington Haven Church. Dedicated to Celtic missionary St Gennys. Norman origins. C12 font of Purbeck stone. Bench ends. Headstone inscribed by Eric Gill. (D6)

Launcells Church. Fortunate to be the only Cornish church not tampered with by the Victorians. Wall painting and 60 carved bench ends shown off in the light interior. Monument. Fine wagon roof. A haven of solitude beside the little stream in a wooded valley. Magical. (J2)

The Beach ss

Sandy Mouth

On The Turn

Outdoor Adventure ss

XTREME SPORTS...

Big Blue Surf School, Summerleaze Beach.
Learn, improve, excel at one of Europe's top schools with National Team coach, Jon Price. Open to all, no matter your age, size and ability. Open all year. (G1) 01288 331764 www.bigbluesurfschool.co.uk

Cold Water Surfer

Bude Surfing Experience, Summerleaze Crescent.
Surf and SUP lessons, board hire & private lessons. (G1) 07779 117746 www. budesurfingexperience.co.uk

Outdoor Adventure, Atlantic Court.
Activity centre for the ultimate coastal experience: coasteering, surfing, coastal traversing, sea cliff abseils, rock climbing, sea kayaking. Activity Weekends. Accommodation. Tuition. (F5) 01288 362900 www.outdooradventure.co.uk

Raven Surf School.
Mike Raven is a former surf champion whose school caters for all levels; from beginners' groups to 1 to 1 tuition. Groups out of season. (G1) 01288 353693 www.ravensurf.co.uk

BOSCASTLE
A charming and attractive village within a steep valley leads down to a sinuous and dramatic harbour. A safe haven on a treacherous coastline, but despite this, it remains an extremely difficult destination to navigate into (especially on a stormy night). More recently, featured in the national news following the horrific flooding on the 16th August 2004. Cars and caravans were swept into the sea. Houses and shops were destroyed. The Royal Naval helicopter squadron from Chivenor was magnificent in its efforts to save life and limb. There are two cafés down by the harbour if you need a bite to eat: The Pilchard Cellar Café (National Trust) and the Harbour Light Café, beside the YHA. October Festival. (B9) www.boscastlecornwall.org.uk www.visitboscastleandtintagel. com

Entrance to Boscastle

WHAT TO SEE & VISIT...

Boscastle's Farm Shop & Café. Home reared Devon cattle and livestock produce award-winning beef, lamb and pork. All-day breakfasts, lunches, teas in café. A mile out of the village beside the B3263. Open 9-5. (B8) 01840 250827 www.boscastlefarmshop.co.uk

Boscastle's National Trust Visitor Centre, Shop & Café. If you are visiting this corner of North Cornwall there is no better place to begin your adventures. More a hive of fascinating facts and information, with attractive tableaux illustrating the coast and its natural phenomena. Books and gifts galore, plus the delightful, Pilchard Cellar Café. Open daily, all year. (B9) 01840 250010

Museum Of Witchcraft. A long established museum, of 50-years, holds the world's largest collection of genuine witchcraft, related artefacts. With over 3,000 books and, since 2000, the Richel Collection. Open daily Easter to Halloween, 10.30-6, 11.30-6 on Su. (B8) 01840 250111 www.museumofwitchcraft.com

Valency Valley (NT). There's a circular walk from Boscastle. A place of romance and literary history, where Thomas Hardy met his first wife, Emma Gifford. He was to return here after her death in 1913, and to write some of his finest poetry. It is rich in wildlife with meadows of wild flowers, oak woodlands and a flowing stream. (C9)

WHERE TO EAT & DRINK...

Napoleon Inn (the 'Nap'), High St. (Upper Village). A full range of beers feeds three beer gardens and two bars - public and officers. Boney's Bistro provides fresh fish, homemade soups and puddings. Children (restaurant) and dogs welcome. Friday music nights. (B9) 01840 250204 www.napoleoninn.co.uk

The Wellington ('Welly') - The Harbour. A traditional Cornish hostelry that has seen much renovation since the floods, yet, maintains its character with log fires, a cosy bar, and a warm welcome. You can eat in the bar or the restaurant. 14-bedrooms with bath/shower. (B9) 01840 250202

WHERE TO STAY...

Reddivallen, Trevalga. Farmhouses don't come more solid than this one. It's straight out of Poldark! The Brewers breed fine Hereford cattle and produce organic beef on their 300-acre farm. The bedrooms are bright and comfortable enjoying splendid views. (A9) 01840 250854 www.redboscastle.com

The Old Parsonage, Forrabury. This is an elegant Georgian property providing 5-star quality B&B, art courses, and spacious bedrooms of great style and comfort. Out of High Season evening meals are an option. (B9) 01840 250339 www.old-parsonage.com

The Old Rectory, St Juliot. This is where Thomas Hardy (poet and novelist) met his beloved Emma Gifford who later became his wife, and where he returned on her death to write some of his greatest

1086   The Domesday Book records that Robert controls 277 Cornish manors

1086   The Domesday Book records there are 340 manors in the county, 5,500 working males and a population of 27,000

Widemouth Sand

poetry. If you seek a luxurious B&B with Green credentials and literary connections, none better. (B9) 01840 250225 www.stjuliot.com

Trevigue B&B. A solid C18 farmhouse (hamlet) on the North Cornish cliffs. With bright bedrooms, log fires and slate floors, all surround a cobbled courtyard. Restaurant. Self-catering. 01840 230492 www.trevigue.com

COASTAL FOOTPATH...

Bude to Boscastle
Ascend to Compass Point for extensive views northwards. The path overlooks reefs, buttresses and pinnacles. Easy going to Widemouth Sands. Through car park, up Penhalt Cliff and on to Millook Haven with cliffs of contorted slate. Rough ascent to Dizzard Point (500ft), prone to landslides, so beware, on to the contorted rock forms of Pencannow Point. What follows is an easy descent to Crackington Haven. It's a hard slog up to Cambeak - rewarded with views across from Hartland Point to Trevose Head. Climbing beside further land-slipped sections, passing jagged cliffs, and The Strangles (beach), scene of many shipwrecks, to High Cliff, at 731ft the highest cliff in Cornwall (although slumping has created a massive sloping undercliff so it lacks the drama of a precipice)

and supposedly a favourite courting and riding spot for Thomas Hardy and his first wife, Emma Gifford. Then to Beeny Cliff, the only headland carved from Chert, a tough black flint-like rock, and often below, basking seals. Along to Pentaragon Waterfall, falling 100ft down a deep chasm. And, then, to Boscastle Harbour for refreshments, via Penally Point, and below fine views of the tortuous, harbour entrance.

BEACHES AND SURFING...

Bude - Crooklets Beach.
Spacious firm sands at LT, bathing HZ at LT. S-B hire, café, Rosie's Kitchen, LG. Surfing - Fine, short breaks for body boarders. With hollow sandbanks waves flow at all stages of tide. At HT Tower Rock produces a good shallow wave. Try Wrangles Rocks to N at LT. (G1)

Bude - Summerleaze Beach.
Popular surfing beach, roomy firm sands and bathing pool at LT. S-B hire. Access. Surfing - HT sheltered from SW wind. R breaks into harbour. Take care, can be steep. Beware strong rips. Ls at LT. Hollow fast wave off the Barrels. (G1)

Bude - Middle Beach. Surfing - Good Ls and Rs with swells up to 6ft. Popular with locals. (G1)
Bude - Upton. Surfing - Good Rs and Ls on the N and S side.

Difficult access down cliff. (G1)
Widemouth Sand. Large sandy beach, rock pools, HZ at LT. Tent and S-B hire/WC/P/café. Surfing - A popular break for all abilities, at all stages of the tide. Best up to 6ft. (G4)

Millook Haven. Secluded cove, shelves steeply - HZ bathing. (F4)

Crackington Haven. Popular bathing beach, sands and rocks. HZ at LT. S-B hire/WC/cafés. Surfing - Sheltered from N winds. Holds big swells. Good waves break off at HT. (D6)

The Strangles. Steep descent down 700ft cliffs. Rocks, sand at LT, swift currents; bathing very HZ. (C7)

Bossinney Haven. P in village, steep 1/2 mile descent to little coves below huge cliffs. Popular surfing. (B8)

WHAT TO SEE & VISIT ON EDGE OF MAP, NEAR LAUNCESTON...

Tamar Otter & Wildlife Centre. Set in 20 acres of mature woodlands where you will see Asian and British otters in semi-natural enclosures, as well as deer, owls, wallabies and waterfowl. Tearoom with homemade food. Gift shop. Open daily Apr-Oct 10.30-6. (L10) 01566 785646 www.tamarotters.co.uk

0   1   2 miles
0   1   2   3 kilometres

The Mouls
Newland   Rumps Point
Por
Com
Head
Pentire Point
Pentire
New
Polzeath
Hayle Bay   Tren
Padstow   The Waterfron
Bay
Stepper   Polzeath
Crams   Point   Tregli
Butter Hole   Mowhay Café   Trebetheric
Daymer   St Moritz Hotel
Gunver Head   Bay   Trewiston
Lellisick   Brea Hill   ST ENODOC
Pityme
Merope   Porthmissen   Crugmeer
Rocks   Bridge   Rock
Trevose Head   Mother Ivey's   Tregirls   St Enodoc Bar & Hotel
Quies   Bay   Porthmissen   Prideaux   Penr
Dinas Head   Mother Ivey Cottage   Harlyn   Trethillick   Place
Trevose   Bay   Farm Shop   Stoptide
Booby's Bay   Trevone   Treator   Porthilly   Gallery
Ancient Burial   Harlyn   Padstow Museum   Cove   Porthilly   Co
Ground   Windmill   Padstow
St Constantine's Chapel   Rick Stein's Café   Cant
Constantine Bay   Constantine   Seafood Restaurant   National Lobster Hatchery   Hill
Bay   St Petroc's Hotel   Dinas
Treyarnon Bay   Cornish Arms   ST MERRYN   No6 Restaurant   Treretherh
Towan   Trerethern   Camel
Pepper Cove   Treyarnon   St Merryn   Tregonce   Trail
Shop   Tregavone   Halwyn
Fox Cove   Trehemborne   Trevarrick   Bodelli
Minnows Islands   Carnevas   Rosken   Molesworth
Porthcothan Beach   Cornish   Manor   Burgois
Trescore   Way   Tregonna   ST PETROCK   Trevance   Per
Islands   Trevean   Roscullion   The Old Mill House
Porth Mear   Porthcothan   Little Petherick   ST IDA
Park   Old Macdonald's   Mellingey   St Issey   Trewince
Head   Pentire   Farm   Trenance   Hawksf
Tumuli   Trevemedar   Treburrick   Penrose

Long Island

1

The Sisters
Willapark
Barras Nose

Trethevey

Tintagel
The Old Post Office (NT)
King Arthur's Great Halls
Visitor Centre

Tintagel Castle
The Island
Tintagel Head

Bossiney
St Nectan's Glen

Lye
Rock

62►

ST MATERIANA

Halgabron

Dunderhole Point

Glebe Cliff

Tintagel

Treven   Trenale

2

Hole Beach

Tregatta

Truas

Treknow

Trebarwith

Gull Rock   **Strand**
Dennis Point   Mill House Inn
  Port William Inn

Trewarmett

Backways Cove
Start Point

Trebarwith

3

Trecarne

Tregonnick Tail

Treligga

Rockhead

Tregardock Beach

Delabole
ST JOHN

4

Trerubies Cove

Tregardock

Slate Quarry
Pengelly

Jacket's Point

Tregragon

Delamere

Westdowns

PORT ISAAC
Nathan Outlaw
The Old School Hotel
The Slipway Hotel

Port Isaac Bay   Delabole Point
Ranie Point

Dannonchapel

Trewalder

5

Kellan
Head

Scarnor
Point

Varley Head

Tresungers
Point
ST PETER

Bounds Cliff

Dinnabroad

Trewennan

yden
oint

Port Isaac

Portquin

Roscarrock

Port Gaverne
Cellars

Treore

St Teath

ST TETHA

Knightsmill

Trefreock
Pottery

Trewetha

Treburgett

Tregreenwell

6

Bee Centre
Wave 7 Studio

orteath
Mesmear

Longcross
Victorian
Garden

Cross Shaft

Trelights

Tresungers

Pendoggett

Tregeare Rounds
Trekee

Trewiggett
Trevorrian

Cornish Tippi Holidays

Whitewell

Trewethan

Treveighan

ST ENDELLIENTA

Plain Street

B3314

St Endellion

Treharrock

Trewane

Pengenna

44►

Gunvenna

Trevathan Farm
Trevathan

Trentinney

Poltreworgey

Trelill

7

18
anger

St Minver

Tregellist

Pennytinney
Lanow

Penvose

Tregwarmond

Trewethern

ST JAMES

Bokelly

Trewen

rizzick

Trevine

Rooke

St Kew

Trequite

St Kew Inn

St Tudy Inn

St Tudy

ST TUDIAS

8

Blakes
Keiro
Old Windmill

Tredower

Maltsters
Arms

**Chapel
Amble**

Pellengarrow

**St Kew
Highway**

Kellygreen

Wetherham

Amble

Lower
Amble

18

Trethevan

Palglaze

Penhale

elver

Dinham

Treworman

River

Benbole

Cross
Hill

9

Tregunna
Camel Trail
Trevanson

Burniere

Bodieve

Tregorden

Kelly

Castle Killibury

Three Holes
Cross

Tregarden

Tregaddock

Hendra

St Mabyn

Longstone

onton
itecross

A39(T)

C15 Bridge

Trenant
ST CONAN

Trevarner

Trevilder

ST
MABENA

Menkee

Trequites

St Breock

Royal Cornwall
Showground
ST BREOCK

Wadebridge

Eglos Pottery

Egloshayle

Clapper
Sladesbridge

Lower
Croan

Croanford

Tredethy

C15 Bridge

Hellandbridge
Pottery

10

Inscribed
Stone

Polmorla

Nanscow

Treneague

Treraven

Pendavey

Wood Design
Tredannick

Trescowe
Pencarrow House
& Gardens

Park

Helland

71

Padstow Harbour

PADSTOW

A labyrinth of narrow alleyways and picturesque houses, and a safe haven on the treacherous North Coast. May Day heralds the arrival of the Hobby Horse ('Obby 'Oss) who prances and dances the streets, taunting young, and not so young, maidens. A celebration of spring fever and the coming of summer. C16 Raleigh's Court House on South Quay. C15 church. Boat trips. Centre of fine cuisine with many restaurants, notably Rick Stein's various enterprises. Some have labelled the town Padstein. Understandable, but a little unfair. True, he may have dominated our TV screens for an age but his success has rippled out across Cornwall and made this old county a destination for lovers of sea food and local produce. It is worth walking away from the crowded harbour front and exploring the side streets or heading out for the coastal footpath to the nearby beaches. The Camel Trail starts here and you can hire a bicycle from one of the hire centres located beside the car park at the bottom of the hill. (E8) www.padstow.com www.padstowlive.com

WHAT TO SEE & DO...

Beyond The Sea, Middle Street. Demelza Prettejohn has built her reputation by having the eye for an investment, and for gaining the trust of her artists. Paintings, glass and furniture. Open daily. (E6) 01841 533588 www.beyondthesea.co.uk

Drang Gallery, 8-9 Drang. It's different. The artwork tends to be brash, and it makes a statement. Very contemporary (not your Giotto or Modigliani), more likely to be a Damien Hirst print, or Peter Blake etching. 01841 533114 (E8) www.thedranggallery.com

Jane Reeves Gallery, 11 Lanadwell St. Housed in a 200-year old Cornish town house, the gallery features Jane's beautiful painted fused glass plus ceramics, jewellery and paintings, locally sourced. Open daily. (E8) 01841 533435 www.janereevesgallery.co.uk

National Lobster Hatchery, South Quay. The fascinating world of lobsters and their environment, and importantly, pioneering marine conservation, research and education. Sponsor a Lobster. Open daily from 10. Visitor Centre. (E8) 01841 533877 www. nationallobsterhatchery.co.uk

Padstow Museum, Market Place. Maritime, local interest - 'Obby 'Oss, WW1 memorabilia and ephemera. Open East to Oct M-F 10.30-4.30, Sa 10.30-1. (E8) 01841 532752 www.padstowmuseum.co.uk

Prideaux Place. Home of the Prideaux-Brune family since 1592. Filled with treasures, pictures, portraits, porcelain and exquisite furniture. Location for many of Rosamund Pilcher's TV series. Open Easter week, then 8 May - 6 Oct Su-Th 1.30-4. Grounds and Tearoom 12.30-5. (E8) 01841 532411 www.prideauxplace.co.uk

Stein's Fisheries, South Quay.
The ultimate fishmonger where you can buy fresh fish and crustacea, and freshly made sandwiches. Your introduction to Padstein! Open daily from 10. (E8)

WHERE TO EAT, DRINK & BE MERRY IN PADSTOW...

Burger & Fish Charcoal Grill, 1A The Strand. BBQ style cooking on an open charcoal fire; cream teas, lobster bakes, delish burgers, Open daily 12-9.30pm. (D9) 01841 532884 www.burgersandfish.com

Rick Stein's Café, 10 Middle St. Light lunches, coffees, pastries and a reasonably priced three-course dinner each evening. B&B. (E8) 01841 532700 www.rickstein.com

Padstow Farm Shop, Trethillick Farm. In need of organic beef, fresh lamb and pork sausages, cakes, ale and Cornish wines? Then, make a trip down a country lane to this emporia of delights. (D8) 01841 533060 www. padstowfarmshop.co.uk

Padstow Seafood School, South Quay. He's done it again! All you ever wanted to know about preparing a good lunch - from filleting a plaice, to stir-frying squid. A delight for all amateur chefs, and their ever grateful dinner guests. (D9) 01841 533250 www.rickstein.com/school

Prawn On The Lawn, 11 Duke Street. A fishmonger and seafood bar, in one, and what a brilliant combination, breaks up Mr Stein's monopoly on seafood sales. Open Tu-Sa 10-10. (E8) 01841 532223 www.prawnonthelawn.com

Stein's Deli, South Quay. Treat yourself to hot takeaway seafood dishes and stir fries. A great destination to head to after a night under canvas, a rip tide surf, or a head-butting gale on the coast path. Open daily 10-5. (E8)

Stein's Fish & Chips, South Quay. Cod is sourced from well-managed Icelandic stock, haddock is line caught, plus plenty of locally-caught fish. Breakfast 10-11.30, Lunch 12-2.30, Dinner 5-8pm. (E8)

St Petroc's Hotel & Bistro, New St. Stein's smaller hotel has been renovated to provide a light and airy feel. As you'd expect, there's plenty of seafood, and meat and veggie dishes, too. (E8) 01841 532700

No 6 Restaurant & Rooms. Paul Ainsworth's smart, chic dining establishment no doubt taking advantage of the Stein-Effect. Private dining rooms available for parties etc. (E8) 01841 532093 www.number6inpadstow.co.uk

The Seafood Restaurant. Needs no introduction. Rick Stein's restaurant has established a reputation since opening 40 years ago. The fish comes, literally, straight off the boats in the harbour (via a judicious by-your-leave in the Kitchen) and onto your plate.

Essential to book unless you have the self-confidence and charm of my late Father, Derek, who refused to book - he was rarely turned away. (E8) 01841 532700 www.rickstein.com

LIGHT BITES...

Ben's Crib Box Café, South Quay Car Park. You can't miss it. Eat in breakfast or take away burgers and baps. The alternative to posh fresh fish! Open Tu-Sa. (D9) 07851 604350

Bin Two, South Quay. If you are searching for that special cup of coffee, or if you believe Champagne can be drunk at any time of the day, then pop in to Bin Two. Opens at 10am till late. (D9) 01841 532022 www. bintwo.com

Rojanos, 9 Mill Square. Italian style coffee shop, or if you want a simpler meal, or a takeaway; pasta and pizzas, or smaller portions for children, this is it. Open daily 10am 'til late. (D9) 01841 532796 www. rojanos.co.uk

The Basement, 11 Broad St. Watch the world go by in their large tent affording harbour views. Coffee, cakes, wines; lunch and dinner. Open daily. (D9) 01841 532846 www.thebasement.co.uk

The Great Hall, Prideaux Place ss

The Seafood Restaurant ss

1189   **Prince John given Cornwall with the exception of Launceston Castle**   1201   **King John grants a Royal Charter to protect and exempt the tinners from normal laws and taxes**

WHERE TO STAY...

Althea House (Library), 64 Church St. Set in the oldest part of town opposite the Church this B&B has all the latest mod cons, and comfy bedrooms, too. No children or pets. (D9) 01841 532579 www.altheahouse-padstow.co.uk

Coswarth House, 12 Dennis Rd. Escape the hustle and bustle of Padstow to this historic house affording breathtaking views across the Camel Estuary. This luxurious and friendly B&B provides charm, style and delicious breakfasts. (D9) 07907 626084 www.coswarthhouse.com

Rick Steins. They have 40 plush bedrooms scattered around Padstow; in the Seafood Restaurant, St Petroc's Hotel, St Edmunds House, Rick Stein's Café, Bryn Cottage and Prospect House. All have crisp linen, superb bathrooms and indulgent beds. The ultimate Restaurant with Rooms experience. 01841 532700 www.rickstein.com

OUTSIDE PADSTOW...
WHERE TO STAY, EAT, DRINK & BE MERRY...

Cornish Arms, St Merryn. Simple Cornish pub run by – wait for it – Rick Stein. Pub grub and St Austell Brewery beers abound. (C9) 01841 532700

Trevathan Farm. Strawberry farm with shop and restaurant. Fruit in season. Pets corner. Self-catering cottages. Open daily. (J7) 01208 880248 www.trevathanfarm.com

Mother Ivey Cottage, Trevose Head. Former 'Fish Cellar' used for processing the day's catch stands on the cliff edge in an enviable position overlooking an emerald-turquoise sea. The interior style reminds me of a Victorian fishing lodge. Hunting prints adorn the walls. Two simple guest rooms. Evening meals an option. The East Wing provides self-catering accommodation for 8. (B8) 01841 520329 www.trevosehead.co.uk

PORT ISAAC

A charming north coast fishing inlet and old port made famous by the TV series, Doc Martin. Hence, the new restaurants, tea rooms and gift shops. A plethora of rental cottages, and exodus of locals who cannot afford to live here anymore. A steep street runs down to the beach and harbour, hazardous when a northerly wind blows. Lobster fishing centre. Trips for mackerel and parking (charge) on beach at LT. **Just Shellfish** sell fresh fish, dressed crab and lobster, beside the Slipway. Three restaurants to choose from down by the harbour. St Endellion Music Festival in Aug. (H5) www.portisac-online.co.uk

WHAT TO SEE & VISIT...

Doc Martin's Surgery. This pretty little house overlooks the harbour and is a few steps up the hill past the Pottery. It looks empty, as do many of the houses used in the TV series. Large's Restaurant and the school teacher's (Martin's wife) cottage, all appear isolated and await the clapper sound of "Action" and coats of new paint. (H6)

Port Isaac Pottery. Individual one-off stoneware pots influenced by the sea and Cornish landscape. Seascape paintings by Barbara Hawkins. Chapel Café and self-catering. Open daily East-Oct 10-4. (H6) 01208 880625 www.portisaacpottery.co.uk

WHERE TO STAY, EAT, DRINK & BE MERRY...

Port Gaverne Restaurant & Hotel. This is a formidable hostelry of style that offers delish food, comfort, a great ambience in a super location overlooking a quaint beach. (J5) 01208 880244 www.portgavernehotel.co.uk

Restaurant Nathan Outlaw, 6 New Rd. New restaurant overlooks the sea and car park at top of town. A La Carte menu, yet specialises in local fish and meat dishes. His, simpler, Fish Kitchen is down in the Harbour. (J6) 01208 880896 www.nathan-outlaw.com

The Old School Hotel & Restaurant. The location for Doc Martin's school is set half way down the steep hill, the position invites grand views across the pretty harbour. A hotel of character, for each wacky bedroom is different. No better place to relax and enjoy the slow tempo of a Cornish fishing village. Attractive restaurant with bright works of art, and a fair portion of fish dishes. (J6) 01208 880271 www.theoldschoolhotel.co.uk

The Slipway Hotel & Restaurant. Set in the middle of the village opposite the harbour and the local fish merchant who supplies the restaurant. Comfortable bedrooms, a bar and al fresco dining area will relax and endear you to this enchanting old fishing village. (J6) 01208 880264 www.portisaachotel.com

LIGHT BITES...

Starting from the top of the village, leading away from the car park, the café **Ruby Tuesday**. Take the right fork, and on your left Takeaway **fish'n chips** etc, and as you descend towards the harbour, the **Golden Lion Inn**, lovely unspoilt Cornish pub serving fine ales. Enter the harbour and on your left is **Outlaws Fish Kitchen**.

HARBOURS OF INTEREST...

Port Quin. A hamlet with few cottages on an inlet, pebble beach and C19 folly, Doyden Castle (NT). Invigorating clifftop walks. (G6)

Port Gaverne. C14 fishing village and C19 pilchard fishing and boat building centre, and exporter of Delabole slate. Remains of large pilchard cellars. Tiny cove. The Port Gaverne Hotel for refreshments, and a bed. (J6)

ROCK

This seaside community may well take on the mantle as the Cornish "Hamptons" or Cape Cod equivalent. It is where the chattering classes network, meet up with old friends and where families congregate, year on year. More recently the well off have bought into this village and new builds are, aplenty. Its location and popularity may well be because of the close proximity to the surf breaks of Polzeath, the ease of reaching the coastal footpath, the safe family beach at Daymer Bay, the gastronomic excesses of Padstow, the golf courses, the spa at St Moritz, and the Sailing Club. It has something to amuse, and retain the interest of all ages and temperaments, and if you are of a literary bent then the poetry and humour of John Betjeman may awaken your sensibilities. (F8)

WHERE TO STAY, EAT, DRINK & BE MERRY...

Mesmear, St Minver. Three chic, boutique-style barns are available to rent for holidays and short breaks. Ideal for parties of up to 10, 4 and 4.

Swimming pool. Private cook. (G7) 01208 869731 www.mesmear.co.uk

Mowhay Café & Restaurant, Trebetherick. Great place to stop for coffee, lunch or evening meal. Always interesting arts and crafts for sale. Open daily in season. (E7) 01208 863660

St Enodoc Hotel. Family-friendly hotel noted for its great location, comfort and superb cuisine, courtesy of Nathan Outlaw. Look out for the Special Breaks. (E8) 01208 863394 www.enodoc-hotel.co.uk

St Moritz Hotel, Trebetherick. Spanking new hotel, apartment and spa complex provides all the amenities you would expect from such a venture: gym, indoor pool, saunas etc, bar, games room and more. (E7) 01208 862242 www.stmoritzhotel.co.uk

LIGHT BITES...

Within the confines of the village you have the restaurant, **The Dining Room**, 01208 862622 www. thediningroomrock.co.uk and the Inn, the **Pityme Arms**. For those seeking a cofffee, and deli style substances, there is **Malcolm Barnecutt's** salad bar/coffee shop...and **Lewis's Deli & Coffee Shop**. Heading westwards towards the beach, on your right, **The Mariners**, public house and part of the Outlaw empire, opposite the Sailing Club. Further down towards the car park is another pub, **The Rock Inn**, open all year. Bottoms Up!

WHAT TO SEE & DO...

St Enodoc Church. C13 origins with a crooked spire. This church lay hidden beneath the dunes until it was dug out in 1863. The grave of Sir John Betjeman, poet and lover of North Cornwall lies here, too. I visited John's grave with my Irish Water Spaniel, Sam, a few weeks following his death. Flowers, post cards and the mound were still freshly dug, and before I could explain to Sam the richness of his verse and his quirky humour, he had cocked his leg on the postcard. Amused, John? (E7)

Porthilly Gallery. (F8) The location will inspire you to paint, and perhaps take home a signature of Cornwall's landscape. Open daily in season. Don't miss the cute Church! (F8) 01208 863844 www.porthillygallery.co.uk

XTREME SPORTS...

An increasing popular adrenaline sport that has found its natural home along the rugged extremities of Cornwall is, coasteering. Not for the faint hearted, the sport involves swimming, climbing and jumping along a section of coastline, exploring caves and gulleys along the way. Surely there is no better place to do this than along the nearly 300 miles of Cornish coastline.

Era Adventures, Polzeath. Try your hand at coasteering, stand-up paddle surfing, sea kayaking, rock climbing, kite surfing or plain old traditional surfing with this organised and knowledgeable company. (F6) 01208 862963 www.era-adventures.co.uk

Daymer Bay

| 1259 | Walter de Bronescombe, Bishop of Exeter dedicates 19 parish churches | 1256 | Glasney College is made the centre of ecclesiastical scholarship. |

TINTAGEL

Tintagel village itself, composed of a long and rather uninspiring high street peopled with gift shops and tearooms, exists solely to service visitors to Tintagel Castle. The setting is spectacular and strange and it's easy to fantasize about Merlin and magic. For remarkable views and a sense of Nature's violence, take a walk onto the Island and around the Castle, then out to both neighbouring outcrops: to Barras Nose and Willapark. Particularly spectacular on a stormy day. This is the perfect place to immerse yourself in Arthurian legend (enthusiastically patronised by German and Dutch visitors, but largely ignored by UK residents), as inspired by Geoffrey of Monmouth in the C12, and later by Tennyson's 'The Idylls of the King.' Summer Carnival. (M2)
www.tintagelweb.co.uk

SPECIAL PLACES TO VISIT IN TINTAGEL...

King Arthur's Great Hall & Hall of Chivalry.
A magnificent hall built in memory of King Arthur and his Knights, using 50 types of Cornish stone and 70 stained glass windows. The Arthurian Experience tells the story of Arthur and his Knights. Dogs welcomed. Open daily, summer 10-5, winter 11-dusk. (M2)

The Old Post Office, Fore St (NT).
A miniature C14 manor house used in the C19 as a Post Office. Open daily mid-Mar to Oct 11-4 (5 in April/May, 5.30 June-Sept). (M2) 01840 770024
www.nationaltrust.org.uk

Tintagel Castle (EH).
An early Celtic settlement 350-800 AD, later developed into an island fortress by the Earls of Cornwall in the C12 and C13s. Fragments of the great hall c.1250, and the gate and walls survive. The wild and windswept coast married with the romantic legends of King Arthur and encouraged by Geoffrey of Monmouth and Tennyson's 'Idyll' (although doubted by scholars) provide an atmosphere of mystery and wonder. Café/shop. Open daily Apr-Oct & 1/2 terms, plus winter W/Es, 10-4. (L2)
www.english-heritage.org.uk/tintagel

Tintagel, St Materiana.
Of Norman origin, and Catholic empathy, this church defies erosive nature and the storms she encounters in its isolated clifftop position. Sailors' graves. Rood Screen, bench ends and monument. Visit on a moody day, and be impressed. (L2)

Tintagel Visitor Centre.
In an age where Information Centres are closing down daily, it's encouraging to find a thriving centre. Housed in an interesting contemporary building with a museum exhibiting local artefacts. (L2)

LITE BITES...

Charlie's, Bossiney Rd.
Its a café/deli/restaurant that empathises with Cornish produce, family values and toddlers. (M2) 01840 779500
www.online-deli.co.uk

The Olive Garden, Atlantic Rd.
Italian restaurant serving pizza, pasta and Cornish seafood. Open F-W from 6pm. Closed in winter. (M2)
01840 779270
www.olivegardentintagel.co.uk

JUST OUTSIDE TINTAGEL... TO STAY...TO DRINK & EAT...

Mill House Inn, Trebarwith Strand.
A welcome retreat tucked away in a secluded coastal valley, a short distance from one of Cornwall's finest beaches. A working mill until the 1930s, the laid-back hotel is a charming building made cosy with comfy bedrooms, wood fires and flagstone floors. New restaurant on the up. (L3)
01840 770647
www.themillhouseinn.co.uk

The Port William Inn, Trebarwith Strand.
Location, location Darling! This has it. Nestling into the cliff edge affording superb beach and sea views. 8-bedrooms. Good pub-grub. (L3) 01840 770647
www.theportwilliam.co.uk

SPECIAL PLACES TO VISIT OUTSIDE TINTAGEL...

Delabole Slate Quarry.
1.5 mile circumference at a depth of 500ft, 375 million years of geological history. Worked continuously since the C16, and possibly by the Romans. Showroom. Tours of Quarry May-Aug M-F at 2pm. (M4)
01840 212242
www.delaboleslate.co.uk

WADEBRIDGE

A busy and feel-good market town that has seen much recent development; new shops, eateries and cycle hire have brought a buzz and liveliness to this old, sleepy town, and venue for the Royal Cornwall Show in June. Magnificent C15 bridge with 17 arches. Superb views from the New Bridge on the A39. Mid-point for cycling the Camel Trail. Cinema. E/C W. (H10)
www.visitwadebridge.co.uk
www.royalcornwallshow.org

WHERE TO EAT, DRINK & BE MERRY...

Relish, Foundry Court.
Members of the Guild of Fine Food Retailers, this café/deli opens M-Sa from 9-5 for breakfast and lunch and a range of delicious drinks and light snacks in between times. The deli specialises in tried and tested produce. (H10)
01208 814214

1280 The Mappa Mundi depicts Cornwall as one of the 4 constituent parts of Britain

1305 The Stannary Charter decrees that Cornish tin must be administered

Tintagel Castle ss

Hewitt's, 33 Molesworth St. This cute coffee bar is all the rage. Open for music nights Friday and every 2nd Wednesday. Its all a buzz with a friendly crowd. Open M-Sa 9-6. (H10) 01208 368191 www.picturesandcoffee.com

Glasshouse, The Piazza. A café-bar-restaurant that encourages al fresco dining in summer. Food is Italian and English, and life passes you by. Close to the bike hire, ensemble. (H10) 01208 814800 www. glasshousewadebridge.co.uk

Raj Bar & Restaurant, 1 Eddystone Place. Tasty Indian restaurant and takeaway which is a favourite of the locals. Bright, contemporary interior. (H10) 01208 895453 www.therajwadebridge.co.uk

The Dancing Taipan, The Platt Cantonese and Chinese restaurant with takeaway that serves local produce with an oriental twist. Good for groups and families. (H10) 01208 816623

PLACES OF INTEREST IN AND AROND WADEBRIDGE...

Egloshayle Bells & Clocks. For all lovers of clocks, it will be the tall spire that first draws you to approach the church, and on entering, the Wagon Roof and font, are wonders

to behold. The pointing is a disappointment. But, if you are able to, do climb the Bell Tower to view the Bells and Clock. Thirsty, walk a left into the village to the C12 inn, The Earl of St Vincemt, and behold more clocks, aplenty. A traditional inn, in a village of too many holiday homes. (J10)

Clapper Yard Gallery, Egloshayle. Penny McBreen's pottery studio displays her ceramic work and paintings, and other artwork of artists she admires. Open daily. (J10) 01208 813308 www.pennymcbreen.net

Wave 7 Studio Gallery, Trelights. Enthusiastic gallery displays a fine mix of arts and crafts. Art Day courses. Open daily Tu-Su 10.30-4.30. (H7) 01208 880605 www.wave7gallery.co.uk

Wood Design. Sladebridge. Stephen Roberts makes made-to-order custom pieces of contemporary furniture. Showroom open daily from 10. (J10) 01208 813305 www. wooddesignfurniture.co.uk

Yvonne Arlott Studio. Wood turning artist at work creating traditional and contemporary artwork from a mixture of carving techniques. Open daily. (J10) 01208 832315 www.yvonnearlott.com

WHERE TO STAY, NEARBY...

Cornish Tipi Holidays, Tregeare. Something different. Hire a traditional North American tent amidst a haven of birdsong, wild flowers, buzzards and rabbits. Trout fishing. No cars on site. Warden on hand. (L6) 01208 880781 www. cornishtipiholidays.co.uk

Longcross Hotel & Victorian Garden. Refurbished boutique-style hotel with 4-acres of lake, maze-walkway, herbaceous plants, cream teas. Plant sales. Disabled facilities. Large decking area for al fresco dining. Open daily 11-dusk. (H6) 01208 880243

Hawksfield, Atlantic Highway. This is a newish, exciting business and visitor attraction that has; a great café, Strong Adolfos (open daily from 8.30-4.30), an art gallery, Circle Contemporary, the Goose Shed, for vintage interiors, the Arc, a speciality food store, Jo & Co, a lifestyle store, The Paddock Room for yoga, pilates, dance and creative workshops, and CMBL, a growing brand of classic surf and motorcycle culture, indeed a site that is developing and gaining much local attention, and worth watching. (F10) 01208 816899 www.hawksfieldcornwall.com www.strongadolfos.com www.circlecontemporary.co.uk www.thearcfoodstore.co.uk

St Enodoc Church

POLZEATH

The main surf and family beach for Rock patronised by generations of families who own, or rent, property here during the summer months. It is where generations have learnt to surf before moving onto the more tricky breaks of Booby's and Constantine Bays. If it was a ski resort you would be cruising the greens and blues of Tignes, rather than the Reds and Blacks of St Anton/Val d'Isere. It, thus has its fair share of cafés/bars and the like. The local art gallery is:-

Whitewater Gallery, 1a The Parade. Sea and landscape paintings in oils and gouache, as well as ceramics, sculpture and glass objects. Open daily from 10. (E6) 01208 869301 www.whitewatergallery.co.uk

LIGHT BITES...

Galleon Café, Polzeath. Long established family friendly café that is great for breakfast or an energy top up between waves. Ideal if you need somewhere for an evening meal that caters for children. 01208 862362 (E6)

Oystercatcher Bar. Up the hill on the right, for panoramic views from their sun terrace. Bar and dining. Apartments to rent. (E6) 01208 862371 www.oystercatcherpolzeath. co.uk

St Kew Church

Sandbar Café/Deli, Polzeath. Overlooks the beach in enviable position. Opens for late breakfast/brunch at 10. Al fresco lunches and evening meals. Style more bistro, than restaurant. Proudly serves local produce where possible. Open daily in season. (E6) 01208 862333

The Waterfront, Beach Rd, Polzeath. Bar and café with an extended decking area overlooking the beach. Gets very busy, so best arrive early. Full range of lagers. Bar food. Open for breakfast from 9 am. (E6) 01208 869655 www. thewaterfrontpolzeath.co.uk

ANCIENT CORNWALL...

Harlyn Bay - Ancient Burial Ground. Iron Age cemetery discovered in 1900. Well preserved cists and skeletons unearthed. (C8)

Pawton Quoit. Massive damaged megalithic chamber 7.5ft X 3.5ft. (J1)

Rumps Point. Ramparts and ditches visible. Huts discovered. (E5)

CHURCHES OF INTEREST...

Little Petherick Church. Quaint C14 church in wooded valley. Developed by the

1322   Edward III appoints Piers Gaveston to be the Earl of Cornwall which drives the Cornish gentry to support the Earl of Lancaster to rebel against the king

1338   Edward III, the Black Prince creates the first Duke of Cornwall, a title bestowed on the first-born son of the Monarch

Tractarian, Molesworth family into an Anglo-Catholic centre of worship. (D10)

Minster Church. The mother church of Boscastle overlooks a wooded valley and the sea. Several monuments. (B9)

St Kew Church. Fine C15 interior with wagon roofing and a collection of magnificent stained glass windows telling the story of Christ's Passion. (K8)

St Mawgan-In-Pydar Church. Large with C13 nave and Arundell arms within the tall Rood Screen and family brasses. C15 Bench Ends. (D3)

SPECIAL FAMILY PLACES TO VISIT...

Old Macdonalds Farm. Small farm park, especially for young children. Pet the animals, bottle feed lambs, pony rides, train rides, trampolines, crazy golf, café, camping. B&B.

Open daily East-Sept 10-6. (B10) 01841 540829 www. oldmacdonalds.co.uk

GARDENS TO VISIT...

Japanese Garden. Set in a sheltered valley. Features Water, Stroll and Zen gardens. Woodland garden. Open daily from 10-6. (D3) 01637 860116 www.thebonsainursery.com

WHERE TO STAY...IN LITTLE PETHERICK, CLOSE TO PADSTOW...

Molesworth Manor. Former Rectory offers spacious B & B accommodation. Three Living Rooms. Continental breakfast (no fatty fry-ups). No dogs. (E10) 01841 540292 www. molesworthmanor.co.uk

The Old Mill House. A luxurious B&B set within a former 16 Corn Mill. 7-rooms with bathroom. Garden and Creek teeming with wildlife.

Old Mill Bistro, on site. (E10) 01841 540388 www.theoldmillhouse.com

SPECIAL PLACES TO EAT, DRINK & BE MERRY...

St Kew Inn. Hidden away down narrow lanes. Dine in the RH rooms if you can. Large garden. Specials board - try the fish, or steaks. (K8) 01208 841259 www.stkewinn.co.uk

St Tudy Inn. Emily Scott, the Head Chef/Proprietor is causing quite a stir in North Cornwall. The chattering classes are rushing to this new Inn/Pub/Restaurant to sample her seasonal dishes, and to relax beside a warm fire. (M8) 01208 850656 www.sttudyinn.com

Camel Trail. An Hens Camhayl. 18-mile trail from Bodmin to Padstow; suitable for jogging, walking, cycling and birdwatching. Cycle hire in Padstow and Wadebridge. (E9)

Trebarwith Strand

1342 The retiring Archdeacon of Cornwall, Adam de Carlton, observes "the folk of these parts are quite extraordinary, being of a rebellious temper and obdurate in the face of attempts to teach and correct"

79

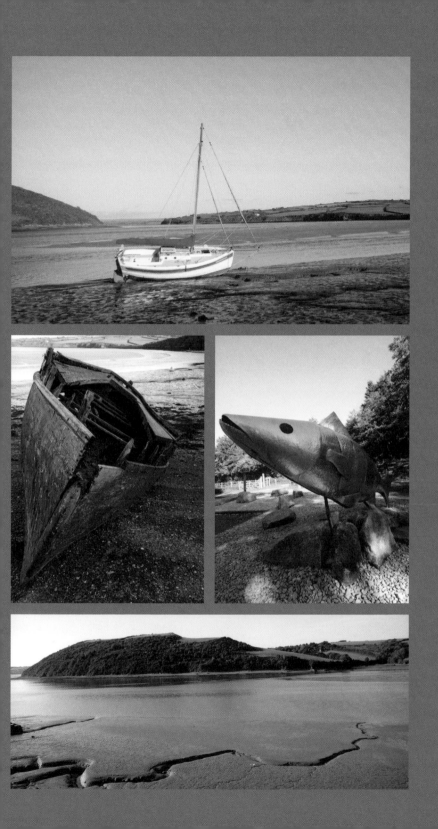

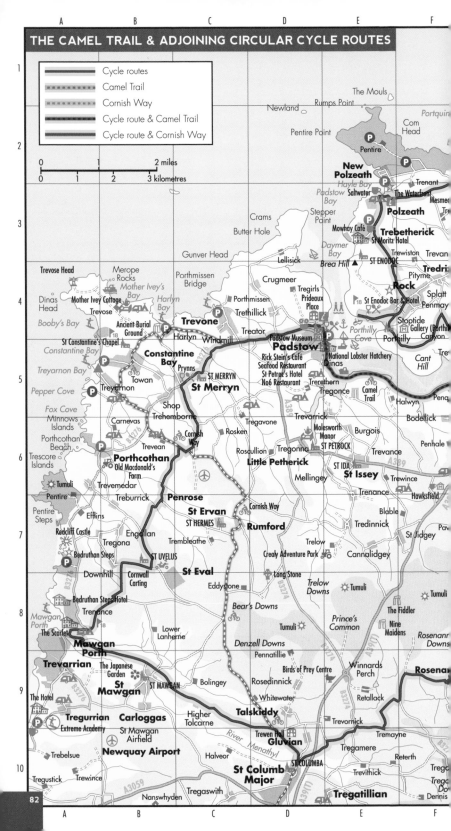

THE CAMEL TRAIL & ADJOINING CIRCULAR CYCLE ROUTES

Legend:
- Cycle routes
- Camel Trail
- Cornish Way
- Cycle route & Camel Trail
- Cycle route & Cornish Way

0 ___ 1 ___ 2 miles
0 ___ 1 ___ 2 ___ 3 kilometres

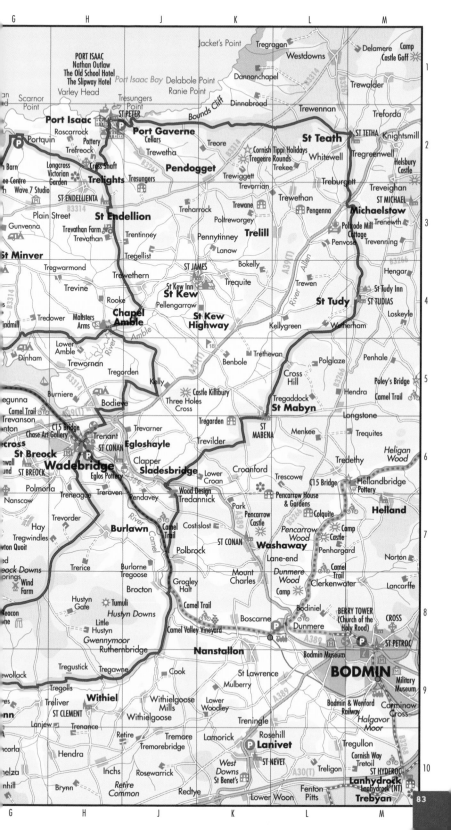

RNLI Lifeboat Station, Trevose Head

COASTAL FOOTPATH...

Boscastle to Park Head
Approx. 46 miles. The cliff walk to Tintagel along springy turf with spectacular views seaward to jagged rocks is quite superb. Worth a diversion inland to visit Rocky Valley, and St Nectan's Kieve, a 60 ft waterfall, and ancient hermitage. Return to the coast path; offshore Lye Rock was renowned as a puffin colony; now the cliffs are nesting sites for fulmars, guillemots, razorbills and shags. The landscape is wild and remote, a place of legends, and the romantic setting for the C13 Tintagel Castle and the mass of older remains on Tintagel Island. On leaving the castle ruins, the path climbs sharply to the cliff top church of St Materiana, guardian of many shipwrecked sailors. Along Glebe Cliff past numerous old slate quarries to Trebarwith Strand, a lovely beach to freshen up before the switchback path to Port Isaac. Choice of strenuous coastal or gentler inland route as far as Port Quin. For inland route: from Pine Haven follow the path for a half mile, then it turns westwards, passing Roscarrock Farm, south of Reedy Cliff to Port Quin, a tiny hamlet, mostly owned by the National Trust. On the headland beyond stands Doyden Castle, a Gothic folly built as a pleasure house and drinking den in C19. Below are black

fearsome rocks stained with green. The path west passes rocky-sandy surfing coves of Epphaven and Lundy, and the dramatic collapsed sea cave of Lundy Hole, before heading out to the headlands of The Rumps (with remains of Iron Age cliff castle) and Pentire. Now the path follows the Camel Estuary, past Polzeath and Daymer Bay and across the dunes to ferry at Rock for crossing the Camel to Padstow. What follows is a coastline dotted with superb sandy beaches and pounded by mighty Atlantic rollers but best appreciated out of season. Splendid views at Stepper Point, then on past caves and sheer cliffs at Butter Hole and Pepper Hole. Passing by the surf beaches of Trevone and Harlyn Bay, then to overlook the turquoise waters of Mother Ivey's Bay, passing the Lifeboat Station. The path continues to hugs the coastline past camping sites and beaches ideal for a quick dip, or if you have a board to hand, a surf. The coastline is peppered with stacks and islands and none more spectacular than at Bedruthan Steps just below Park Head.

BEACHES AND SURFING...

Trebarwith Strand. Popular family beach, especially at low tide. S-B hire/WC/P/Café/Inn. **Surfing** - Beach submerged at HT. Average breaks with consistent waves.

S end good Ls, and is protected from N winds. (G6)

Hayle Bay, New Polzeath. Wonderfully spacious family beach, S-B hire/P/WC/Café/access. Surfing - Crowded and popular beach break. Picks up most swell. RH wave off Pentire Point produces big swells (E6) **Cornish Rock Tors.** For coasteering, New Ecocoasteering, rock climbing, sea kayaking, wild swimming and more adventures. 07791 534884

Daymer Bay. Sheltered with firm golden sands, dunes and bathing safest at HT. Very popular with young families. WC/P. (E7)

Porthilly Cove, Rock. Spacious sands, ferry to Padstow, access/WC/Café. (E8)

Padstow, St Georges Cove. Sheltered inlet, 10 minute walk from town. (E7)

Padstow, Harbour Cove. Spacious sandy cove 20 minutes walk from town. (E7)

Trevone Bay. Sands, rock pools, Round Hole - collapsed cave. WC/LG/Café. (C8)

Harlyn Bay. Firm sands sheltered from south westerlies. WC/P/LG/Inn/Café. Surfing - Popular beach with strong SW winds and big swells. Can be fast and hollow at all stages of tide. Best with incoming tide. (C8)

Harlyn Surf School, Higher Harlyn Caravan Park, St Merryn. For coasteering, paddleboarding and surf lessons. 01841 533076 (C8)

Mother Ivey's Bay. Private beach with access from the caravan park. Effervescent, turquoise sea. Spacious sands at LT. (B8)

Booby's Bay. Spacious sands,

Treyarnon Bay

swirling currents, HZ bathing, rock pools at LT, access/P/LG. Surfing - Good R reef break from low to mid tide. Strong rips, for experienced only. (B8)

Constantine Bay. Spacious sands, swirling currents, HZ bathing, rock pools at LT, access/P/LG. Surfing - One of the best swell magnets. In the middle are good Rs and Ls. At S end break L off the reef. Strong rips, for the experienced only. (B9)

Treyarnon Bay. Sheltered, popular family beach with tidal pool, bathing is HZ near rocks. Access/WC/LG/P. Surfing - Popular beach. Good at mid to HT. Various peaks. LH wave for experienced with breaks off reef at LT. Tidal Pool. (B9)

Bedruthan Steps. One of Cornwall's most dramatic and spectacular beaches. Firm golden sands and massive rocks, and caves. Steep, cliff staircase (closed in winter) descends

to beach. Solar panelled café above beach. NT shop/WC at P. (C1)

Trethias, Pepper Cover & Fox Cove. Access by foot to inlet with sandy patches. (A9)

Porthcothan. Sandy bay, bathing HZ at LT. P/WC. Surfing - L & R beach breaks. (A10)

Bedruthan Steps

Harlyn Bay

Mounts Bay, The Lizard II

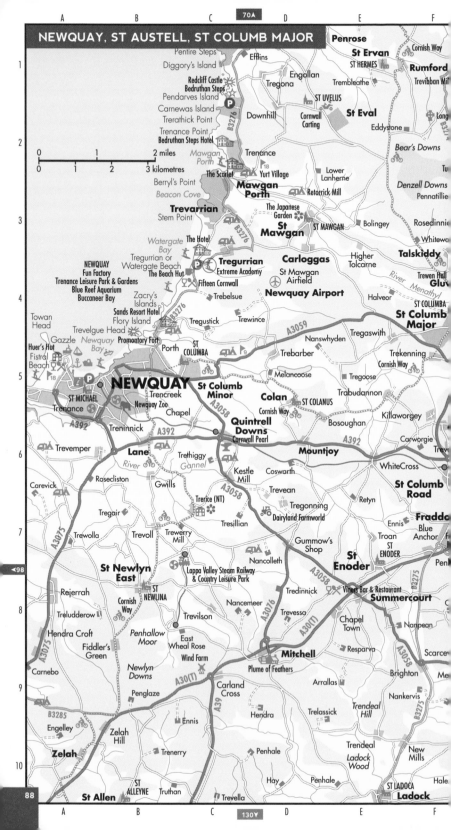

NEWQUAY, ST AUSTELL, ST COLUMB MAJOR

Penrose

St Ervan
Cornish Way
ST HERMES
Rumford
Trevibban Mil

Pentire Steps
Efflins
Engollan
Tregona
Trembleathe

Diggory's Island
ST UVELUS
St Eval
Long

Redcliff Castle
Bedruthan Steps
Pendarves Island
Downhill
Cornwall
Carting
Eddystone

Carnewas Island
Trerathick Point

Trenance Point

Bedruthan Steps Hotel

Trenance
Bear's Downs
Tu

Mawgan
Porth
Lower
Lanherne

Berryl's Point
The Scarlet
Yurt Village
Denzell Downs
Pennatillie

Beacon Cove
Mawgan
Porth
Retorrick Mill

Trevarrian
The Japanese
Garden
Rosedinnie

Stem Point
St
Mawgan
ST MAWGAN
Bolingey
Whitewa

Watergate
Bay
The Hotel
Carloggas
Higher
Tolcarne
Talskiddy

NEWQUAY
Fun Factory
Tregurrian or
Watergate Beach
Tregurrian
Extreme Academy
St Mawgan
Airfield
Trewen Hall
Glu

Trenance Leisure Park & Gardens
Blue Reef Aquarium
Buccaneer Bay
The Beach Hut
Fifteen Cornwall
Newquay Airport
River
Menathyl

Zacry's
Islands
Trebelsue
Halveor
ST COLUMBA

Towan
Head
Sands Resort Hotel
Flory Island
Trebarwith
St Columb
Major

Trevelgue Head
Promontory Fort
Tregustick
Trewince
Tregaswith

Huer's Hut
Gazzle
Porth
ST
COLUMBA
A3059
Nanswhyden
Trekenning
Cornish Way

Fistral
Beach
Newquay
Bay
Trebarber
Trebarber

NEWQUAY
St Columb
Minor
Melancoose
Tregoose

ST MICHAEL
Trencreek
Colan
Trabudannon
Killaworgey

Trenance
Newquay Zoo
Chapel
ST COLANUS
Bosoughan
Carworgie

Treninnick
A392
Quintrell
Downs
Cornish Way
Trev

Trevemper
Lane
Trethiggy
Cornwall Pearl
Mountjoy
WhiteCross

River
Gannel
Kestle
Mill
Coswarth
St Columb
Road

Carevick
Rosecliston
Gwills
Trevean
Retyn
Fraddo

Tregair
Trerice (NT)
Tregonning
Ennis
Blue
Anchor

Trewolla
Trevoll
Trewerry
Mill
Tresillian
Dairyland Farmworld
Troan
ST
ENODER
Pen

Gummow's
Shop
St
Enoder
Viners Bar & Restaurant

St Newlyn
East
Lappa Valley Steam Railway
& Country Leisure Park
Nancolleth
Summercourt

Rejerrah
ST
NEWLINA
Tredinnick
Nanpean

Treludderow
Cornish Way
Trevilson
Nancemeer
Trevessa
Chapel
Town
Resparva
Scarce

Hendra Croft
Penhallow
Moor
Mitchell
Me

Fiddler's
Green
East
Wheal Rose
Wind Farm
Plume of Feathers
Brighton

Carnebo
Newlyn
Downs
Arrallas
Nankervis

Penglaze
Carland
Cross
Trendeal
Hill

B3285
A39
Hendra
Trelassick

Engelley
Zelah
Hill
Ennis
New
Mills

Zelah
Trenerry
Penhale
Trendeal
Ladock
Wood

St Allen
ST
ALLEYNE
Truthan
Trevella
Hay
Penhale
ST LADOCA
Ladock

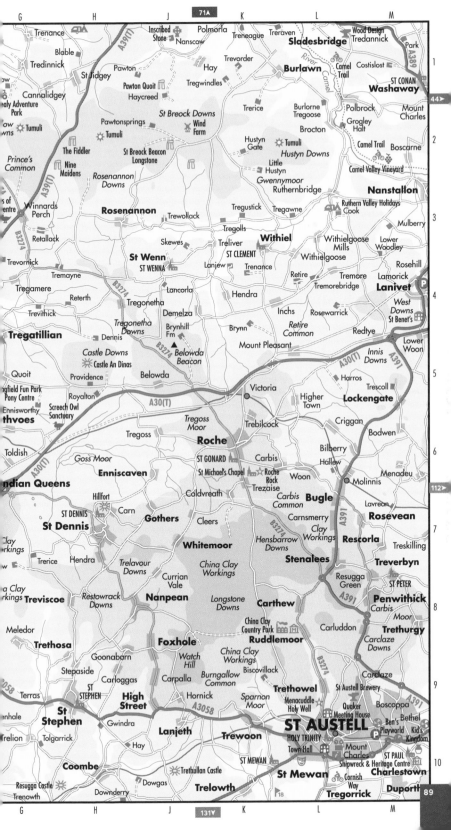

Trenance
Blable
Tredinnick
St Jidgey
Cannalidgey
aly Adventure Park
Tumuli
Prince's Common
The Fiddler
Nine Maidens
Winnards Perch
s of entre
Retallack
Trevornick
Tregamere
Tremayne
Reterth
Trevithick
Tregatillian
Quoit
gfield Fun Park
Pony Centre
thvoes
Ennisworthy
Toldish
ndian Queens
Clay
rkings
Trelion
enhale
Treviscoe
Meledor
Trethosa
Terras

Inscribed Stone
Nanscow
Polmorla
Treneague
Treraven
Sladesbridge
Wood Design
Tredannick
Costislost
Park
A389

Pawton
Hay
Tregwindles
Trevorder
Burlawn
Camel Trail
ST CONAN
Washaway

Pawton Quoit
Haycreed
Burlawn
Burlorne Tregoose
Polbrock
Grogley Halt
Mount Charles

Pawtonsprings
Tumuli
Wind Farm
Trerice
Brocton
Camel Trail
Boscarne

Tumuli
St Breock Beacon
Longstone
Hustyn Gate
Tumuli
Hustyn Downs
Little Hustyn
Gwennymoor
Ruthernbridge
Camel Valley Vineyard
Nanstallon

Rosenannon Downs
Trewollack
Tregustick
Tregawne
Ruthern Valley Holidays
Cook
Mulberry

Rosenannon
Tregolls
Treliver
Withiel
Withielgoose Mills
Lower Woodley
Rosehill

St Wenn
ST WENNA
Skewes
Lanjew
ST CLEMENT
Trenance
Withielgoose
Lamorick
Lanivet

Lancorla
Hendra
Retire
Tremore
Tremorebridge
West Downs
St Benet's

Tregonetha
Demelza
Inchs
Rosewarrick
Redtye
Lower Woon

Tregonetha Downs
Dennis
Brynhill Fm
Brynn
Retire Common
Mount Pleasant
Innis Downs
A30(T)
A391

Castle Downs
Castle An Dinas
Belowda Beacon
Providence
Belowda
Victoria
Harros
Trescoll
Lockengate

Royalton
Screech Owl Sanctuary
Higher Town
Criggan
Bowden

Tregoss Moor
Tregoss
Trebilcock
Bilberry
Hallew
Menadeu

Roche
Carbis
Woon
Molinnis
Lavrean

Goss Moor
Enniscaven
Hillfort
ST GONARD
St Michael's Chapel
Roche Rock
Trezaise
Bugle
Rosevean

ST DENNIS
Carn
Gothers
Coldvreath
Cleers
Carbis Common
Carnsmerry
Clay Workings
Rescorla
Treskilling

St Dennis
Whitemoor
Hensbarrow Downs
Stenalees
Treverbyn

Trerice
Hendra
Trelavour Downs
Currian Vale
China Clay Workings
Resugga Green
ST PETER

Restowrack Downs
Nanpean
Longstone Downs
Carthew
Penwithick
Carbis
Moor

China Clay Country Park
Carluddon
Trethurgy
Carclaze Downs

Goonabarn
Foxhole
China Clay Workings
Ruddlemoor
Carclaze

Stepaside
Carloggas
Watch Hill
Biscovillack
St Austell Brewery

ST STEPHEN
High Street
Carpalla
Burngallow Common
Trethowel
Menacuddle Holy Well
Quaker Meeting House
Boscoppa
Bethel

St Stephen
Gwindra
Hornick
Sparnon Moor
ST AUSTELL
HOLY TRINITY
Town Hall
Mount Charles
Ben's Playworld
Kid's Kingdom

Tolgarrick
Lanjeth
Trewoon
ST MEWAN
ST PAUL
Shipwreck & Heritage Centre
Charlestown

Coombe
Hay
Trethullan Castle
St Mewan
Cornish Way
Duporth

Resugga Castle
Trenowth
Dowgas
Downderry
Trelowth
Tregorrick
Duporth

River Camel
Burlorne Tregoose

B3274
B3274
A30(T)
A39(T)
A3058
A391

NEWQUAY

A popular seaside resort where the superb beaches give it the edge as Cornwall's foremost surfing centre. It has, thus, all the facilities of a modern resort: indoor and outdoor pools, cinema, fishing/boat trips from the Quay. Huer's Hut on headland (an ancient lookout for pilchards). The mainstream popularity of surfing has encouraged billions of pounds worth of property development. Tacky, old hotels and guesthouses are being pulled down (sadly, not all of them) to make way for luxurious apartments at Fistral and Lusty Glaze. Despite this influx of money, and the growing understanding among many that it is necessary to raise your game to compete successfully in today's holiday market, the town still gets its fair share of stag/hen parties and suffers the blight of unruly or anti-social behaviour. The town's development is suffering as a consequence, or perhaps it is no different from the norm of English towns? North and south of the town are a choice of quieter beaches. And, as the following selection shows, there is an increasing number of top end places to stay, and a great selection of eclectic foodie places to eat. You also have a fair share of budget hostels and camp/caravan sites that surround the town not listed here. Carnival Week – end May/early June.(B5)
www.newquayguide.co.uk
www.newquay.com
www.visitnewquaycornwall.co.uk

WHERE TO EAT, DRINK & BE MERRY...

Amity, South Quay Hill. Seafood takeaway like no other - Katy calls it: "Street food with a roof." Seafood sandwiches, oysters in batter, lobster in a brioche roll. All mouth-watering. Open daily except Tu. (A5) 07813 792968

Boathouse,The, South Quay Hill. Tucked away down in the harbour, is this bright and breezy eatery. Friendly and laid-back, and host to sophisicated "sexy fish and chips." Lunch 12-4.30pm, dinner from 7pm. 01637 874062
www.finns2go.com

Bush Pepper, 6 Fore Street. A little slice of Oz, who describe themselves as quirky, and of Today. Opens at 10 for breakfast. (A5) 01637 852530
www.bushpepper.co.uk

Fistral Beach Complex. In superb position overlooking the beach. There are three restaurants to whet your appetite. Upstairs, **The Stables Pizza, Pie and Cider Eatery**. They call it English rustic. Its a fab view and informal. 01637 878311
www.stablepizza.com Below, the **Fistral Beach Bar & Cafe**. All the nourishment a surfer needs after romanticizing a barrel, or two. Below, **The Fish House** run by Paul Harwood, formerly a chef with Steins. This is a small eatery supplied by Newquay fisherman, e.g. fresh lobster. You can dine al fresco on the balcony, accompanied by fine wines and take in the amazing sea view. 01637 872085.
www.thefishhouse-fistral.com
And, next door, **Rick Stein Fistral**. It's an up-market beachside chippy with Indian Takeaway. All comes in carry-out boxes. Open daily 9-9. (A5)

FSC Surf Diner, 19 Cliff Road. These guys have been feeding hungry surfers above their store sincer 1989. Overlooks Newquay Bay. Open for breakfast, lunch and dinner. (A5) 01637 498040
www.fistralsurfco.co.uk

The Scarlet, Mawgan Porth.
Eco, green, sustainable living…and pure hedonism. This is what separates this multi-million pound investment from its peers. It is an expensive place to play and relax…a pity that their fine example has yet to translate into cheaper, more plentiful, options. Better try it anyway, before your kids take the first option. Adults only. (C2) 01637 861800
www.scarlethotel.co.uk

| 1351 | Tin production drops by 80% due to bubonic plague | 1400-1500 | Intense church building programme across the county |

Gilmore's, 11 Tower Road.
Mini-golf is now cool again,
especially when associated
with this taco and cocktail bar.
Opens daily for breakfast. (A5)
01637 872995
www.gilmoresnewquay.co.uk

**Gusto Deli Bar, South Quay
Hill.** Lunch boxes to whisk
away; salads, wraps, roasts,
Middle Eastern chicken, spiced
flatbreads - all great beach
food. Open 11.30-3.30. (A5)
07415410734

**Jam Jar Cafe, 2 Broad
Street.** A wee, little cake shop
and cafe serving homemade
gluten-free delicacies. Open
daily 8-4. (A5)

**Lewinnick Lodge, Pentire
Headland.** If you seek
isolation, heady seaviews
and to escape to a blustery
headland with a fine bar, locally
caught seafood and boutiquey
bedrooms, or to pop by for
breakfast at 8am after a surf.
(West of A5) 01637 878117

WHERE TO STAY...

The House in The Sea.
Do you long for a romantic
interlude on your own private
island, then this location with
breathtaking views, may be for
you? Luxuriously decorated and
surrounded by sea at High Tide.
Sleeps 2. Civilisation is reached
via a 70ft-high suspension
bridge. (A5) 01637 881183
www.houseinthesea.
uniquehomestays.com

**WHERE TO STAY & RELAX
(WITH KIDS)...**

Bedruthan Steps Hotel.
One of Cornwall's great family
hotels set high on the cliff's
edge overlooking Mawgan
Porth beach. Awarded a Green
Tourism Gold Award. It uses
solar panels and light sensors,
helps clean the local beach and
uses local suppliers. Art & Craft
exhibits. Cinema. Associated

with **The Scarlet.** (C2) 01637
860860 www.bedruthan.com

**Headland Hotel, Fistral
Beach.** Majestic, Awesome,
Imposing ... describes this family
owned, and run hotel, since
1989. Built in 1900 to be the
South-West's finest. It overlooks
Cornwall's premier surf break,
and if you can afford it, nowhere
better to hang out and learn this
difficult sport. (A5)
01637 872211
www.headlandhotel.co.uk

Sands Resort Hotel. Family/
spa hotel offering modern
facilities with many sporting
options, spacious suites, health
and beauty centre and children's
clubs. (B4) 01637 872864
www.sandsresort.co.uk

The Hotel, Watergate Bay.
A family-style, boutique hotel
overlooking this stunning
beach with separate restaurant.
The Brasserie is yet another
destination for foodies to
unleash their waistlines. The
start-off point for enjoying the
Great Outdoors and varying
degrees of extreme sports. (C3)
01637 860543

**ALTERNATIVE PLACES
TO STAY...**

Retorrick Mill. If you seek
some rustic camping on a grassy
knoll, in a horsebox or sailing
boat coupled with Scott & Babs
finest wood fired food (much
is grown on Wilf's farm) and
dancing to an 8-piece French
Reggae band, you may well
have found your Shangri-La.
(D2) 01637 860460
www.scottandbabs.com
www.retorrickmill.co.uk

**The Park Mawgan Porth
Yurt Village.** 4-luxurious yurts
with all the comforts of home.
(D2) 01637 850322

**WHAT TO VISIT IN
NEWQUAY...**

Blue Reef Aquarium.
Overlooking one of England's
most popular surfing beaches
- houses the creatures which
live beneath those crashing
waves! Journey through the
wonderful underwater worlds
from the Cornish coastline to
the undersea gardens of the
Mediterranean. Café/gift shop.
Open daily, 10-5. (B5)
01637 878134
www.bluereefaquarium.co.uk

Watergate Bay

Extreme Academy, Watergate Bay ss

Newquay Fun Factory, 1 St Georges Rd. Adventure play centre for children, 2 to 12 years old. Coffee shop. Open daily Jul-Aug 10-9, Sept-Jul 10-6. (B5) 01637 877555

Newquay Zoo. Experience the wildlife amongst the exotic lakeside gardens live 100s of animals from around the world. Highlights are feeding times and animal encounters. Café. Open daily Apr-Sept 9.30-6, Oct-Mar 10-5. (B5) 01637 8733342 www.newquayzoo.org.uk

Trenance Leisure Park & Gardens. Multi-leisure park with Zoo, Waterworld, mini railway, tennis courts, crazy golf and boating lake, all set in lakeside gardens. Open daily. (B5) 01637 854020

Pirate's Quest. Life-size figures and scenes capture Cornwall's exciting and legendary past: smugglers, giants, sea creatures, highwaymen, mermaids. Open East-Oct Su-F & BHs 10-dusk. (B5) 01637 873379 www.piratesquest.co.uk

FAMILY FUN PLACES TO VISIT OUTSIDE NEWQUAY...

Cornish Birds Of Prey Centre. Falcons, hawks and owls. Waterfowl lake. Flights twice daily at 12 & 2.30. Open daily Apr-Oct 10-5. (G3) 01637 880544 www.cornishbirdsofprey.co.uk

Cornwall Pearl. Exhibition centre/workshop/gemstore selling a complete range of jewellery. Tea house. Champagne & Oyster Bar. Open daily 9.30-5.30. (C6) 01209 203280 www.cornwallpearl.com

Crealy Adventure Park. Megaslides, twisters, water slides. Shire horses, farm museum, 120-acres to wander. Restaurant. Open daily East-Oct 10-5. (G1) www.crealy.co.uk

Dairyland Farmworld. Milking Parlour, Cornish Countrylife Museum, 12,000sq. ft indoor play area, Nature Trail & Playground and the county's friendliest farm animals to pat, feed & pet. Open daily 1/2 terms & Apr-Oct 10-5. (D7) 01872 510246 www. dairylandfarmworld.com

Lappa Valley Steam Railway. Steam railway giving a two-mile return trip along a 15" gauge line to a pleasure area with boating lake, crazy golf, maze, two miniature railways, walks and film show. Café and gift shop. Open daily East-Oct & 1/2 term 10.30-5.30. (C7) 01872 510317 www.lappavalley.co.uk.

Screech Owl Sanctuary. Rescue and rehabilitation centre for sick and injured owls. Guided tours. Open daily 1/2 terms & Apr-Oct 10-6, winter 10-4.(G6) 01726 860182. www.screechowlsanctuary.co.uk

Springfields Fun Park & Pony Centre. Pets corner, bottle feeding, tractor rides and play areas. Café. Open daily East-Sept 10-6 , Oct-Nov 10-4. (G5) 01637 889123 www. springfieldsponycentre.co.uk

HOUSES & VINEYARDS TO VISIT...

Camel Valley Vineyards. Award-winning wines from 8,000 vines growing on the south-facing valley. Tasting, shop and pre-booked tours. Open M-F 10-5 (Sa East-Sept). (M2) 01208 77959 www.camelvalley.com

Trerice (NT). A delightful, small secluded Elizabethan manor house rebuilt in 1571, containing magnificent fireplaces, plaster ceilings, oak and walnut furniture. Small lawn mower museum. Refreshments. Open daily late Feb to Oct from 10.30.

THE BACKGROUND TO THE CHINA CLAY INDUSTRY...
William Cookworthy. The Plymouth chemist discovered kaolin at Tregonning Hill in 1768, a substance to form the basis of England's porcelain industry. Later, extensive finds were discovered around Hensbarrow Downs close to St Austell which became the centre of the industry. Kaolin is a product of changed granite; the rock is extracted from enormous pits, 300ft deep and 1/2 mile across. Only a portion is used, the rest is piled in great white heaps, hundreds of feet high, like towering snow mountains, the 'Cornish Alps' on which vegetation scarcely grows (unless the Alp is part of the Eden Project).

1437 Fowey's importance as a port attracts emigrants from Brittany, Holland, Ireland and Flanders making up one-third of the population

1470 Edward VI initiates a Royal Commission to stop the piratical seafarers of Fowey, Polruan and Bodinnick from going to sea

(C7) 01637 875404 www.
nationaltrust.org.uk/trerice

Trevibban Mill Vineyard & Orchards. You can take the Sunday (pre-booked) 3-hour walking tour, or just sample a dry, elegant white suffused with citrus aromas, or a punchy, lengthy, red full-bodied and balanced, accompanied by cheese or charcuterie. Open daily in summer, 12-6, winter W-Su 12-5. (F1) 01841 541413 www.trevibbanmill.com

Camel Valley Vineyard ss

SPECIAL PLACES TO VISIT OUTSIDE ST AUSTELL...

China Clay Country Park. Mining and Heritage Centre. New exhibition: Work Horse to War Horse, open air displays, historic nature trails with spectacular views of modern clay pit. Children's challenge trail, licensed café and shop. Open daily mid-Jan to 23 Dec 10-5. (K8) 01726 850362 www.wheal-martyn.com

ST COLUMB MAJOR
Isolated town of slate-hung houses noted for its superb C14 church. Hurling competition every Shrove Tuesday and Saturday of following week. Also, a venue for Cornish wrestling. (F4)

Church of St Columba. One of Cornwall's major churches that is visible from a great distance. C14 font, bench ends and brasses of the Arundell family. (F4)

Fraddon Pottery. Stoneware pots of Celtic design made from local materials. Tuition on hand. Open Tu-Sa 10-4. (F7) 01726 860206 www.fraddonpottery.co.uk

WHERE TO STAY...

Ruthern Valley Holidays, Ruthernbridge. Nestling in a wooded valley this site offers traditional facilities for tents and caravans but also log cabins, wigwams, camping huts and bungalows. (L3) 01208 831395 www.ruthernvalley.com

PUB TO VISIT...

Plume Of Feathers. A remodelled C16 Inn midway within Cornwall's holiday routes, and a perfect stop-off point for families seeking a friendly welcome, and wholesome food. Cream teas, log burners, large garden, dogs welcome. B & B. Sister to Lewinnick Lodge, Newquay. (D9) 01872 510387 www. theplume.info

ANCIENT CORNWALL...

Castle An Dinas. Four massive concentric rings, crowned by 'Roger's Tower.' an C18 folly. Iron Age pottery found. (H5)

Roche Rock. C15 St Michael's chapel/hermitage is a granite construction perched on top of jagged rocks affording fine views. (K6)

WATERGATE BAY
Extreme Academy. It's all beach action: kitesurfing, traction-kiting, buggying and kite-boarding, waveski, mountain boarding, and of course surfing. Tuition and kit hire. Beach Hut Bistro. Annual events. (C3) 01637 860840 www.watergatebay.co.uk

Jamie Oliver's Fifteen Cornwall. One of Cornwall's most desired 'foodie' experiences, to bag. Launched with the 'Jamie Oliver' flavour - they call it modern, Italian, influenced food. Profits go to the Cornwall Foundation of Promise - assisting young people from difficult backgrounds. Open daily for breakfast, lunch and dinner from 8.30 am. (C4) 01637 861000 www.fifteencornwall.co.uk

The Beach Hut. Fresh, simply cooked food in a sensational location. What more could you ask for? Fish and burgers feature strongly. Daily Specials. Open from 8.30 till late. (C3) 01637 860877 www.watergatebay.co.uk

Jamie Oliver's Fifteen ss

Fistral Beach

Watergate Bay

BEACHES AND SURFING...

Mawgan Porth.
Popular family beach, fine
bathing and access/S-B hire/
LG/WC/Café. Surfing - Good
beach break favouring Ls into
River Menathyl. Beacon Cove
less crowded. (C2)

Watergate Bay. Two miles
of glorious sands and access to
hotel, surf-canoeing. S-B hire/
WC/P/Cafe. Surfing - Good
beach break. Popular with
Newquay locals. (C3)

The Cribber. Big wave spot
for the experienced big wave
surfers only. Very dangerous
rips. Beware! (B4)

Newquay - Porth Beach.
Flat spacious golden sands. Fine
surfing and bathing (avoid river).
Blow Hole at Trevelgue Head.
P/LG/WC/Café. (B4)

Newquay - Lusty Glaze.
Sands sheltered by cliffs, access
via steps from cliff top, surfing
S-B/LG/WC. (A5)

Newquay - Tolcarne Sands.
Suntrap below Narrowcliff
Promenade, surfing. (A5)

**Newquay - Great Western
Beach.** Sheltered suntrap,
access via path beside Great
Western Hotel, surfing S-B
hire/LG. (A5)

Newquay - Towan Beach.
Ideal family beach; golden
sands, good bathing. Near
harbour and town centre. S-B
hire/LG/WC. (A5)

Newquay - Fistral Beach.
Surfing Venue for European
Championships. Consistent
swell across beach with peaky
barrelling Ls and Rs. South
Fistral breaks L, better at HT.

North and Little Fistral break
L and R. North breaks at HT.
The LT barrels have made the
waves at N end a crowd puller.
(A5)

COASTAL FOOTPATH...

Park Head to Newquay
Approx 12 miles. Southwards,
the tremendous view of the
Bedruthan Steps where legend
so claims the stacks (or rocks)
were used as stepping stones by
the Cornish giant, Bedruthan.
In summer, you can walk the
cliff tops beside carpets of wild
flowers for the air is bursting
with the scent of burnet rose
and gorse. Reaching Stem
Point it's possible to walk the
sands to Newquay at low tide,
alternatively the headland path
is easy going.

Huer's Hut, Newquay

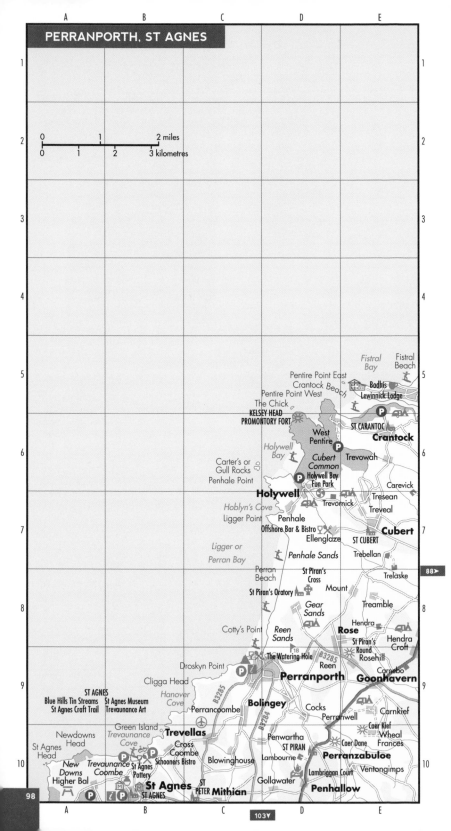

0 1 2 miles
0 1 2 3 kilometres

Fistral Bay
Fistral Beach

Pentire Point East
Crantock Beach
Pentire Point West
The Chick
KELSEY HEAD PROMONTORY FORT
Bodhis
Lewinnick Lodge
ST CARANTOC
Crantock

West Pentire
Cubert Common
Trevowah

Holywell Bay
Carter's or Gull Rocks
Penhale Point
Holywell Bay Fun Park
Carevick

Holywell
Trevornick
Tresean
Treveal

Hoblyn's Cove
Ligger Point
Penhale
Cubert
ST CUBERT

Ligger or Perran Bay
Offshore Bar & Bistro
Ellenglaze
Trebellan

Penhale Sands

Perran Beach
St Piran's Cross
Mount
Trelaske

St Piran's Oratory
Gear Sands
Treamble

Cotty's Point
Reen Sands
Hendra
Rose
St Piran's Round
Rosehill
Hendra Croft

The Watering Hole
B3285
Reen
Carnebo

Droskyn Point
Cligga Head
Perranporth
Goonhavern

ST AGNES
Blue Hills Tin Streams
St Agnes Craft Trail
St Agnes Museum
Trevaunance Art
Hanover Cove
B3285
Bolingey
Cocks
Perranwell
Carnkief

Newdowns Head
Green Island
Trevaunance Cove
Perrancoombe
Trevellas
Penwartha
ST PIRAN
Caer Kief
Wheal Frances

St Agnes Head
New Downs
Higher Bal
Trevaunance Coombe
St Agnes Pottery
Cross Coombe
Schooners Bistro
Blowinghouse
Lambourne
Caer Dane
Perranzabuloe
Ventongimps

St Agnes
ST AGNES
ST PETER
Mithian
Gollawater
Lambriggan Court
Penhallow

PERRANPORTH

The glorious 3-miles of sand has made this beach into the popular surfing and holiday centre with all the hangers on, that that entails, which has thus epitomized the worst excesses of Cornwall; haphazard and dour, ugly architecture behind the beach. The main street is festooned with surf and gift shops, and multiples. Now buried beneath the dunes, the St Piran's Oratory, a site reached by a 30-minute walk. The cliffs on the southern edge of the beach have restricted access, are dangerous and must not be climbed due to constant erosion. More interesting, The Poldark novels were written in the late 1940s from a bungalow (long gone) amidst the sand dunes. (D9) www.perraninfo.co.uk

SPECIAL FAMILY PLACES TO VISIT...

Holywell Bay Fun Park. All action outdoor fun park - go karts, battle and bumper boats, laser day pigeon shooting, café. Open daily East-Oct 10-5. (D6) 01637 830095 www.holywellbayfunpark.co.uk

HISTORIC INTEREST...

St Piran's Round. The ancient amphitheatre where plays were performed in the C17. (E9) www.stpiran.org

WHERE TO EAT, DRINK & BE MERRY...

The Watering Hole, The Beach. Its actually situated on the sand, backed by dunes and fronted by the sea. A great view if you can see past the hoards on sunny days. It just may be the nearest you get to a slice of Oz. Weekend music events. (C9) 01872 672054 www.thewateringhole.co.uk

ST AGNES

A former mining community that left the skyline jagged with disused engine houses. There is an arty ambience to this corner of Cornwall, quite different from other parts, perhaps more akin to Penwith. It is hilly, with three parts; Churchtown (the top end), Peterville (X-roads) and Trevaunance Cove. With no shortage of foodie places and fine, independent shops; baker, butchers etc., the town is a popular and convenient location for Truro's medics to live. Hence, the high house prices. The birthplace of John Opie in 1761, Cornwall's most famous painter who became a Fellow of the Royal Academy at 26 and who is buried in St Paul's Cathedral. A family resort, centre for dramatic coastal walks, and tricky surf break. Arts and Crafts Trail. HQ for SAS (Surfers Against Sewage) and Finisterre, a cold water surf company. (H1) www.stagnes.info www.st-agnes.com

LIGHT BITES...

For ease of navigation, **St Agnes** is split into three (3) areas:**Vicarage Road/Churchtown** (Top End), **Peterville** and **Trevaunance Cove** (Beach).

Entering **St Agnes** from the Truro road you pass the public car park on your L, and enter Vicarage Road. On the corner, **Taste Restaurant**, 40 Vicarage Road. An ideal spot for morning coffee, a light lunch, perhaps alfresco, to people watch. Open Tu-Sa 10.30-2, 6-9 and Su for lunch 11-2. 01872 552194 www.tastestagnes.co.uk. If you seek ale and good-value pub-grub try the **St Agnes Hotel** opposite the Church. A little further on, on the corner the **St Agnes Bakery** and **KT's Coffee Shop**. I always stop here for a pastry pork sausage roll, or pasty - they come in all combinations, and the best I have eaten. And, make for a substantial picnic.

01872 552308 www.stagnesbakery.co.uk

Peterville: Now, if you seek a venue for a special occasion, or are just flush with some cash, it has to be **No. 4** in Peterville. The Starters could be; Scallops, Quail or Grilled Figs, the Main Course; Roasted Partridge, Monk Tail, Hake and Smoked Pork Shoulder - Sunday Brunch, that's just for starters. Summer open Tu-Su, winter W-Su. 01872 554245 www.no4peterville.co.uk Next door, **The Taphouse**, Peterville Square. Their passion is live music and surf, and many front line artists have played here: Ben Howard, Angus and Joss Stone, to name a few. The ambience is laid-back, the decor; wild and colourful, the food; nachos, pizzas, burgers, local fish. 01872 553095 www.the-taphouse.com Then, head R for the beach, soon to come to the **Studio Tea Room Gallery**, Quay Road. For all-day breakfasts, Cornish tea and cakes, artworks for sale. Open all year. 01872 857045 www.tearoom.co.uk **Trevaunance Cove**: There's quite a choice: **The Driftwood Spars** is a well-known C17 inn, popular with locals and families, alike ... Across the road, the **Brewery** with Visitor Centre and proud to show you their award-winning ales. Next door, the glorified fish'n chip shop, **Lewsey Lou's** open W, Th & F 5-8.30 pm, W/Es 12-3, 5-8.30 pm. 01872 552126 www.lewseylous.co.uk And, to the beach we descend. Overlooking the majestic sands, and tricky surf break, **Schooners**, the ideal spot for breakfast, coffee/tea and cakes, seafood platters. Reggae Nights in summer evenings, Open daily in summer, W/Es in winter. 01872 553149 Above, the **Breakers Surf School** serves burgers and ice creams. 01872 553811.

WHERE TO STAY...

Lambriggan Court B&B, Lambriggan, Penhallow. Boutique-style B&B and S/C cottages set in a group of beautifully converted Cornish barns with Mediterranean flavours. Tranquil and inviting. (D10) 01872 571636 www.lambriggancourt.com

GALLERIES & MUSEUMS TO VISIT...

Blue Hills Tin Streams. The skills of the ancient tinner, from rock to metal. Giftware. Open mid-Apr to mid-Oct Tu-Sa 10-4. (B10) 01872 553341 www.bluehillstin.com

Churchtown Arts, 5 Churchtown. C15 building houses arts and crafts gallery. Workshops and studios to view. Open 9.30-5.30, Su 10-5. (B10) 01872 553229

Little Feathers Gallery, 18 Churchtown. More a crafty gift shop; jewellery, local paintings, sculpture. Open daily. (B10) 01872 554303 www.littlefeathersgallery.co.uk

St Agnes Museum. Tin mining to turtles, fishing to folklore. Free. Open daily East to Sept 10.30-5. (B10) 01872 553228 www.stagnesmuseum.org.uk

St Agnes Pottery. Wide range of hand-thrown stoneware, earthenware and porcelain by John Vasey. Open M-Sa 9.30-5. (B10) www.studiopottery.com

CHURCHES TO VISIT...

Crantock Church. This religious community was established by St Carantoc in the C6, The Norman carved font is exceptional, Chancel rebuilt in C15, C15 sculpture inside south wall. Village stocks. The four great windows of Victorian stained glass and the

Trevaunance Cove, St Agnes

Rood Screen tell the story of man's fall and redemption. (E6)

Cubert Church. C14 tower, pulpit made of old bench ends. Original wagon roofs. Attractive slate monuments. (E7)

St Piran's Oratory. Ruins of C7 church and burial place of St Piran the early Celtic missionary. Now buried beneath sand for protection. (D8)

CRANTOCK
An early religious centre from the C6 with origins dating back to Languroc, "The Dwelling of the Monks" until closed by Henry VIII in his Dissolution Of The Monasteries, 1536-1541, and formerly a busy port until the Gannel estuary silted up. Superb beach. Old Albion Inn. Cosy Nook tea gardens. (E6)

SPECIAL PLACES TO EAT, DRINK & BE MERRY...

Bodhi's Café, Fistral Beach (South side). Building a reputation for imaginative cuisine and a location for superb views of the surf. Pudding Nights. (E5) 01637 850793 www.bodhisfistral.co.uk

Offshore Bar & Bistro, Holywell Rd, Cubert. Angus McNair's full 25-years experience in the kitchen is to the benefit of all who drop by here, beit, for brunch, the tapas, or supper. Open Tu-Su (lunch) (D7) 01637 830505 www. offshorecornwall.co.uk

BEACHES AND SURFING...

Crantock Beach. Spacious golden sands sheltered by Pentire Point. Bathers must avoid The Gannel, and take the pedestrian ferry to Newquay. S-B hire/LG/WC/P. Surfing - long hollow Rs at S end over the sand bank. Protected from N and NE winds. Good Ls when S end has big swell. Fern Pit café. (E5)

Porth Joke (Polly Joke). 15 minutes walk from P to a suntrap of yellow sand, nestling between low cliffs. Seals laze opposite on the Chick. Tidal Pool. (D6)

Holywell Bay. Popular family beach, dunes, bathing HZ at LT. Access P/WC/LG/Café.

1534   Parliament passes the Act of Succession, sanctioning the annulment of the King's marriage to Catherine of Aragon   1535   Cornwall is considered a separate state in Polydore Vergill's Anglia Historia

Surfing - Average beach break. Protected at S end. 10 minute walk from P. (D6)

Penhale / Perran Beach, Perranporth. The ideal family beach, a vast 3 mile stretch of sand with dunes behind, bathing HZ at LT and near Chapel Rock. S-B hire/WC/LG/Café at southern end. (D7)

Penhale. Surfing - Rs peel off at N end. (D7)

Perranporth. Surfing - Good at mid-tide with long rides. Watch your position with strong tidal flow. Ls break off the headland. (D8)

Trevaunance Cove (St Agnes). Smallish sandy beach, effervescent blue sea and strong currents on ebbing tide. S-B hire/WC/P/LG/Café. Surfing - SAS HQ. Yet water quality still poor. Mid-tide produces powerful surf. SW wind unusually creates waves. Can be crowded. (B10)

Koru, Trevaunance Cove. Why not go for a guided 2-hour kayak, and discover caves, archways and seals? Wetsuits available. Tuition on hand. 0779 4321 827 Also, on the Helford River. www.korukayaking.co.uk

COASTAL FOOTPATH...

Newquay To Chapel Porth This section is a very busy holiday area with many camping sites and seductive beaches. First cross the Gannel by the tidal bridge or ferry (in summer). Out of season, follow the road to Trevemper (or cross the Trethellan tidal bridge at low water). Worth a detour to visit pretty Crantock. Then easy going around Penhale Point; alternatively, a route via Holywell Bay, Ellenglaze, Mount and Gear. At Penhale Sands one sees the first sign of Cornish tin mining, desolate engine houses and chimneys on hill tops, silhouettes which

appear increasingly frequently as one walks westwards. Climbing out of Perranporth the path is relatively easy-going and follows the cliff edge to Trevaunance Cove. From Perranporth the coast is quite magnificent. Around St Agnes Head, a profusion of heather, gorse and sea pinks, and much evidence of tin workings with the ruins of many old mine shafts. Rounding the headlands the views are distant and dramatic, bare cliffs and rolling heathland stretching westwards, the sea below all sparkling blues and turquoise. Scramble up St Agnes Beacon (630ft) for spectacular views west down the coast and inland to Bodmin Moor, and across the peninsula to Falmouth and St Michael's Mount.

St Piran

Towanroath Shaft, Wheal Coates Mine

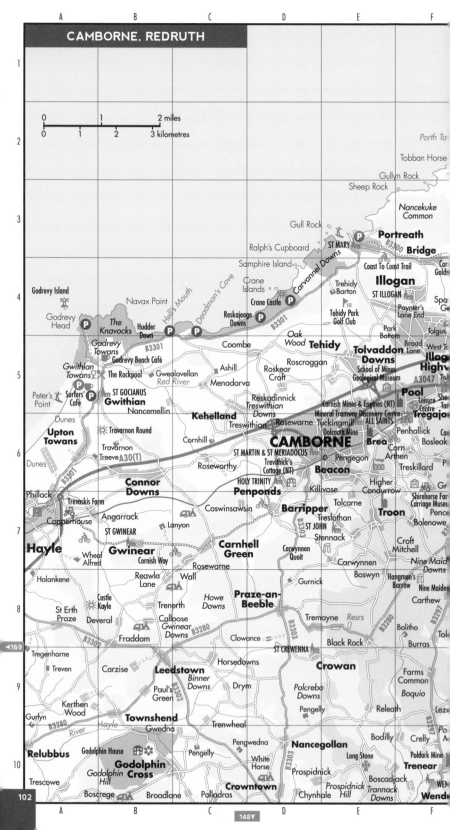

Porth To

Tobban Horse

Gullyn Rock

Sheep Rock

Nancekuke Common

Gull Rock

Ralph's Cupboard

ST MARY

Portreath

Bridge

B3300

Coast To Coast Trail

Cor Golds

Samphire Island

Carvannel Downs

Illogan

ST ILLOGAN

Spa

Deadman's Cove

Crane Islands

Trehidy Barton

Paynter's Lane End

18

Godrevy Island

Navax Point

Hell's Mouth

Crane Castle

Reskajeage Downs

Tehidy Park Golf Club

Park Bottom

Tolvaddon Downs

Broad Lane

West To

Illog High

B3301

Godrevy Head

The Knavocks

Hudder Down

Oak Wood

Tehidy

School of Mines Geological Museum

Tolgus

Gadrevy Towans

Coombe

Roscroggan

A3047

Pool

She Tar

Godrevy Beach Café

Ashill

Roskear Croft

Cornish Mines & Engines (NT)

Leisure Centre

Gwithian Towans

The Rockpool

Menadarva

Reskadinnick

Mineral Tramway Discovery Centre

Tregajo

Peter's Point

Gwealavellan

Red River

Treswithian Downs

Roswarne

Tuckingmill

ALL SAINTS

Penhallick

Ca

Surfers' Café

Gwithian

Kehelland

Treswithian

Dolcoath Mine

Brea

Bosleak

Nancemellin

CAMBORNE

Carn Arthen

Gr

Cornhill

ST MARTIN & ST MERIADOCUS

C. Pengegon

Treskillard

Upton Towans

Travarnon Round

Roseworthy

Trevithick's Cottage (NT)

Beacon

Shirehorse Far Carriage Museu

Dunes

Travarnon Treeve

A30(T)

HOLY TRINITY

PENPONDS

Killivose

Higher Condurrow

Pence

Dunes

Connor Downs

Coswinsawsin

Barripper

Tolcarne

Troon

Gr

Phillack

Angarrack

Lanyon

B3303

ST JOHN

Treslothan

Croft Mitchell

Bolenowe

Trevaskis Farm

Stennack

Copperhouse

ST GWINEAR

Carnhell Green

Carwynnen Quoit

Carwynnen

Boswyn

Nine Maid Downs

Hayle

Wheal Alfred

Gwinear

Cornish Way

Rosewarne

Gurnick

Hangman's Barrow

Nine Maider

Halankene

Reawla Lane

Wall

Praze-an-Beeble

Tremayne

Resrs

Carthew

B3280

St Erth Praze

Castle Kayle

Trenerth

Howe Downs

Bolitho

Tol

Deval

Calloose Gwinear Downs

B3280

Clowance

ST CREWENNA

B3303

Black Rock

Burras

◄169

Fraddam

B3302

Horsedowns

Tregenhorne

Treven

Carzise

Leedstown

Binner Downs

Drym

Crowan

Farms Common

Boquio

Gurlyn

Kerthen Wood

Paul's Green

B3302

Polcrebo Downs

Releath

Lez

B3280

Townshend

Gwedna

Trenwheal

Pengelly

Bodilly

Crelly

Nancegollan

River Hayle

Pengwedna

Long Stone

Trenear

Relubbus

Godolphin House

Pengelly

White Horse

B3303

Prospidnick

Poldark Mine

WEN

Trescowe

Godolphin Hill

Godolphin Cross

Prospidnick Hill

Boscadjack Trannack Downs

Wend

Boscrege

Broadlane

Polladras

Crowntown

Chynhale

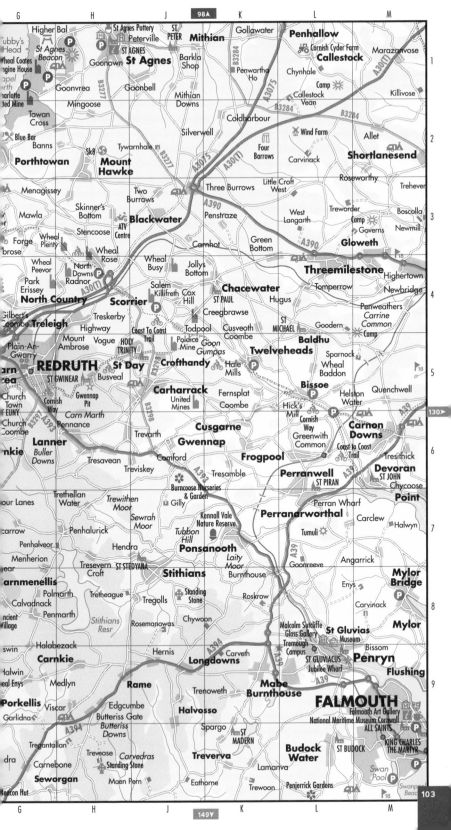

CAMBORNE & REDRUTH

These two towns appear as one. Formerly a mining centre, and the hive of great industry and skill. The birthplace of Richard Trevithick, 1771 - 1833 designer of the high-pressure steam pump which revolutionised mining, enabling water to be pumped out at great depths. Tin mining halted in the 1930s due to imports of cheap Malaysian tin. There are some handsome buildings to be seen and many pretty rows of terraced houses, which if up country, would be in great demand. Cinema. (E6 & H5) www.camborneonline.co.uk

CORNWALL'S INDUSTRIAL HERITAGE - WHAT TO SEE & VISIT...

Coast to Coast Trail. 11 miles/18 km. Linking the harbour of Portreath on the Atlantic coast and Devoran near Falmouth, this mostly off-road trail passes through ancient woodland, heathland and historic mining sites being overrun by nature like ancient temples. A beautiful walk or cycle ride with plenty of B&Bs and dining options at either end. (E3)

East Pool Mine & Taylor's Engine House (NT). These two great beam engines built in 1892, were used for pumping water, and winding men, and ore, up and down, from depths of over 550 metres. Site includes the Industrial Discovery Centre at East Pool. Open daily except M & Su late Mar to Oct 10.30-5. Mitchell's Engine House open 12-4. (F5) 01209 315027 www.nationaltrust.org.uk

Dolcoath Mine. At 3,500 ft below the surface, Cornwall's deepest mine. Shut down in 1921 following the tin slump after WWI. (E6)

Kennal Vale Nature Reserve CWT. A former gunpowder factory was located in this reserve of broadleaf woooodland, waterfalls, open glades and footpaths. Easy access. (K7)

Mineral Tramways Discovery Centre, Penhallick. Cornwall's industrial past revealed by following the Portreath Tramroad, the 11km and the Great Flat Lode trail of 10km. Interpretation Centre. The King Edward Mine. Open all year Tu-Su 10-4, Sa 1-4. (F6)

Poldark Mine. Underground exploration with easy and difficult routes. Suitable for elderly and the fit and fearless. Poldark museum and film. Surface fun for the family. Open East, then all year 10-5.30. (F10) 01326 573173 www.poldarkmine.org.uk

Trevithick's Cottage (NT). Richard Trevithick, the Cornish engineer and inventor of the high-pressure steam engine, lived here between 1810-1815. Open Apr-Oct W 2-5, donations welcome. (D6) www.nationaltrust.org.uk

SPECIAL PLACES TO VISIT...

Burncoose Nurseries & Garden. 30 acre woodland garden. Also nursery with 3,000 varieties of trees, shrubs and unusual plants. Light refreshments. Open daily 8.30-5 (Su 11-5). (J6) 01209 860316 www.burncoose.co.uk

Cornish Cyder Farm. 40 varieties of fruit products made, from scrumpies to chutneys. Open daily. (L1) 01872 573356 www.thecornishcyderfarm.co.uk

Godolphin House (NT). Romantic Tudor and Stuart mansion, c.1475. The Godolphin family's courtly ambitions and taste are expressed in the evolving design of the house. Tin mining provided wealth for this family of entrepreneurs, soldiers, poets and officials. C16 and C17 English furniture. Estate open daily. Conservation work is being undertaken, yet, the house is generally open the first Sa-Th of every month Feb-Oct (not Aug), plus part Dec. Gardens open daily 10-5. (B10) 01736 763194 www.nationaltrust.org.uk/godolphin

Penjerrick Gardens. Essentially a spring flowering garden of 16 acres: camellias, azaleas, rhododendrons and tree ferns. Magnificent trees, pond

Gwennap Pit

1542 Andrew Boorde's First Boke records there are two speeches in Cornwall: naughty Englysshe, and Cornysshe Speche

1549 Edward VI's Act of Uniformity whereby church services are to be held in English, as opposed to Latin, starts the Prayer Book Rebellion

Godolphin House

gardens, bamboo. Woodland walk. Open Mar-Sept W, F & Su 1.30-4.30. (L10) 01872 870105 www.penjerrickgarden.co.uk

Mount Hawke - Sk8. Skateboarding park undercover. BMX club. Youth Group charity status. Open daily. (H2) 01209 890705 www. mounthawkeskatepark.com

Shire Horse Farm & Carriage Museum. A special experience awaits those who love horses; especially Shire and Suffolk Punches. Horse-drawn, agricultural and private vehicles. Open East-Oct Su-F 10-4. (F6) 01209 713606 www. shirehorseandcarriagemuseum. co.uk

GWENNAP
A district with an abundance of disused mines, engine houses, and engine tracks from former copper and tin mines. (H5)

Gwennap Pit. Amphitheatre caused by mining subsidence. Landscaped in 1803. Has excellent acoustics, and is known as the Methodist 'Cathedral'. Open all year. John Wesley first preached here in 1762, and in 1773, to a congregation of 32,000. How on earth did they all fit in? Annual Methodist Meeting - Spring BHM., when Visitor Centre opens to Sept M-F 10-4.30, Sa 10-1. (H5) 01209 822770 www.gwennappit.co.uk

WHERE TO STAY...

Treglisson, Wheal Alfred Rd. For all lovers of industrial archaeology, why not stay in the former mine owner's house which is a comfortable and relaxed farmhouse B&B. Swimming pool. Adjacent, a small caravan and camping site. (A7) 01736 753141 www.treglisson.com

PORTREATH
Harbour built by Francis Bassett to serve local mines. In 1809 the terminus for one of the country's first railway lines. Many interesting industrial remains. (E3) www.portreathslsc.co.uk

Cycling Couple

ANCIENT CORNWALL...

Carwynen Quoit. Fine specimen, three legs and large capstone. (E7)

Carn Brea. Traces of neolithic settlers. Focus of legends and giants. Site of C15 castle. A 90ft Obelisk built in c.1836 in memory of Lord de Dunstanville, at 783ft, a superb viewpoint. (F6)

BEACHES AND SURFING...

Chapel Porth. Spacious sands at LT, but beware of fast-flowing incoming tides along this coast and strong currents, bathing can be HZ. Bass fishing/caves, S-B hire/LG/P/WC. Surfing - Submerged at HT. Powerful surf. Beach café open daily in summer and winter W/Es. (G1)

Porthtowan. Surfing - Fine beach break. HT protected from SW winds. Crowded in summer. (G2)

Portreath. Popular family beach with golden sands, fast HZ incoming tides, caves, S-B. hire/LG/P/WC/Café. Surfing - On beach beginners keep L and surf the beach break. Can be crowded. The harbour's N end produces good breaks in a fair swell. (E3)

Godrevy Towans. Sand, rocks and dunes. Enter beside Red River. WC/LG/Cafés. (A5)

Gwithian Towans. Surf, dunes and P/WC/LG/Café. Surfing - Peaks suitable for novices. At HT cut off by rocks. (A5)

SEAVIEW CAFÉS...

Blue Bar, Porthtowan. Surfers' bar attracts all ages and serves freshly cooked food. Live bands and discos at weekends. Opens from 10. (G2) 01209 890329 www.blue-bar.co.uk

Godrevy Beach Café, Godrevy Towans. Serves breakfast, lunch, dinner. Choose from organic cakes, take-aways and barbeques. Great views of sunsets from the decking area on stilts. Open from 10, seven days a week. (A5) 01736 757999 www.godrevycafe.co.uk

Sunset Surf (Surfer's Café/Bar), Gwithian Towans. A fun family-friendly hang-out, great food and facilities. Surf school and hire. Open daily from 10 for breakfast. (A5) 01736 752575 www.sunset-surf.com

The Rockpool Seafood Café/Bar & Grill, Gwithian Beach. Après-surf fun; baps, burgers, omelettes and fresh fish dishes, and live music. Next door, the Gwithian Academy of Surfing. (A5) 01736 449990 www.therockpoolbar.co.uk

COASTAL FOOTPATH...

Trevaunance Cove (St Agnes) to Hayle (& St Ives): Approx 30 miles. From Perranporth to Godrevy Point the coast is quite magnificent. Around St Agnes Head, a profusion of heather, gorse and sea pinks, and much evidence of tin workings with the ruins of many old mine shafts. Rounding the headlands the views are distant and dramatic, bare cliffs and rolling heathland stretching westwards, the sea below all sparkling blues and turquoise. Scramble up St Agnes Beacon (630ft) for spectacular views west down the coast inland to Bodmin Moor, and across the peninsula to Falmouth and St Michael's Mount.

From Chapel Porth to Porthtowan: The path climbs up over Mulgram Hill past Great Wheal Charlotte. On to Portreath and for much of the way a barbed wire fence on your left marks the perimeter of Nancekuke Airfield.

From Portreath to Godrevy Point: Along North Cliffs there's superb cliff scenery and invigorating walking. The lonely stretch from Bassett's Cove to the savage Hell's Mouth has been a graveyard of many ships over the centuries; a place of drama, and melancholy, and fierce crashing seas. The path passes inland to Gwithian then returns seaward to follow the edge of the towans (sand dunes) to Hayle. Thereafter it follows the road round the Hayle estuary and returns to the coast for the last stretch into St Ives.

Portreath Beach

1582 The Cornish fleet has grown to 88 ships

1584 The war with Spain determines 5,000 troops to be stationed at St Michael's Mount

Looking South West from Tubby's Head

Towanroath Shaft, Wheal Coates

| 1584 | Cornwall is represented by 44 MPs(39 more than today) | 1585 | Nicholas Prideaux builds Prideaux Place in Padstow |

Lobster Curgurrell Farm, Portscatho

For Chic Hotels, Culture, Glorious Gardens, Harbours, Shopping, Stylish Living, Watersports, Waterside Pubs & Cafés

This is the affluent heart of Cornwall. The great harbour of Falmouth visited by the Romans and Phoenicians is today a centre of maritime excellence. The magnificent Fal Estuary, home to thousands of sailing craft, is a playground for water sports. Connected by water, Truro lies twelve miles up river and is Cornwall's only Cathedral city. It's busy and attractive with designer shops, flea markets, restaurants and art galleries, and host to a food and drink festival on Lemon Quay in late September.

Across the estuary from Falmouth lies the sedate village of St Mawes and the exquisitely beautiful Roseland Peninsula. Not to be missed is the church at St Just. The coastal footpath is now tamer and the landscape gentler. It passes some fine chic hotels and pretty harbours on its journey towards St Austell and Charlestown. Hereabouts, is Eden, visited by many hundreds of thousands. This project has brought prosperity to this area, and has reminded many (who may have forgotten in their search for Mediterranean or Caribbean sun) of the hidden delights of Cornwall. Fowey has benefited too, and here the gastronome is spoilt for choice, for the many sophisticated eating and drinking holes on offer. It is also a fine place to stay. Take a trip up the Rivey Fowey and you will reach Lostwithiel, a small, charming town often overlooked by the traveller in a hurry. Or, you may continue eastward along the coast; the delightful fishing harbours of Polperro and Looe await you. Not far away are many great gardens to visit: Caerhays Castle, Heligan, Trelissick and more. Spring is the best time, for on display are the camellias, azaleas, magnolias and rhododendrons.

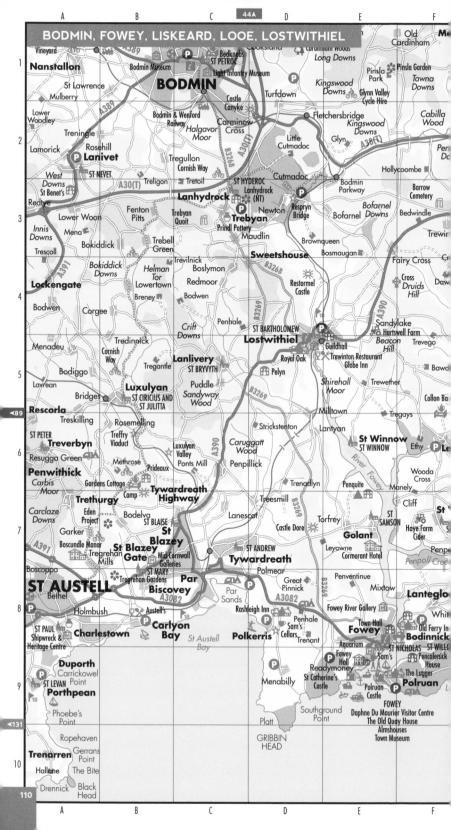

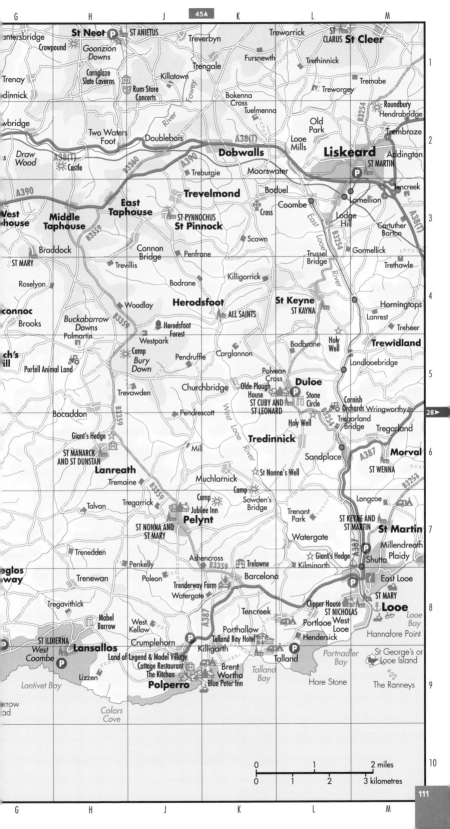

BODMIN

The County town of Cornwall is positioned in the centre of the county just off the busy A30. It is worth a stop-over to explore the interesting museums and the C15 St Petroc, the largest Parish Church in the County. It does not have the chic shops of Truro or the dramatic locations of Falmouth and Penzance. It is a quiet, country town full of history. Witness the historic prison, scene of public executions until 1862, and keeper of the Crown Jewels in WWI. The Information Centre is set in the old Court House where the ghosts and spirits of unlucky souls foundered. A good start-off point for the Camel Trail. Indoor swimming pool. E/C W. (C1)
www.bodmin.gov.uk
www.bodminlive.com

Woods Cafe

SPECIAL PLACES TO VISIT...

Bodmin & Wenford Railway, Bodmin General Station. Standard gauge steam railway. Café at Bodmin and a buffet car on most trains. Open Feb-Oct but Timetables vary throughout the year – Enquire for details. (C2) 01208 73555 www.bodminrailway.co.uk

Bodmin Museum, Mount Folly. Exhibits of local history, Victorian kitchen. 'Echoes of Bodmin Moor!' Open Apr-Sept M-F 10.30-4.30, Sa 10.30-2.30, Oct M-Sa 10.30-2.30. (B1) 01208 77067

Cardinham Woods. Just off the A30 and A38 is this wilderness of off-road cycling trails and walking trails of 1.5 to 4 miles. Graded leaflet available. 01594 833057. **Woods Café** for daily baked cakes and savouries, delectable home-made food. Log fires in winter, Al fresco in summer, child and dog friendly. Open daily 10-4.30. Holiday Flat to let. 01208 78111 www.woodscafecornwall.co.uk (D1)

Duke of Cornwall's Light Infantry Museum, The Keep. Three hundred years of military history, including weapons, medals, uniforms, memorabilia and extensive archive/research facilities. Open M-F 9-5. (C1) 01208 72810 www.cornwalls-regimentsmuseum.org

Prindl Pottery. Japanese inspired pots; some are of enormous size and originality, others are simply shaped in stoneware or porcelain. Open M-F 10-5. (C3) 01208 269493 www.prindlpottery.co.uk

St Petroc's Church, Bodmin. In C6 Cornwall's patron saint, St Petroc, founded a priory

Lanhydrock House (NT). Cornwall's grandest house was built in the C17 but following a fire in 1881 was largely rebuilt. It has superb Victorian kitchens and some magnificent plaster ceilings depicting scenes from the Old Testament, and a Long Gallery 116 feet long. C17 Gatehouse. Fine shrub and formal gardens. Woodland walks. Restaurants. Shop. Open daily 15 Mar-2 Nov except M when House only closed, but open BH Ms 11-5.30 (-5 in Oct), Gardens open all year 10-6. (C3) 01208 265950 www.nationaltrust.org.uk

here. Later, in the C9, a monastery was established, and in the Middle Ages the town became an important religious centre. The present large church was built mainly in the C15. Norman font, monuments and Wagon roof. (C1)

WHERE TO STAY...

Bedknobs at Polgwyn, Castle St. A large detached Victorian villa tastefully furnished and set in an acre of woodland. The bedrooms have massive beds, baths and power-showers. Walkers and cyclists are made, most welcome. (C1) 01208 77553 www.bedknobs.co.uk

CHARLESTOWN
There's a nostalgic atmosphere about this C18 china clay harbour built by Charles Rashleigh for the export of coal, tin and china clay. Home port for the famous tall ships of the Square Sail Shipyard Company. Diving centre. Location for TV series and films, notably; Poldark, Jane Austen's Persuasion, The Three Musketeers, The Onedin Line and The Voyage of Charles Darwin. Dogs are banned from the small beach, and you can only view from afar, not close to, the tall ships beside the harbour wall. Parking fee. (A8)

SPECIAL PLACE TO VISIT...

Shipwreck and Heritage Centre. The largest shipwreck artefact collection in the UK. Titanic display. Hands-on rescue equipment and lots more. Nelson Gallery. Open daily Mar-Oct 10-5. (A8) 01726 69897 www. shipwreckcharlestown.com

LIGHT BITES...
ACCOMMODATION...

Descending into Charlestown, on your R is **Charlies**, for breakfast, coffee and cakes.

Open most days. Then for more substantial fare, and a bed, **The Rashleigh Arms**, Charlestown Road. Log fires smoulder in winter below photos of times gone by, and in the dining area, its all contemporary and fresh. The food is burgers and hot dogs with chilli beef, etc. (A8) 01726 73635. www. rashleigharms.co.uk
Continue towards the harbour to, **Wreckers**, a bistro serving fresh fish and try the Seafest Special; moules mariniere, Tiger Prawns and Calamaris. Open 10-4, 6-9, winter from 11. 01726 879053 www.wreckers. me.uk For an alfresco drink and harbour view, it can only be from **The Pier House Hotel**.

FOWEY
Pronounced Foy. Fowey is a chic and fashionable town of narrow streets and brightly coloured houses, that overlook the superb natural harbour. A haven for yachtsmen, a commercial seaport and centre of many inns, restaurants, galleries and shops. Look out Padstow, you have serious competition. One of England's busiest towns in the Middle Ages, and home of the 'Fowey Gallants,' a bunch of reckless and invincible pirates who raided French and Spanish shipping. Still a busy exporter of China Clay. Fishing trips and passenger ferry to Polruan. Festival of Words & Music - May. Royal Regatta & Carnival week - Aug (2/3 week). (E8) www.fowey.co.uk

SPECIAL PLACES TO VISIT...

Daphne Du Maurier Literary Centre, 5 South St. Explores Fowey's literary connections with among others, the Du Mauriers, Kenneth Grahame, Leo Walmsley and Arthur Quiller-Couch. Houses the Information Centre. Open daily, all year. (E8) 01726 833616 www.dumaurier.org

Fowey Aquarium. Wide collection of marine life taken from our in-shore waters. Open daily East-Sept. (E8) 07753254736 www. foweyaquarium.co.uk

Fowey River Expeditions. Travel the river upstream by kayak, canoe or motorboat. Stopping off at Golant or Lerryn for lunch. Accompanied by staff and safety boat. Runs from Whitsun to mid-Sept. (E8) 01726 833019 www. foweyriverexpeditions.co.uk

Fowey River Gallery, 38 Fore St. Cornish contemporary paintings and crafts: ceramics, glass, jewellery. Open M-Sa 10-5, Su 11-4. (E8) 01726 833828 www.foweyrivergallery.co.uk

Fowey River. Rises on Bodmin Moor, especially beautiful between Lostwithiel and Doublebois - richly wooded riverbanks. Trout and Sea Trout fishing. (E6) www. ukriversguidebook.co.uk/fowey www.foweyriversailing.com

Luxulyan Valley. Wooded ravine overgrown with flowers and fauna. Watered by nearby clay pit. (B6)

Town Museum, Trafalgar Square. Local history and bygones. Open May-Sept M-F 10-5. (E8)

WHERE TO STAY...

Cormorant Hotel & Riverview Restaurant, Golant. Just the place to unwind after fretful days in the City. The gentle sway of the tidal Fowey River (which this hotel so spectacularly overlooks) will calm and rebuild your nerves. Small, comfortable bedrooms, a restaurant (lunch & dinner) with an award-winning wine list, and al fresco seating. (E7) 01726 833426 www.cormoranthotel.co.uk

View of Polruan from Fowey.

Fowey Hall Hotel, Restaurant & Spa.

This is a luxurious hotel designed for families with an entourage (Nannies and Au Pairs). Set in a quite superb hilltop location overlooking Fowey. It's thus child-friendly and has masses of things to do (and suggestions) on offer. It could be described as an expensive nursery. I loved the children's bright paintings adorning the walls. Dogs (teddies, rabbits, ponies?) (and mothers-in-law) welcome, too. In the off-season their lunches are great value. (E9)
01726 833866
www.foweyhallhotel.co.uk

Old Quay House, 28 Fore St.

Set in one of the most beautiful estuaries in Cornwall with a resplendent waterside location offering stylish accommodation which is chic, welcoming and relaxed. Award-winning restaurant. Open all year. (E8)
01726 833302
www.theoldquayhouse.com

Pencalenick House, Lanteglos-By-Fowey.

Perfect for that one-off, once-in-a-lifetime house party. This is luxury, par excellence - for you get 5-Star treatment: luxurious bedrooms, your own chef and full time house manager. Sleeps up to 16. Minimum stay: three nights. (F8) 020774 76858
www.pencalenickhouse.com

LIGHT BITES...A SOUPCON...

Descending into Fowey, on your L, the **Life Buoy Café**. Quirky and vintage with a nautical theme. Opens at 9 for breakfast and bacon butties. (E8) 07715075869
www.thelifebuoycafe.co.uk
and bearing L at **the Ship Inn**, for sandwiches/picnics, **Kittows of Fowey**, the fifth generation butcher and deli, for handmade pies and quiches, cakes and pastries.
01726 832639

Charlestown Harbour

Across the road is **Brown Sugar**, 2 South St. Opens at 8 for breakfast and Cornish roasted coffee. Home-made cakes. (E8) Around the corner for a harbour view, **King of Prussia**, Town Quay. Excellent pub grub: local fish, burgers with a view to match. B&B. Open daily. (E8) 01726 833694
www.kingofprussiafowey.co.uk

Now visit the main thoroughfare, Fore Street, for a cuppa, **Dwelling House**, 6 Fore St. Traditional tea room serving scones, home-made cakes. B&B. 01726 833662 (E8)
www.thedwellinghouse.co.uk....
Fancy a burger? **Sam's**, 20 Fore St. The original bistro, bar, lounge serving fresh fish, homemade burgers, and cocktails. Open daily. (E8) 01726 832273
www.samscornwall.co.uk

Its a long street, so you may be in need of a comfy sofa and another cuppa. It has to be the **Pinky Murphy's Café**, Ferry Road. A blaze of colour greets you, as do images of Elvis, Marilyn and surfing. Veggie. Comfy, snoozing chairs, upstairs. Dog/child friendly. Wifi. (E8) 01726 832512
www.pinkymurphys.com

MORE SUBSTANCE...

You have two options. Either take the Ferry to Bodinnick where a pre-prandial in the Old Ferry Inn may settle your nerves and digestion, or if in need of exercise return by foot to the town's centre and take the ferry to Polruan, and follow the coast path north east which will bring you to Bodinnick after a 60-90 minute trek where you will have earned your feast.

Old Ferry Inn, Bodinnick.

The chef, Pascal, is heavily influenced by French cuisine, and the seafood, duck and meat dishes will not disappoint you. 12-bedrooms with nautical objects and old photos. Free house. (F8) 01726 870237
www.oldferryinn.co.uk

Views of Looe

LISKEARD

Once an important Stannary Town surrounded by prosperous copper mines. Today, it's a busy market town for the agricultural community with attractive Georgian and Victorian cottages. Impressive large C15 Church, carnival - June (3rd week). Fat stock show - Nov (2nd week). (M2)
www.liskeard.gov.uk

WHERE TO EAT, DRINK & BE MERRY...

Olde Plough House, Duloe. A warm welcome awaits you in this neat and well laid out hostelry. Interesting mixture of seating. Food from local suppliers - delicious sausages and hams. Fine ales. Dogs welcome (Jack Russells rejoice). Smart modern bedrooms. (L5) 01375 891592
www.yeoldeploughhouse.co.uk

LOOE

You may well think you have entered a time-warp (with Dr Who and the Tardis) but, no, Looe is still an active and scruffy fishing village with a bustling quay, tidal harbour and off it, on either side, a web of narrow streets provide an unforgettable tableaux of Cornish life. Today, a popular embarkation point for deep-sea fishing. Perhaps, too many gift shops selling unnecessary junk, and too many pasty/fish'n chip parlours. You can forget all this by setting out to walk the Looe Valley Line, where a number of way-marked trails lead off along 8-miles of railway track, from Looe to Liskeard - leaflets available from the local Information Centre. Fish Market on East Looe Quay, Sub-Aqua club, boat trips. (M8)
www.looe.org

LIGHT BITES...

If you are self-catering, or camping, then get down early to the harbour and buy fresh fish from **Simply Fish**, or **Pengellys**. For breakfast you could try the greasy spoon, **the Harbour Café**, with a view over the harbour, or if you prefer a more sedate style, the locals recommend **Café Fleur** for tea/coffee and cakes, child and dog friendly, too. **Sarah's Pasty Shop** on Buller Street will gladly fill your stomach with the Cornish Miner's lifesaver. Beside the harbouth mouth and the RNLI Station is the seaview **Pier Café**. Over on the West side, the **Jolly Sailor**, oldest inn in Looe, but there's little evidence of its age. If you are in a mood for a Promenade, or Passagata, then follow the coast path on the West side, and after half-a-mile you will come to the **Island View Café** beside the Tennis Club.

Luxulyan Valley ac

| 1608 | The death of Sir Francis Godolphin, the man who did so much for Cornish mining and who added £1,000 per year to the Queen's coffers | 1620 | Sir Richard Robartes, Truro tin and wool merchant buys Lanhydrock Estate |

Polruan Boatyard

Pengellys Fishmongers, East Looe

Restormel Castle ss

| 1642-46 | English Civil War | 1643 | Cornish hero Sir Bevil Grenville is killed at the Battle of Lansdown, near Bath fighting for the Royalists |

WHERE TO STAY...

Clipper House, Dawn Rd., Hannafore, West Looe.
With panoramic views tucked away on a private road there is Clipper House providing self-catering accommodation for large groups of up to 22, or two family groups of 5 and 6. (M8) 01503 265607
www.clipperhouse.co.uk

LOSTWITHIEL

A charming town, and a great favourite of mine, often overlooked because travellers fail to drive off the main road into the side streets. It became the C13 capital of Cornwall and as the Stannary Court oversaw the administration of the medieval tin industry. The town has many beautiful buildings - the C13 Duchy Palace on Quay St., C13 Parish Church with splendid spire, C17 and C18 Georgian houses on Fore St. and the C18 Guildhall. Also, not to be missed, the important early C20 corrugated iron, army drill hall. C13 bridge. Boat trips to and from Fowey along the beautiful Fowey Valley. May Making ceremony, 'Beating the Bounds' - May (1st Monday) Carnival week - late July. E/C W. (D5) www.lostwithiel.org.uk

WHERE TO EAT, DRINK & BE MERRY...

Trewithen Restaurant, 3 Fore St. An intimate eatery that has built a fine reputation. Roast peppers glazed with Cornish Brie, or King Scallops drizzled with black pudding, and that's just for starters. Open Tu-Sa for brunch, from 11am. Lunch till 2pm. Supper from 6.30pm. (D5) 01208 872 373 www.trewithenrestaurant.com

LIGHT BITES...TO REST...

Lighting on Fore Street you will find a selection. First up on your R, the **Duchy Coffee Shop**. Opens from 10 M-Sa. Moving down the street for some herbaceous aromas, it has to be the **County Flowers Coffee Shop**. Open M-Sa from 10. Next door, for a bit of Italian style, **Calogero's**, 35 Fore St. Open for breakfast, lunch and dinner. For homemade pasta, soupa, cappucinnos. 01208 873 070 www.calogeros.co.uk
In need of a bed, then try **The Globe Inn** for accommodation on 01208 872501 www.globeinn.com

WHERE TO STAY...

Collon Barton, Lerryn. Fortress-like country house, high on a hill (like a lonely goatsherd, lahee-ho, lay-hee-ho lay he he...) overlooks a pastoral landscape of pastures green and emerald. Family portraits of the Grenville-Fortescues adorn the walls, the furnishings and bedrooms are comfortable and understated. Ideal centre for circular walks, canoeing and biking (from the village). (F5) 01208 872908

Hartswell Farm, Lostwithiel. Conveniently situated just outside the ancient capital of Cornwall. This C17 farmhouse has witnessed Civil War battles and much more. Today, a Twitcher's delight with farm trail, birds (feathered variety) galore and rare breeds. (E4) 01208 873419

SPECIAL PLACES TO VISIT...

Golitha Falls. Trail starts at Redgate Bridge. Follows riverbank and profusion of wild flowers to tranquil resting place. (K1) 01872 265710 www.english-nature.org.uk

Lostwithiel Church. Unusual octagonal spire and tower. Norman, octagonal font. C15 monuments. Clerestory windows. (D5)

Restormel Castle (EH). A model of military architecture, classically symmetrical with circular moat, and strategically positioned allowing breathtaking views across the River Fowey. Built c.1100 with C13 additions. Owned by Simon de Montfort and Richard, Earl of Cornwall. Open daily Apr-Oct 10-6 (5 in Oct). (D4)

Fowey

Polperro Reflections

POLPERRO

The quintessential and "Pretty As A Picture" idyll of a Cornish fishing village. It is, yes, picturesque, for indeed a timeless ambience pervades the narrow streets, pastel-shaded cottages and busy fishing harbour. It can be crowded during the day, and its a long slog from the top end car park. Best visited in the evening and you can enjoy a quiet pint at the Blue Peter Inn, and if, in luck, listen to the Fisherman's Choir practicing. Tea/gift shops, aplenty. Fishing trips. Regatta mid-July. Park above the village. (J9) www.polpero.org

WHAT TO VISIT...

Ebenezer Gallery, The Coombes. East Cornwall Society of Artists members exhibit here, plus two floors of paintings and ceramics. Open daily Apr-Oct. 10-5.30. (J9 www.ebenezergallery.org.uk

Land of Legend and Model Village. Replica of Polperro, built locally with animated display of Cornwall's history and legends. Open daily East-Oct 10.30-6 (9 high season). (J9) 01503 272378

Heritage Museum of Smuggling & Fishing, The Warren. Set in the old pilchard factory, a collection of C19 photos and C18 memorabilia. Open daily 10.30-5. 01503 272423 (J9)

Polperro Arts, Quay Road. An arts foundation with a gallery showcasing locally sourced arts and crafts. Open daily. (J9) www.polperroarts.org

WHERE TO EAT, DRINK & BE MERRY...

Blue Peter Inn. You can't miss it, and you won't want to. It overlooks the harbour and is an ideal spot to succour fine ales,

good pub-grub, tasty sandwiches and, a most pleasing view. Music nights: jazz to rock. (K9) 01503 272743 thebluepeterinn.yolasite.com

Couch's Restaurant. Richard McGeown will proudly tell you he has cooked at Marco P Whites, Le Manoir al Quatre etc and Ramseys, so be prepared for a feast of Cornish delights. (K9) 01503 272554 www.couchspolperro.com

The Kitchen, The Coombes. Park at the top of village and walk down to this snug fisherman's cottage for Looe Bay Scallops, Fillets of Lemon Sole and 28-day hung Ribeye Steaks. Dinner 7-9.30. (J9) 01503 272780

LIGHT BITES...

The action is around the Harbour so that's where you want to be (amongst the

1644 Sir Richard Grenville blocks Plymouth but is soon pushed west across the Tamar by the Earl of Essex's forces

1644 The Earl of Essex takes Bodmin

crowds, eh-ho?). Two spots: **The Wheelhouse** opens for breakfast/coffee, and serves fresh fish and gourmet burgers. Across the water, **the Museum Café**, with al Fresco dining, cream teas and cakes.

WHERE TO STAY...

Talland Bay Hotel. Boutique-style family run hotel with fine sea views close to the coastal footpath. You can choose to eat between fine dining in the Terrace Restaurant, or the bar-like Brasserie. Both do 'Catch of the Day.' Art and sculptures liven the bright surroundings. Dog friendly. (K8)
01503 272667
www.tallandbayhotel.co.uk

Trenderway Farm, Pelynt. The farm is 900 years old, the farming is of mixed arable, and the building is granite. The outside bedrooms are bright, and luxurious, and the breakfasts are organic and mammoth, the mood is tranquil. (K8) 01503 272214
www.trenderwayfarm.co.uk

POLKERRIS

Former pilchard fishing port. Harbour breakwater built by the Rashleighs of Menabilly. Remains of huge pilchard 'palace'. (D8)

WHERE TO EAT, DRINK & BE MERRY...

Sam's On The Beach, The Old Life Boat. Laid-back and family oriented; freshly made pizzas, burgers and shellfish. Its a cool place to be. Open all day. 01726 812255 www.samscornwall.co.uk/fowey

The Rashleigh Inn. Butting up to the beach, this is an ideal spot to linger over fresh fish and a glass of ice-cold cider. Hair ruffled by the sea breeze, blood pressure lowering. Easy to find, hard to leave. (D8)
01726 813991

POLRUAN

Attractive village with busy boatyard. The main street plunges almost vertically to the small quay on Fowey estuary. Cars not encouraged. Superb views from hill-top car park and walks east to Lantic Bay. Pedestrian ferry to Fowey. (F9)

LIGHT BITES...

The Lugger. Famous Inn noted for its pub-grub and fine ales. Dog friendly. Worth the ferry trip. (E9) 01726 870007
www.luggerinnpolruan.co.uk

At the bottom of the hill, **Crumpets Teashop**, 1 Fore Street. Open daily from 9 for all-day breakfasts, coffees, lunches and cream teas. Kids portions. 079968 502644 (E9)

ST AUSTELL

A major route centre which has seen much recent development and prosperity since the opening of first, Heligan Gardens and then, the Eden Project. Brewing centre and formerly an old tin mining village whose prosperity later relied very much on the china clay industry. The hinterland is made up of white mountainous pyramids, man-made lakes, and palm trees. There is a fine C15 perpendicular church, the Holy Trinity, an C18 coaching inn, The White Hart Hotel and a Georgian Quaker meeting house built in 1829. (A8)
www.staustelltown.co.uk

WHAT TO VISIT...

Kidzworld. 20,000 sq ft of mega-slides, giant tubes, assault course... fun for kids. Café. Open daily 10-6.30. (A8)
01726 815553
www.kidzworldcornwall.co.uk

Church of the Holy Trinity. The exterior is more interesting than the restored interior. The tower has sculptures set in the niches and the south porch has interesting open work tracery. Original wagon roof Carvings of Cornish saints. (A8)

Eden Project. Major multi-million pound project to turn old china clay pits into vast steel-framed domes (biomes) housing a tropical rain forest and a Mediterranean climate. This project of enormous vision, and ambition, has been an outstanding success, and has drawn visitors in their millions since opening in Spring 2000. It has also opened the floodgates of new architecture into the county. YHA and camping. Open daily from 10. (B7)
www.edenproject.com

Mid-Cornwall Galleries, St Blazey Gate. A fabulously successful gallery showcasing new collections of paintings, ceramics, blown glass, sculptures and jewellery. Open M-Sa 10-5. 01726 812131
www.midcornwallgalleries.co.uk

St Austell Brewery Visitor Centre. Traditional brewers for 140 years. Guided tours and beer sampling at 11am and 4pm. Licensed shop. Open M-F 10-5.30, Sa 10-4. (A8)
www.staustellbrewery.co.uk

Tregrehan Garden Cottages and Nursery. Woodland garden created in the C19 by the Carlyon family. Nursery. Camellias. Self-catering cottage. Open mid-Mar to end-May W-Su & BH Ms 10.30-5. (B7) 01726 812438
www.tregrehan.org

WHERE TO STAY...

Boscundle Manor, Tregreham Mill. Small, C18 country house hotel, restaurant and spa. Luxuriously furnished in contemporary designs, perhaps boutique style. Impressive wine list. 5 acres of private grounds. (B8)
01726 813557
www.boscundlemanor.co.uk

WHERE TO EAT, DRINK & BE MERRY...

Austell's, 10 Beach Road, Carlyon Bay. Brett Camborne-Paynter has a fine pedigree having cooked at The Ivy, The Waldorf and The Four Seasons. Modern British cuisine is his recipe for a succulent meal. Open Tu-Su 6-9 pm., Su lunch 12-2. (B8) 01726 813888 www.austells.net

Sam's On The Beach, Carlyon Bay. Another outpost of this successful pizza and burger bar. Open in season. (B8)

SPECIAL PLACES TO VISIT...

Carnglaze Slate Caverns. Famous subterranean lake with crystal clear blue-green water in huge underground chamber. Open all year M-Sa 10-5 & **The Rum Store,** Classical and pop concerts put on in underground 400-seat auditorium. Superb acoustics. (H1) 01579 320251 www.carnglaze.com

Cornish Orchards. Handmade apple juices, ciders and honeys from West Country orchards. Open W 10-3.30. (L5) 01503 269007 www.cornishorchards.co.uk

Haye Farm Cider, St Veep. Real, traditional, local farm scrumpy cider matured in wooden barrels. Open daily. (F7) 01208 872250 www.hayefarmcider.com

Herodsfoot Forest. Deer park, walks and cabins for self catering holidays. (J4) 03330110495

Porfell Animal Land. Designed for all ages to enjoy domestic and exotic wild animals, play area and walks in lovely countryside. Open 1/2 terms, then daily Apr-Oct 10-6. (H5) www.porfellanimalland.co.uk

Lanreath Church

CHURCHES OF INTEREST...

Lanreath Church. Norman cruciform, medieval screens and carved figures, and colourful monuments of the Grylls family. (H6)

Lanteglos-By-Fowey. Norman origins. C13 font. Brasses of the de Mohuns. C16 bench ends. (F8)

Liskeard Church. Separated from the town by slim valley. It is perpendicular and the second largest in the county. 13 consecration crosses - a unique feature, and undistinguished new tower. (M2)

St Martin-By-Looe Church. Norman origins with C15 additions, and ceiled wagon roof. Parclose Screen and C17 monuments. (M7)

St Neot's Church. Imposing building in scenic valley famous for the 15 medieval stained glass windows. Restored in 1830 by John Hedgeland. Perhaps only outshone in the West Country by those of Fairford in Gloucestershire. Wagon roof. Monuments of William Bere and family. The font is C13 and C15. (H1) www.stneot.org.uk

St Winnow. In an idyllic location overlooking the River Fowey. Superb bench ends; a ship with wood carver's mistake and a Cornishman drinking a flagon of cider. St Winnow settled here in 670 AD. Next door, a small agricultural museum serves tea. (E6)

BEACHES AND SURFING...

Charlestown. To west of harbour, sand and pebbles, strong currents. No dogs.(A8)

Carlyon Bay. Spacious golden sandy beach with all amenities in adjacent leisure centre.

The Rum Store, Carnglaze Caverns

1653 Parliamentary representation turned from 44 to 12 MPs 1661 Founding of Flushing village

Lantic Bay

Polgaver Bay. Cornwall's first official naturist beach. Boat hire, water skiing etc., P/WC/Café/ Bars. No dogs. (B8)

Par Sands. Large extensive sandy bay. Very popular with children, seaside amusements, boating lake, easy access, private harbour, china clay works, effluent on west side. P/WC/ Café/Huts. (C8)

Polkerris. Small sandy family beach sheltered by curving harbour wall. Safe bathing, S-B hire/P/WC/Café/Inn. Surfing - Popular. Big swell required. (D8)

Poldridmouth Cove. 15 mins walk fron P. Sheltered sandy cove. (D9)

Fowey - Readymoney Cove. 20 mins walk from town centre. Small sandy beach at LT. Good bathing, sheltered. WC/Tea rooms. (E9)

Lantic Bay. 10 mins walk from NT P. Follow path across fields, and down a steep 400ft climb to a lovely beach at LT. (F9)

Lantivet Bay. 15 mins walk from Lansallos, secluded beach with pebbles and shingle. (G9)

Talland Bay. Access via a steep narrow lane, shingle, rocks and sand at LT flanked by cliffs. P/WC/Café. (K9)

Portnadler Bay. Follow the coastal footpath for 1 1/4 mile from West Looe to a quiet sandy beach with rock pools. (L9)

West Looe - Hannifore. Rock pools and pebbles, sandy patches at LT. WC/Café/ Kiosk. (M8)

East Looe - Banjo Pier. Suntrap behind pier, sands and pebbles, good bathing. (M8)

East Looe - Plaidy Beach. Access by foot from Banjo Pier. Rock pools and shale. WC/ Café. (M8)

COASTAL FOOTPATH...

Porthpean to Looe: Approx 30 miles. It is worth exploring the port of Charlestown and seeking out a cup of coffee.

You may be in luck and be able to admire a tall ship in the dry dock. The path is easy going across Carlyon Bay, the coast does become more built-up as you approach Par Sands, past the thriving china clay harbour of Par. Lovely walk through pretty Polkerris, then up to the impressive cliffs of Gribbin Head (224ft) and an 84ft landmark, erected by Trinity House in the 1820s. There are fine views across towards the Lizard and Rame Head. At Polridmouth, you will come across sub-tropical flora, and on following the path, you will soon spy fine views of Fowey and its busy Harbour. Soon to pass the remains of St Catherine's Castle. Follow road into Fowey where there is a regular ferry to Polruan. Then, six miles of magnificent, lonely, cliff-top walking to Polperro. Inland are grazed fields and gentler contours, but the coast path is often steep and hard going in places. Polperro must first be explored before setting out again along a well maintained path that follows the cliff edge to Looe.

Brass of Thomas de Mohun, Lanteglos-By-Fowey

Jester, St Nonna, Altarnun

Noah Window, St Neots

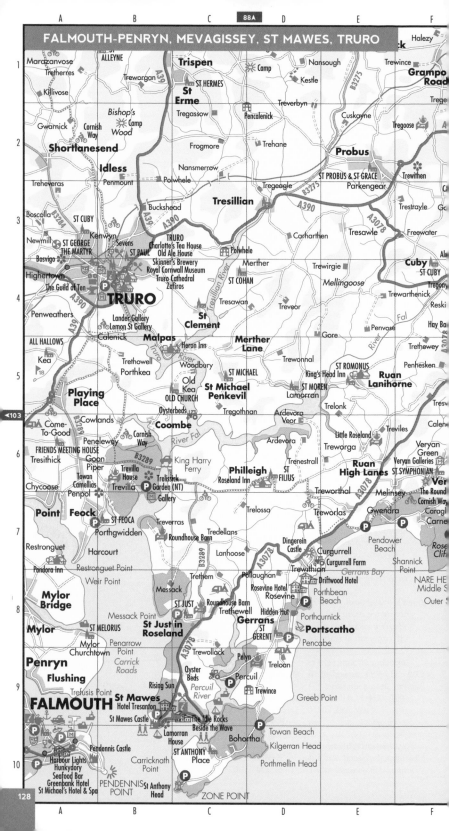

Falmouth ff

FALMOUTH

The site of the third deepest natural harbour in the World, and haven for international yachtsmen. The Phoenicians and Romans came here in search of tin. In the late C16, Sir Walter Raleigh persuaded the piratical, Killigrew family to develop the harbour's potential, and for 200 years Falmouth became the centre of the Mail Packet Trade, smuggling and piracy. Falmouth (Aberfal) is a busy and likeable town with many places in which to share a coffee, sink a pint or take a snack or meal. There is a lively café culture and we list some of the best in "Light Bites". The town has some new architectural developments, notably the National Maritime Museum and adjacent area. Outside the town, there is the Penryn Campus containing departments from the Universities of Exeter and Falmouth. At Wood Lane, the Universities Fine Art and Graphics departments. Popular yachting centre. Cinema and 3 beaches. Regatta week - mid Aug. E/C W. (A10) www.falmouth.co.uk

Falmouth ff

GALLERIES & MUSEUMS TO VISIT... WHAT TO SEE & DO...

Beside The Wave, 10 Arwenack St. Established in 1989 to provide an outlet for Cornwall's leading contemporary artists and craftsmen. Open M-Sa 10-5, Su 11.30-4. (A10) 01326 211132 www.beside-the-wave.co.uk

Fal River Links, The Quay. Travel by ferry or take a cruise up river to Trelissick or Truro. Cross to St Mawes. (A10) 01326 741194 www.falriver.co.uk

Falmouth Art Gallery, The Moor. Maritime pictures and quality temporary exhibitions. Work by J W Waterhouse and Henry Scott Tuke. Open all year M-Sa 10-5. (A10) 01326 313863 www.falmouthartgallery.com

Falmouth School of Sailing, Boat Park Grove Place. Courses range from dinghy, to keelboat, to powerboats, taking you to varying levels of seamanship. (A10) 01326 211311 www.falmouthschoolofsailing.co.uk

National Maritime Museum. With breathtaking views from the 29m tower, one of only three natural underwater viewing locations in the world. Hands-on inter-actives, A/V immersive experiences, talks, special exhibitions, and the opportunity to get out onto the water. This new generation of museum has something for everyone. New Viking Voyagers. Open daily 10-5. (A10) 01326 313388 www.nmmc.co.uk

Orca Sea Safaris, Discovery Quay. Your chance to see dolphins, seals and seabirds galore, a spectacular coastal safari. (A10) 01326 214928 www.falriver.co.uk

The Poly, 24 Church St. Arts centre devoted to cinema, comedy, dance, music, paintings and theatre, since 1833. Bar. Open daily. 01326 319461 (A10) www.thepoly.org

WHERE TO EAT. DRINK & BE MERRY...

Hunkydory, 46 Arwenack St. If art, the young and beautiful, chic decor, and sumptuous food (especially fish) feed your desires, this is it. Dinner 6-10. (A10) 01326 212997 www.hunkydoryfalmouth.co.uk

Hooked On The Rocks, Swanpool. They focus on 'What can be done with quality Cornish seafood, and a talented chef.' Set in a location with views to die for, with al fresco dining. Open daily from 10, lunch 12-2.30, dinner 5.30-late.

01326 311886
www.hookedcornwall.com

Olivers, 33 High St. Run by a well-known local family, and popular, indeed, with inhabitants of the locale, this bistro provides wholesome Cornish-inspired dishes. Open Tu-Sa for lunch and dinner. (A10) 01326 218138 www.oliversfalmouth.com

The Wheelhouse Crab & Oyster Bar, Upton Slip. You need to book well in advance to bag a table. The service is funny and friendly, and the food; crustacea, in all its arthropodic forms, is eaten with relish, and gusto. (A10) 01326 318050

LIGHT BITES...

Take a trip through Falmouth. Starting from the **Boat House**, great views and real ales, above the entrance to the the **Old High Street**. On your left the **Star & Garter**, for coffee and cakes, or lunch (more later) with fabulous harbour views, then on your right; **Kacho**, an authentic Japanese restaurant. All, simple dishes, cooked to order, Ramon wheat noodles, a speciality. Open Tu-Sa for lunch, F & Sa Saki evenings. Further down, **Café Cinnamon**, at 6 Old Brewery Yard, a licensed vegatarian café and coffee shop, with vegan and gluten free options. Open Tu-Sa 9.30-4.30. Descending on your left to: **Stones Bakery**, 28a High St., Falmouth's finest bakery, and coffee shop serving artisan bread, homemade cakes, pizzas and savoury tarts, baked on the premises. Open M-Sa. www.stonesbakery.co.uk

Soon to enter **The Moor**. Bear right, then onto Killigrew Street on your left where you are spoilt for choice. First to: **Good Vibes**, 28 Killigrew St., Exceptionally popular with "arty" students for the friendly vibes, and Brunchin Sundays. Its a treat. www.goodvibescafé.co.uk Back on yourself, and right into **Market Street**. Enter Bells Court. **Beerwolf**, for Books & Beer. What a brilliant combination. Arty books on sale, and fine ales and tables to sit, contemplate and restore order to one's soul. Next door: **Courtyard Deli**. Breakfasts, Soups, picnic hampers, tapas bar, afternoon tea. Open daily, all week from 8.30. www.courtyarddeli.co.uk

Moving along to: **Dolly's Tea Room & Wine Bar**, 21 Church St. Above Falmouth's finest bookshop. This is quite a fun experience. English tea coupled with Gin Cocktails after 6pm. For all dog lovers. www.dollysbar.co.uk

Opposite to freshen the palette. **Ciuri Ciuri Italian gelato**, 44 Church St. Smooth, soothing gelato, made on the premises, as only the Italians can do. **The Meat Counter**, 25 Arwenack St. Calling all Carnivores! The burgers relish will drip down your jaw...ecstacy. Onto: **Elixir Soup & Juice**, 42 Arwenack St. Be amazed at the delicate flavours and refined juices available to tempt you. Open daily. www.elixirsoupandjuice.co.uk **Harbour Lights**, Arwenack St. A celebration of the fish'n chip experience. Stuff your face with chips whilst admiring matched by a view to wonder at. Open daily. www.harbourlights.co.uk Further down the street: **The Stables**, Arwenack St. For pizza, pies and cider in the old Custom House. An enjoyable experience. 01326 211199 www.stablepizza.com Through the car park to: **Rick Stein's Fish & Chips**, Discovery Quay. A 130-seat restaurant, takeaway, Champagne and Oyster Bar. Open daily, lunch 12-2.30, dinner 5-9. (A10) www.rickstein.com. Behind, **Pizza Express**, and in the RH corner: **The Shack** (seafood), **The Shed** (Cocktails) and **The Ranch** (steakhouse & grill), all under the same ownership. Moving on to: **Gylly Beach Café**. Loved by students' visiting families for its location and no-nonsense food. Open daily. (A10) And, finally, many of my friends favourite, foodie, destination: **Provedore**, 43 Trelawney Rd. Its small, rustic and always ahead of the game. A basic tapas bar and café that started as a deli, and through acute demand evolved into this modest café. (A10) 01326 314888 www.provedore.co.uk Bon Appetit!

Stones Bakery ff

Mevagissey

AND SLEEP...

Bosanneth Guest House, Gyllynvase Hill. Exceptional value B&B provides smart, modern bedrooms, tasty Cornish breakfasts and supper, if required. (A10) 01326 314649 www.bosanneth.co.uk

The Greenbank Hotel, Harbourside. Falmouth's oldest, and recently refurbished hotel, has sweeping views of the harbour. Ancient stone-flagged floors, leather sofas and polished wood provide an aura of permanence and comfort. Spa treatments. Connected to The Working Boat Inn. For ale, conversation and a fabulous view. (A10) 01326 312440 www.greenbank-hotel.co.uk

Highcliffe Guest House, 22 Melvill Rd. This is a luxurious, family-run B&B in a smart, contemporary-furnished Edwardian villa. Perhaps, more like an intimate hotel. (A10) 01326 314466 www.highcliffefalmouth.com

St Michael's Hotel & Spa. This hotel has undergone a complete makeover to appease those seeking a hedonistic lifestyle. It's all contemporary décor. Flying Fish restaurant (very child-friendly) amidst subtropical gardens. (A10) 01326 312707 www.stmichaelshotel.co.uk

The Rosemary B&B, Gyllyngvase Terrace. A smart Edwardian town house, (comfortably furnished) designed by Ethel Mary Charles, England's first female architect. Sea views, within walking distance of the town, and close to the Woodland and Tremough campuses. (A10) 01326 314669 www.therosemary.co.uk

AND SPECIAL PUBS TO VISIT...

Heron Inn, Malpas. In fine situation overlooking the tidal River Fal. Modern, light decor provides a nautical ambience. Children welcome. Best visited on a warm summer's evening. (C5) 01872 272773

Pandora Inn, Restronguet. C13 thatched pub beside the estuary has a bagatelle of flagstone floors, cosy alcoves and low ceilings. Al fresco pontoon over the river. Children and dogs welcome. (A7)

The Star & Garter, 53 Old High Street. This restored old pub has created quite a stir amongst local foodies. With a self-styled butchery on-hand to produce Family Banquetting (large joints of meat) parties, who enthuse at the fine cuisine, and the harbour views. Opens from 10 for coffee/cakes. (A10) 01326 316663 www.starandgarterfalmouth.co.uk

FLUSHING

Those living on North Parade, Falmouth, and visitors to The Greenbank benefit for having a fine view of Flushing's waterfront lined with tall elegant C18 houses. A former steam packet centre and accessible venue for short and coastal walks to Penryn and Mylor. Two Inns; Royal Standard and Seven Stars, sailing club and pedestrian ferry to Falmouth. (A9)

TO SLEEP, TO DREAM...

An Chy Coth B&B, 37 Kersey Road. "The Old House" is a traditional C17 cottage, but with all the comforts of home. Double and single room. It will charm you. www.flushingbandb.co.uk

PENRYN

An attractive granite town (often overlooked) at the head of Penryn Creek. Picturesque steep main street with handsome restored, Georgian houses, and off it, run 'opes' and alleys with quaint cottages - just some of the 250 listed buildings, hereabouts. Granted Charter in 1236. Hence, a much older town than its more famous neighbour, Falmouth. In the C17, England's busiest port after London. The granite from Penryn's quarries helped to build New Scotland Yard, four London Bridges and the Fastnet Lighthouse. The home of Falmouth (& Exeter) University at Tremough Campus. A place of creativity and artistic endeavour where there is an undercurrent of bohemia at play. Town Fair - Aug BH W/E. (L9)

PLACES TO VISIT...

Caroline Fricker Bridal Wear & Makery, 13 Broad St. Hand-made, bespoke gowns from Modern to Vintage styles illustrate her exceptional craftmanship. Open by appointment. (L9) www.carolinefricker.com

Enys Gardens. The oldest garden in Cornwall, and home of Robert de Enys who lived here during the reign of Edward 1. Bluebells galore. An ambitious project is underway to restore this ancient garden to its former glory. Open Apr-Sept Tu Th & Su 2-5. (L8) www.enysgardens.org.uk

Fannie & Fox Gallery, 7 Broad St. A friendly co-operative with an eclectic mix of fine and applied arts: painting, ceramics, jewellery, glass, and they also hold workshops. Open Tu-Sa 10.30-5. 01326 378397 (L9) www.fannieandfox.co.uk

Glasney College, the Collegiate Church. Founded in 1275 by Bishop Bronescombe (of Exeter) to be the leading ecclesiastical powerhouse in medieval Cornwall. It controlled over 16 parishes, and was the setting for miracle plays in Cornish but was looted and destroyed during the Dissolution of the Monasteries, 1536-1545. The scholarship upheld here promoted the Cornish language which then languished, thereafter, and it was the Prayer Book Rebellion of 1549 that was the final nail in the coffin. Just a wall and field remain. (L9)

Jubilee Wharf. A triumphant design by Bill Dunster Architects. This is where Cornwall leads the field: a carbon neutral building that

is sustainable, holistic, green, and built for the community at large. It incorporates art and craft workshops, flats, a toddler group, yoga classes and the **Muddy Beach Café**, Opens for breakfast, lunch and dinner. A family business specialising in Little Plates (tapas) and Beach Boards (shared courses), al fresco, with a view overlooking the estuary. (L9) www.jubileewharf.co.uk

Malcolm Sutcliffe Glass Gallery, 2 West St. Blown studio glass made on the premises by Malcolm Sutcliffe, plus jewellery, paintings and cards. Open Tu-F 10-5, Sa 10-1. (L9) 01326 377020 www.malcolm-sutcliffe.co.uk

Penryn Museum. History of this ancient town established in the C13: Neolithic, Medieval Glasney College, trade and victualling, piracy and smuggling, copper and tin mining. Open M-F 10-3.30. (L9) 01326 372158

Sail Agnes. Charter this 46 ft Pilot Cutter, and explore the Cornish Coast, Isles of Scilly, Brittany and beyond. (L9) 07790 638084 www.workingsail.co.uk

LIGHT BITES & DRINKS IN PENRYN...

Earth & Water Deli, 6 St Thomas St. A friendly café to share a coffee, and to buy fresh bread and healthy foods. Open 9-5. (L9) 01326 259889 www.earthandwater.co.uk

Number 20, 14 Lower Market St. Cocktail and wine bar by night, café by day from noon. W is quiz night, Th backgammon, F guest ales. (L9) www.number-20.co.uk

The Thirsty Scholar, 18 West St. There has been a brewery/hostelry on this site for 600-years where many a rogue and smuggler has caste his

beady eye. Today, the food is wholesome and the ale, always most welcome to one's palette. B&B. (L9) 01326 372996 www.thethirstyscholar.co.uk

MEVAGISSEY
One of Cornwall's most picturesque and unspoilt fishing villages. The fine inner, and more recent outer harbour has been at the centre of the town's history for hundreds of years. A famous shark fishing centre, Ferry to Fowey. Nearby, Heligan Gardens. Feast Week-late June.(L4) www.mevagissey-cornwall.co.uk

SPECIAL PLACES TO VISIT...

Bodrugan's Leap. Sir Harry Trelowth of Bodrugan rode his horse over the cliff to be picked up by a passing fishing boat after fleeing the Battle of Bosworth in 1485. (L4)

Cofro, 14 Fore St. Affordable works of art by 30+ Cornish artists: jewellery, glass, sculptures, paintings. Open Su-F 10.30-5. (L4) 01726 842249 www.cofro.co.uk

Mevagissey Folk Museum, East Quay. Exhibits of local origin; fishing, agriculture and domestic life in an old 1745 building where luggers (fishing boats) were built. Open East-Oct 11-6. (L4) 01726 843568 www.mevagisseymuseum.co.uk

World Of Model Railways, Meadow St. Over 2,000 models, 30 trains controlled in sequence. Model shop. Open daily mid-Mar to Oct (Nov-Feb W/Es). (L4) 01726 842457 www.model-railway.co.uk

WHERE TO EAT, DRINK & BE MERRY...

The Alvorada, 2 Polkirt Hill. Family-run, Portugese restaurant with a lively atmosphere. Dinner 6.30-12. (L4) 01726 844327

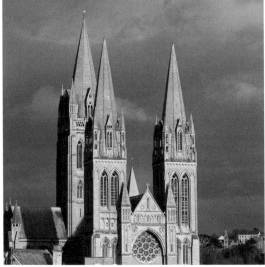

Truro Cathedral

TRURO

Cornwall's Cathedral city
and administrative centre is
spacious and has some elegant
and beautiful buildings of the
Georgian and Regency period.
In Lemon Street the Assembly
Rooms of 1772, and the
Mansion House and Prince's
House in Princes Street, and the
Cathedral, 1880-1910. The city
has seen much development of
late; there are multiple stores
and offices and flats overlooking
the river, and a wealth of
contemporary architecture as
in Truro College and the new
hospital buildings. Always a
busy town, it has the finest shops
in the county, and is abuzz with
cocktail bars for the after-work
crowd. Educational centre.
Cinema. (B4) www.truro.gov.uk

SPECIAL PLACES TO VISIT...

**Guild Of Ten, 19 Old
Bridge St.** Co-operative of
craftsmen and women living in
Cornwall. They seek to produce
workmanship of the highest
quality: knitwear, designer
clothing, glass blowing, ceramics
etc. Open M-Sa 10-5.30 (B4)
01872 274681
www.guildof10.co.uk

Lander Gallery, Lemon St.
Spacious open gallery displays -
C19 and C20 Cornish masters
to contemporary fine art and
crafts. Coffee shop. Open M-Sa
9-6. (B4) 01872 275578
www.landergallery.co.uk

**Lemon Street Gallery,
Lemon St.** Quality gallery
whose aim is to introduce the
British Art Scene to Cornwall.
Modern, contemporary art and
ceramics. Sculpture Garden.
Open M-Sa 10.30-5.30. (B4)
01872 275757
www.lemonstreetgallery.co.uk

**Royal Cornwall Museum,
River St.** World-famous
collection of minerals,
archaeology, ceramics, paintings
and old master drawings. Open
M-Sa 10-5 (except BH's).
(B4) 01872 272205 Next
door, the **Arts Café**. www.
royalcornwallmuseum.org.uk

Truro Cathedral. The first
English Cathedral to be built
after St Paul's. An imposing
building designed by John
Pearson, in the Gothic style,
1880-1910. Three soaring
spires, and an unrivalled
collection of stained glass

windows. Refectory for light
meals, 10-4. Open daily 8-6,
shop and Chapter House from
10. (B4)
www.trurocathedral.org.uk

LIGHT BITES AND DRINKS...

As Cornwall's only City, and
premier shopping destination its
no surprise that your choice is a
cornucopia of pleasures.

Truro's main shopping
thoroughfare, Boscawen Street,
runs East to West, and at each
end you will find most of the
cafés/tea rooms described
below. But, first, enter from the
South:-

The top of Infirmary Hill is a
good place to start. Opposite
the Richard Lander Monument
you will find the pub, **The
Thomas Daniell**, Infirmary
Hill. For Thomas Daniell was a
man of notoriety, and head of a
merchant's dynasty in the late
C18. This fine contemporary
pub/wine bar is popular with
the Ladies, too, and serves
breakfast 10-11.30, coffee and
cake, lunch 12-5 and supper
5-10. 01872 858110
www.tdtruro.com

1720   Ralph Allen, born in St Blazey, devises the first
cross-country postal service   1720   Botallack Mine, St Just brought into
operation

Descending Lemon Street, enter the **Lemon Street Market** (open M-Sa 10-5) (bakery, Illustrated Living gift shop, Fig Café, Oscars) and upstairs the **Lander Gallery** - see above. Walk through to, on your right, the Cornish Food Box Co. where you can purchase goods from over 120 local farmers and producers. Coffee shop. Open M-Sa from 9.30. Return to Lemon Street and make your way to the centre, Boscawen Street, bear R and immediately you will find the **Café Uneeka**, the King of Cafés. Downstairs, a gift shop selling all manner of gifts and cards. Upstairs is the café; homemade cakes and soups, wifi, lunch 12-3 and takeaways. www.uneeka.com

For a more traditional tea party, take a R and enter Coinage Hall to **Charlotte's Tea House**… below, **Pizza Express**. Bear R on leaving into Duke Street, the **Duke Street Sandwich Deli**, for sarnies, salad boxes, paninis, soups and takeaways. 01872 320025

Walking towards the bridge, on your L **Janosik** for Polish hams and sausages. Go back on yourself, bear R into St Mary's Street. Fancy a gelato ice cream or milk shake with an Italian pastry, try **Angelato**. Moving on, to manys favourite Truro eatery, **The Old Grammar School**, 19 St Mary's Street, sister to The Thomas Daniell. The eccentric layout may tease you, the coffee/cakes and café lunches will surprise you, and the tapas/cocktails/music will endear you, to linger. 01872 278559 www.theoldgrammarschool.com

If rustic ales are to your liking, and you feel a thirst coming on, and time to assuage your condition then turn around, cross the x-roads into Quay Street and head along to **The Old Ale House**. To savour

the flavours and delights of the West end of Boscawen Street. Passing Waterstones and Lloyds Bank to bear R at fork, and its 100 metres to the **Arts Café**, 25 River Street beside the Royal Cornwall Museum. In summer alfresco eating is a pleasure here, the food is wholesome and the ambience lends itself to combing the daily papers and art books. In winter a log burner warms your cockles, and a hot drink and toasted panini will soothe you. 01872 274974 www.truroartscompany.co.uk.

On leaving, turn R, then L into Little Castle Street where you will find **Bone China** at No 57, a vintage cocktail café open M-W 11-6, Th-Sa 11-11. An extravaganza of tea drinking, colourful cocktails, vintage crockery and an Alice In Wonderland party. www.bonechinatruro.com. Turn L to junction of Kenwyn Street, and cross to **The Secret Garden Café**, 15 Kenwyn Street. A popular lunch venue; homemade quiches and tarts, especially cater for gluten free, vegan and veggie dishes. Open Tu-Sa 10.30-4.30. 07949 293399 wwwsecretgardencafe. co.uk Across the road, **Archie Browns**, 105 Kenwyn Street. By this time you may will need this health food shop and vegetarian cafe. Open M-Sa 9-4. 01872 278622 www.archiebrowns.co.uk Leave and turn L towards the City centre. Shortly on your L, **The Hubbox**, The Old Chapel, 116 Kenwyn Street. After this coffee/tea shop crawl you may be in need of some hardy sustenance; gourmet burgers, hot dogs, a craft beer or cocktail, all surrounded by walls of derring-do. Open daily 11.30-9. 01872 240700 www.hubbox.co.uk

Now for some retail therapy! In need of some refreshment? Then head to the **Midtown Deli & Café**, 3 King Street for

their homemade soups, quiches, bread, smoothies where you can seek some 5-star treatment. Open daily.

If you follow this trail of excess you will notice not all coffee joints have been included. Its not that I have your digestive systems at heart. Its that I don't have the space! Bon Appetit!

WHERE TO EAT, DRINK & BE MERRY...

Charlotte's Tea House, Colnage Hall, 1 Boscawen St. Step back in time into a sanctuary of Victoriana. Full range of teas, coffees, sandwiches, scones, cakes and a formal, waitress service. Second-hand bookshop - Golf, a speciality. Open M-Sa 9.45-4.45. (B4) 01872 263706

Gravy Boesti, 8 Edward St. Three great mates have pulled together to create a fine dining experience for you to salivate and be seduced by their audacious talents. Open Tu-Sa. (B4) 01872 222237 www.gravy-boesti.co.uk

Mannings, Lemon St. Popular after-work cocktail bar for the ever-affluent professional classes, and their mates. Hotel and restaurant. (B4) 01872 270345 www.manningshotels.co.uk

Old Ale House, Quay St. A great atmosphere pervades this busy town pub. Food produced in full view and it's good, too. Wide range of local and East Anglian ales. Recommended. (B4) 01872 271122. www.old-ale-house.co.uk

Skinner's Brewery, Newham Rd. Visit a working brewery and sample their fine ales. Guided tours & tastings (11 & 2.30), visitor centre and shop. Open M-F (East-Oct). (F4) 01872 271885 www.skinnersbrewery.com

The Hubbox

Truro Arts Café

Cornish Food Box Co

Lemon Street Gallery

THE ROSELAND PENINSULA

In Cornwall the landscape can, in the main, be hard and unforgiving. One thinks of the rugged North Coast and the interior of the county, not known for its aesthetic qualities. But, every now and then, you will come across a gentle, pastoral landscape that is magical. From the country lanes switching back and forth from the Fal and Tresillian Rivers taking you through woodland to the little ports of Portloe and Portscatho. It is a place to travel slowly and to succour the isolated churches and views across the brooding creeks. The road from Truro to St Mawes seems to take an age for the traveller in a hurry. More fool him who follows a sat-nav (and misses everything). October Music Festival www.roselandfestival.co.uk

PORTLOE

Little fishing village with a narrow and rocky harbour. A wonderful view from the coastal path to the north. (G6)

The Lugger Hotel. C17 smugglers' inn has been turned into a chic, trendy restaurant. The local boats supply the fish. Accommodation. Lunch 12-2, dinner 7-9. (G6) 01872 501322 www.luggerhotel.co.uk

PORTSCATHO

An old harbour settlement on the Roseland shore with narrow streets beset with pretty cottages (mainly second homers) running down to a tiny pier. Plume of Feathers Inn. (D8)

GALLERIES...

Spindrift Gallery, 8 The Quay. A showcase for Cynthia Greenslade and her friends whose paintings reflect Cornwall and, especially Roseland. Also, hand-painted furniture. Open Th-Su and Tu in summer from 10.30. 01872 580155 (D8)

The Harbour Gallery, 8a The Quay. "Making Art Accessible" is their Raison d'Etre, with regular exhibitions and "Meeting The Artist" evenings. Open Weds-Su from 10.30. 01872 580807 (D8) www.theharbourgallery.co.uk

The New Gallery, 5 The Square. This gallery is the brainchild of Chris Insoll and has ben described as The Cornish Art Colony. It represents established West Country artists, and is a treasure trove of unexpected pleasures. Open Th, F & Sa 10-12.30, 2-5. 01872 580445 (D8) www.chrisinsoll.com

FEASTY BITES...

Curgurrell Farm. The farmer is Portscatho's Harbour Master who owns a bevy of lobster and crab pots. You can drop in and buy freshly caught crustacea, and fish caught off-the-line; bass, plaice etc. Open daily Apr-Oct & Dec 10-5. Self-catering accommodation. (E7) 01872 580243 www.curgurrellfarmshop.co.uk

Hidden Hut, Porthcurnick Beach. Acorns to oak trees - Its amazing that a small, rustic, outdoor beach café with access via the coast path should host Feast Nights - that are now over-subscribed with 30,000 on their email list for a mere 150 covers to fill. Open daily for breakfast, lunch and tea in the season. Cash only. (D8) www.hiddenhut.co.uk

Tatams Stonebaked. These converted loos provide fresh coffee, pastries and fine views of Portscatho's beach. Open daily in season. (D8)

WHERE TO STAY, NEARBY...

Driftwood Hotel. Stylish, tasteful, chic, and a professional expertise to soften the edges of your hard-won battles. Many of the furnishings are sculpted pieces of driftwood: mirrors, table lamps etc. A relaxed ambience pervades, and the sea views are stunning. You can relax in the (natural) garden, or follow the path down to the private beach. The Michelin Star restaurant - one of Cornwall's finest, is impressive. Family-friendly. No dogs. (D8) 01872 580644 www.driftwoodhotel.co.uk

Little Roseland B&B, Treworga. A delightful C18 Cornish house surrounded by an enchanting garden. Your hostess, Didi Vernon Miller has brought all her interior design skills to bear on the gorgeous bedrooms. Quite a find. (E6) 01872 501243 www.littleroseland.co.uk

Roundhouse Barn B&B, St Just in Roseland. Luxurious B&B for adults over 15 who seek the latest techno wizardry, King-size beds, cream teas and quiet. No pets or children. (B7) 01872 580038 www. roundhousebarnholidays.co.uk

Rosevine Hotel. A new style of hotel designed for families and groups. Separate, independent units, offer self-catering but have the added bonus of a top-notch restaurant and hotel facilities to hand. All set within gardens overlooking the sea. Indoor pool. Open to non-residents. (D8) 01872 580206 www.rosevine.co.uk

TO QUOFF FINE ALES & GOOD FOOD...

Roseland Inn. Friendly, crowded pub with log fires and low ceilings. Cornish produce makes up the menu. Daily specials. Booking advised. Micro-brewery. Dogs and children welcome. (D6) 01872 580254 www.roselandinn.co.uk

Jubilee Wharf, Penryn

Panoramic Terrace View, The Idle Rocks ss

ST MAWES

An attractive, sunny haven of bright, mediterranean light popular with yachtsmen and second home-owners, lieing on a tributary of the Fal Estuary. The main centre for the Roseland Peninsula with easy, ferry access to Falmouth. And, a strategic spot from which to explore the eating houses and gardens of Roseland. Boat/fishing trips, Percuil Regatta - Aug. (B9)
www.stmawes.info
www.stmawessailing.co.uk
www.stmawes-ferry.co.uk

WHERE TO EAT, SLEEP & BE MERRY...

Hotel Tresanton. This chic, family-friendly hotel has raised the bar by which all are judged in Cornwall, and elsewhere. Owned by the interior designer Olga Polizzi (of the Forte family) and her husband, the political commentator William Shawcross. It is a superb example of understated good taste. The bedrooms are bright and colourful, and finely tuned with a blend of contemporary and antique furnishings. Note the mosaics in the bathrooms. All have sea views. Sculptures and fine art is everywhere. The service is discreet. The highly acclaimed restaurant is noted for seafood. (B9) 01326 270055
www.tresanton.com

St Mawes Hotel. A (little) sister to The Idle Rocks. Smart and chic, but with less formality. Great sea views. Open for coffee, afternoon tea and cakes, or perhaps, a bucks fizz, or two. (C9) 01326 270266
www.stmaweshotel.com

The Idle Rocks. This is a beautiful and chic hotel, to relax, be seen, and to look out across a blue sea, mirrored by the slick interior designs and artworks lovingly created for your aesthetic sustenance. Enchanting. Open to non-residents, and a perfect venue for an al fresco lunch on the Terrace. (C9) 01326 270270
www.idlerocks.com

LIGHT BITES...

Stepping off the Ferry, you can't miss the **St Mawes Bakery** who have been baking bread every day for 70-years except (and I quote) on the Sabbath. The scones are great value, and the humour light-hearted. Teas, too. Then its a stones throw to, **Café Chandlers & Deli**. A harbour view from which to succour fresh coffee and pastries, made on the premises, and homemade soup for lunch. Open 9-11 for breakfast, teas until 4.15. (C9) 01326 270998
www.caféchandlers.co.uk

Turning L for the only, proper, pub in St Mawes, **The Victory Inn**. A sharp ascent, and a warm welcome to be had with

Caerhays Castle & Gardens ss

1752   Cornish Stannary Court (independent administrators of the tin industry) is suspended by the King

1755   Henry Bone, Cornish born, becomes the Prince of Wales's enamellist

seafaring images on the walls, doom bar to sup and special feast nights of steak/curry/ fish'nchips. For lunch try the 'Medley of Sea Fish.' (C9) 01326 270324 But, if you have kids in tow, and seek space, a tankard of lager, its a few steps to, **The Rising Sun**. A family-friendly, seaside hostelry providing an all-day service. Food is available from the restaurant or bar. Seating areas outside. Dogs and children welcome. B&B in brightly coloured rooms with all mod cons. (B9) 01326 270233 www.risingsunstmawes.co.uk

CASTLES, HOUSES & GARDENS TO VISIT...

Bosvigo. A plantsman's garden, best seen in summer (June-Aug); series of enclosed and walled gardens with herbaceous borders. Nursery. Open Mar-Sept W, Th & F 11-6. (A3) www.bosvigo.com

Caerhays Castle & Gardens. 60-acres of informal woodland gardens created by J C Williams who sponsored plant hunting expeditions to China. Noted for camellias, magnolias and rhododendrons. Garden open daily mid-Feb to late May, 10-5.00. Castle from Mar to late June 12-3 M-F. (J5) 01872 501310 www.caerhays.co.uk

Creed House Gardens. 5-acre Georgian Rectory garden. Tree collection, rhododendrons, sunken alpine and walled herbaceous gardens, trickle stream and ponds. B&B. Open to groups only. (G2) 01872 530372 www. creedhouse.co.uk

Heligan Gardens. Explore 200-acres of Cornish countryside, including award-winning productive garden restoration, atmospheric pleasure grounds, sub-tropical 'Jungle,' valley and estate land incorporating a pioneering wildlife conservation project.

Heligan Gardens ss

Tearoom/Plant Centre. Open daily, all year from 10. (K3) www.heligan.com

Lamorran House Gardens. 4-acre Mediterranean garden overlooking the sea. Water, palms and sub-tropical features. Open Apr-Sept W & F 10-5. (B9) 01326 270800 www.lamorrangardens.co.uk

Trelissick Garden (NT). Extensive park, farmland and woods. Large garden, lovely in all seasons with beautiful views over Fal Estuary and Falmouth Harbour. Woodland Walks beside River Fal. Open daily from 10.30. (B6) 01872 862090 www.nationaltrust.org.uk

Hotel Tresanton vi

St Mawes Castle

Trewithen Gardens. 30-acre garden renowned for its magnificent collection of camellias, rhododendrons, magnolias and many rare trees and shrubs, surrounded by traditional parkland landscaped in the C18. New sculpture fountain. Gardens open daily 10-4.30 Mar-June & Aug BHs 2-5. House open M & Tu 2-4. (F2) 01726 883647 www.trewithengardens.co.uk

Pendennis Castle (EH). Built 1544-46 in the age of the Cannon and gunpowder as one of a chain of castles Henry VIII erected from 1538 to deter French Invasion. Circular keep with drawbridge, portcullis, spy holes and spiral staircase. Superb viewpoint. To the south-east is the blockhouse built on the rocks. Open daily mid-Feb to Oct & winter W/Es, 10-4. (A10)

St Mawes Castle (EH). Built in 1540-43 as a link in Henry VIII's chain of coastal defences. A fortress of striking symmetry; trefoil shaped with gun emplacements, drawbridge and heraldic decorations, and set

in sub-tropical gardens. Superb viewpoint. Great place for a wedding. Open daily mid-Feb to Oct & winter W/Es, 10-4. (B10)

ANCIENT CORNWALL...

Castle Dore. Prehistoric earthwork with inner ramparts. Deserted in AD 100, occupied in C5. Legendary setting for the love story of Tristan and Iseult. (D7)

WHERE TO STAY...

Caerhays Estate Luxury Holiday Cottages. From The Vean (see below) to the Fish Sheds and Lime Kilns overlooking Portholland's beach to the Old Village Hall. (J5) 0800 032 6229 www.nicheretreats.co.uk

Hay Barton, Tregony. Just the perfect accommodation for groups of four. The house is split into two, so the B&B area of two (light and airy) bedrooms is separate from the main house. All the fabrics are Cath Kidston and Colefax & Fowler, the beds are zip-link doubles, the breakfasts of yoghurt, grenola

and farm eggs are made on the premises. Tennis Court. Wi-Fi Internet access. (F4) 01872 530288 www.haybarton.com

Lower Barn B&B, St Ewe. Fabulous bedrooms, fully equipped gym, chill out rooms, therapies on hand, bubbling hot tubs and hedonistic indulgences, all set within beautiful Cornish countryside. (J2) 01726 844881 www.lowerbarn.co.uk

The Vean, Caerhays. This Georgian rectory on the Caerhays Estate has been transformed into a sumptuously decorated country house (for house parties) with all things Cornish thus helping reduce their carbon footprint. B&B. Dinner. (J5) 01872 501310 www.thevean.co.uk

Tregoose B&B, Grampound. This private house exudes old style country house living. Generations of family portraits line the walls, the furnishings are antique and tasteful. The bedrooms are comfortable. Evening meals, an option. Set on farmland belonging to the

1769   Bodmin to Launceston turnpike road in operation

1777   Dolly Pentraeth dies. The last true speaker of the Cornish vernacular (language)

Pendennis Castle ss

Trewithen Estate. WL. (F2) 01726 882460 www.tregoose.co.uk

Trevalsa Court Hotel, School Hill Rd, Mevagissey. An interesting combination of a cosy boutique-style hotel within an Arts & Crafts Movement building. It also has its own secluded cove. (L3) 01726 842468 www.trevalsa-hotel.co.uk

Trevilla House, Feock. The perfect location for garden lovers as it's close to Trelissick. Jinty, your charming hostess, will treat you as a house guest and will become invaluable to you as a mine of local knowledge. Family portraits and photographs adorn the walls, the beds are high with custom-made mattresses, breakfast is taken in the conservatory overlooking Carrick Roads. (B6) 01872 862369 www.trevilla.com

Wild Escapes, Tregothnan Estate. You have a choice; from a Shepherd's Hut beside an idyllic creek to cottages in remote spots on the Lizard Peninsula. The Estate produces its own blended tea, charcoal and trees/shrubs for gardens and nurseries. www.tregothnan.co.uk

CHURCHES TO VISIT...

Creed. Lavish windows in south aisle. C13 trefoil arch. (G3)

Falmouth, St Charles The Martyr Church. Classical C17 with oblong tower. Sir Peter Lely portrait of Charles I. C15 pulpit embellished with vine carvings. Memorials reflect Falmouth's role as a Royal Mail Packet Station. (A10)

Fowey. A mighty church that was sadly sacked by French pirates in the C15. Jacobean pulpit made from a Spanish galleon. Tall tower. C12 font. Rashleigh monuments are exceptional. (E8)

Golant. Beautifully situated C15 church with fine wagon roofs, intricate wood carvings surround the pulpit, and C15 glass. Holy well. (E7)

Mylor. Celtic cross with Norman doorway and superb setting above the creek overlooking hundreds of yachts at anchor. (A8)

Probus. C16 tower, tallest in county of Somerset design (striking and intricate tower) similar to North Petherton, C16 brasses. (E2)

St Clement. C13-14. Above the beautiful Tresillian River. Well restored in 1868. (C4)

St Just In Roseland. An iconic view of a Cornish Church, photographed in a thousand apertures. A quite gorgeous situation overlooking the creek within a tropical garden. Fascinating tombstones. Best visited at high tide so you can see the reflections. (C8)

St Michael Penkevil. Large, statuesque building of late C13-14 in feudal village with C17 & C19 monuments, and later restoration which has covered earlier work of great interest, adjacent to the Tregothanan Estate. (C5)

The Round Houses, Veryan

SPECIAL PLACES TO SEE & VISIT...

Carrick Roads. 4-mile long valley fed by 5 tributaries. Boat trips from Falmouth to Truro and St Mawes from Prince of Wales Pier. At Custom House Quay, trips to Helford Passage and Roseland, in summer season. Popular with yachtsmen. (B6) www.falmouthport.co.uk

Floe Creek. Haven for wildfowl and herons. Start of 6 1/2 mile walk around peninsula:- to Towan Beach, coast path to Zone Point, Carricknath Point, St Anthony and back. Shorter 3 1/2 mile walk:- Westwards direct to Porthmellin Head and St Anthony. (C10)

Loe Beach, Feock. Watersports and the kids club will keep your children amused for hours and days. (B7)

Mylor Churchtown (Harbour). Flourishing yachting centre complete with chandlers and three eateries: or Mylor Harbour Café, open all year, fish restaurant and bistro. Car park. (A8) www.harbourviewfalmouth.co.uk

The Waterside Gallery, 21 Marine Parade. A flourishing little gallery specialising in marine/coastal images, plus ceramics, driftwood sculptures and jewellery. Open daily. 01326 270136 www.watersidegallery.co.uk

Tregony Gallery, 58 Fore St. Contemporary landscapes/seascapes of the Roseland Peninsula by John Brenton, David Rust...Open daily. (F4) www.tregonygallery.co.uk

Trelissick Gallery. Set within the National Trust's garden, it is run in partnership with Cornwall Crafts to show off the best of Cornwall's arts and crafts. Open daily Mar-Dec 10.30-5.30. (B6) www.trelissickgallery.co.uk

Veryan - The Round Houses. Five circular thatched houses built during the days of superstition. Designed with conical roofs, pointed doorways and window arches, so that 'the devil could find no niche in which to hide.' (F6)

BEACHES AND SURFING...

Falmouth - Swanpool Beach. Sandy cove, safe bathing, boating adjacent. Kayak hire. P/WC/Café. (A10)

Falmouth - Gyllynvase Beach. Popular family beach with spacious sands, access P/WC/Gylly Beach Café. (A10)

Falmouth - Castle Beach. Safe bathing, rockpools and sands. All facilities. (A10)

Towan Beach. Sand dunes, shingle, rock pools and unspoilt. P. (D10)

Mylor Harbour

1791 | Charles Rashleigh develops the port of Charlestown

1792 | The founding of Cornwall's county library

Portscatho

Porthcurnick Beach. Sandy patches, facilities in Portscatho. P. Hidden Hut Café. (D8)

Pendower / Carne Beach. Lovely sands extend for 1 mile. Fine bathing and rocks. P/WC. (E7)

Kiberick Cove. Secluded and tricky access, sand exposed at LT. (F7)

Portloe. Good bathing with grey shingle at LT. P/WC/Inn. (G6)

East & West Portholland. Shingle with sand at LT. HZ cliffs to sides P/WC. (H6)

Porthluney Beach. Popular sheltered family beach with extended sands. P/WC/Kiosk. (J6)

Hemmick Beach. Steep 1 in 5 descent to small sandy beach. (K6)

Bow Or Vault Beach. Steep, tricky path down to spacious sands and shingle. A Naturists favourite. (L6)

Gorran Haven. Family resort with fine bathing and spacious sands. P/WC/boats for hire. (L5)

Portmellon. Good bathing off small sandy beach, rocks at both sides. P/WC/Inn/Café. (L4)

Pentewan. Spacious sands, HZ bathing; strong currents, avoid channel. P. Surfing - Sheltered spot. Waves only occur after an enormous swell, rarely in summer. Hollow beach break. (L3)

Porthpean. Popular family beach with safe bathing, rock pools and old fish cellars. P/WC/Café. (M1)

COASTAL FOOTPATH...

Falmouth To Porthpean: Approx. 40 miles. Two ferry journeys are required to continue along the path. The first, a regular ferry trip to St Mawes sails all year, the second in summer only, across the Percuil Estuary from St Mawes to St Anthony-in-Roseland. At other times, it's usually possible to make arrangements with local boatmen. From St Anthony Head and Zone Point, there are superb views south overlooking Carrick Roads, or looking north east towards the coast up to Portscatho. The route is easier along Pendower Beach and up to Nare Head (331ft), slate cliffs and hedgerows of foxgloves and red campion in summer with a lovely descent to Portloe. From this juncture you will come upon sandy beaches, smugglers' coves and evidence of the china clay industry. East past delightful Portholland and remote farmland meeting

the sea, then the steep climb to Dodman Point where there is a granite cross erected in 1896 as a mark for fishermen. Offshore are some notorious currents and the scene of many shipwrecks. The path carries on down to Gorran Haven past the long sweep of Vault Beach. Beyond Chapel Point and Bodrugan's Leap, the path becomes easy going, the landscape has softened. The harsh cliffs and thunderous roar of the north coast, Penwith and Lizard are far behind. Beyond Mevagissey, you are in holiday country as you cross Pentewan Sands, but soon the path is lonely and remote again towards Black Head as it sweeps into St Austell Bay.

Mylor Harbour

Dusk, Mounts Bay

For Contemporary Art, Dramatic Cliffs, Fabulous Beaches, Mediterranean Light, Stone Circles, Sub-Tropical Gardens and Wild Flowers.

A magical spirit embraces these two peninsulas as the elements have shaped the landscape and its hardy people.

From the tall cliffs of Land's End, to the great granite boulders of Nanjizal, to the brilliant white sands of Porthcurno, the interior is a patchwork of treeless fields separated by drystone walls. Yet, on the south east corner are the sheltered harbours, Newlyn and Mousehole, and the valleys, Lamorna and Penberth.

Early Man settled here leaving stone circles and ancient burial mounds. The Early Celts came too, and their ancient crosses remain. For a brief period tin and copper mining brought affluence, and the haunting Engine Houses can be seen at Pendeen and Botallack.

In the C19 and C20 the brilliant Mediterranean light beckoned artists and their followers. The names of Patrick Heron, Barbara Hepworth and Bernard Leach became synonymous with the St Ives movement in the C20. The number of artists increased into the C21, and the towns of Penzance, St Ives and St Just are today thriving centres of art and craftsmanship.

The Lizard is the most southerly point of Britain, and off Lizard Point lie the graveyards of many fine ships. This peninsula shares many characteristics with its neighbour Penwith; a warm, equable climate is rarely touched by frost or snow. The Lizard is a National Nature Reserve of over 4,000 acres, and is a wonderland for botanists, geologists, ornithologists, and the amateur nature lover.

It is also a place of many contrasts, from the thrashing waves of Porthleven Sands to the peace and calm of the Helford River (a mere six miles to the east) overlooked by the sub-tropical gardens of Trebah and Glendurgan.

Not to be forgotten, the fabulous family beaches (Kynance Cove and Kennack Sands) and little harbours (St Anthony and Helford). Whether you choose to beach it, or muck about in boats, you'll be hard pressed to find a safer or better destination for your summer holiday.

HELSTON

The Market town for the Lizard Peninsula, and venue for the Floral Dance (around 8 May) when elegantly dressed couples dance through the streets to welcome the coming of Spring, and locals take the opportunity to sample too much of the Spingo brew in the Blue Anchor. It is possibly the only day in the Cornish Year when you will see such sartorial formality, and a perfect coiffeur, a rare sight indeed - the prevailing winds put paid to this. It is worth exploring Church and Coineagehall Streets, location for fine, sophisticated architecture. Birthplace of Henry Trengrouse, inventor of the rocket lifesaving signals. Boating lake. Cycle hire beside the Penrose Trail. Harvest Fair - Sept (Ist week). (E2)
www.helstone-online.co.uk

WHERE TO GO, WHAT TO SEE IN AND AROUND HELSTON...

Creftow Gallery, Church St. Co-operative of 20 Cornish artists and 3-studios displaying an eclectic mix of paintings, sculpture and ceramics. Open M-Sa 10-5. (E5) 01326 572848 www.creftow.com

Flambards Experience. All weather attraction: Victorian Village and Britain in the Blitz experiences, Space Quest, live entertainment, Science Centre, Wildlife Experience, best thrill rides in Cornwall. Open most days early Apr to end Oct 10.30-5. (E3) 01326 573404 www.flambards.co.uk

Helston Museum & TIC, Market Place. Exhibits of rural life, crafts and industries which flourished in the C19/C20. Open daily M-Sa 10-4, all year. (E2) 01326 564027 www.helstonmuseum.co.uk

Loe Pool & Penrose Estate (NT). The largest natural lake in the West Country inhabited by wildfowl and surrounded by rhododendrons and wild flowers. In evidence since the C14, the River Cober was blocked by silt and the Loe Bar developed to form a bank of flint shingle. Cycling trails for families have been developed around the Estate. Apple Festival in the Autumn. Bridleways are being developed for horse riding. Stables Café open daily in summer, W/Es in winter. (D3) www.nationaltrust.org.uk

Pengersick Castle. Fortified Tudor manor c.1500 with evidence of apothocarian garden in C14, to be renovated. This place of legend and mystery has an uncertain future. (A2) 01736 763975 www.pengersickcastle.com

The Cornubian Arts and Science Trust, 3 Penrose St, Helston. Cornwall's latest edition to the World of Art where studio spaces are occupied by a diverse range of artists. Café at weekends. Open, as advertised on the door. (E2)

Blue Anchor, Coineagehall St. An inn of real character with small, cosy snugs to relax, parley and enjoy fine ales. Brewers of Spingo Beer. Beware on leaving, the gutters beside the pavement can be overlooked and a tumble, or mishap, should be avoided. (E2) 01326 562821 www.spingoales.com

The Craft Box Cafe, 9 Church St. No better place in town than this, for coffee, cakes and savouries. Craft activities. Parties. Open M-Sa 9-5, Su 10-4. 01326 55882 www.thecraftboxcafe.com

CADGWITH

Thatched cottages of darkly mottled serpentine rocks, and boats beached on the shingle cove create a picturesque, yet workaday and iconic scene. Haunt of artists. Superb coastal scenery. Café & Inn. Crow's Nest Gallery. Fresh fish for sale. Suggest you park at the top of the village and walk down, otherwise you may well get stuck in the bottleneck. (H9) www.cadgwith.com

Cadgwith Cove Inn. The inn is 300 years old and is steeped in fishing and smuggling adventures. The fresh fish is literally straight off the boats. B&B. Music nights. (H9) 01326 290513 www.cadgwithcoveinn.com

COVERACK

Charming old fishing village and former smuggling centre. Small protected harbour. Fish (& chip) restaurant in the old lifeboat station. (L7)

Cycling the Penrose Estate, Helston

| 1801 | Richard Trevithick operates the first road-going locomotive | 1802 | Richard Trevithick invents the High Pressure Steam Dredge |

Cadgwith

Grey Seal

GWEEK

Attractive village with shop and pub. It was formerly the port to Helston and the surrounding mining areas until the C19. It lies at the head of the Helford Estuary where you will see the old quays, a busy boatyard and entrance to the Seal Sanctuary. (G3)

WHAT TO VISIT...

National Seal Sanctuary. The UK's leading Grey seal rescue centre. Home to permanent resident seals and sea lions. Feeds and talks throughout the day, real working seal hospital. Cornish coast rock pool, otter creek trail, café & gift shop. Open daily from 10. (G3) 01326 221361 www.sealsanctuary.co.uk

Tolmen Centre, Constantine. A varied arts programme is organically created out of this little build; from movie-making to plays, to choir-making plus vibrant courses on yoga, pilates and todlins. (H1) 01326 341353 www.tolmencentre.co.uk

HELFORD & HELFORD RIVER

Beautiful tree-lined (hollies and oaks) tidal river with romantic creeks (Frenchman's Creek, immortalised by Daphne du Maurier's novel) and inlets. Picturesque villages of Durgan, Helford (passenger ferry) and St Anthony (SailAway organise dinghy hire 01326 231357) popular with 'muck abouters' in boats, and those wishing to rent a holiday home. **The Shipwright Arms** are worthy of a visit.
www.stanthony.co.uk
www.helfordriver.net

Oyster Farm at Porth Navas. On the north shore, a profusion of wonderful gardens, see overleaf for details. (J3)

Gweek

1805   John Opie is appointed Professor of Painting to the Royal Academy   1806   Caerhays Castle designed

St Christopher, Breage

Glendurgan Garden nw/nt

GARDENS TO VISIT...

Glendurgan Gardens (NT).
Valley garden of great beauty.
Fine trees and shrubs, a maze,
a giant's stride, and a wooded
valley of primulas and bluebells
runs down to the Helford River.
Open daily mid-Feb to 30 Oct
10.30-5.30. (L2) 01326 252020
www.nationaltrust.org.uk

Trebah Gardens. Magical
sub-tropical ravine gardens
running down to private beach
on the Helford River; a canvas
of everchanging colour, from
Spring to Autumn. A garden
for the plantsman, artist, family,
and a paradise for children. Art
Gallery holds the Hunting Art
Prizes in Spring. Open daily,
all year 10-6 (or dusk if earlier).
(K2) 01326 252200
www.trebah-garden.co.uk

CHURCHES TO VISIT...

Breage Church. C15 granite
building with fine C15 wall
painting of St Christopher. (C2)

Gunwalloe Church. C14
unusual detached tower with
remains of C15 rood screen
illustrated with paintings of the
apostles. It lies in dunes beside
the beach, and is a popular local
venue for weddings. (E6)

**Landewednack (Church
Cove) Church.** Tower and
Norman doorway of serpentine
stone. (H9)

**Mawgan In Meneage
Church.** C13-C15 wagon roof
and brasses in lovely setting.
(G3)

St Keverne Church. Spacious
interior, C14, with tall spire.
Resting place for many drowned
sailors. (L5)

ANCIENT CORNWALL...

Halliggye Fogou. The largest
underground store chamber in
Cornwall 9ft x 6ft. (H4)

THE LIZARD PENINSULA
The most southerly village
in England. Popular walking
centre. Gift shops galore, many
selling ornaments made from
the purplish Serpentine Rock,
unique to the Lizard. There
are haunting photographs of
shipwrecks in the local pubs. At
Church Cove, pretty cottages
and a converted lifeboat station.
Walks to Lizard Point and
Kynance Cove. Both have cafés.
(G10)

SPECIAL PLACES TO
VISIT ON THE LIZARD
PENINSULA...

Bonython Gardens. All
season interest with Walled,
Potager, Valley and Hot
gardens. Lakes. Tea rooms.
A 'Must' for all garden lovers.
Holiday Lets. Open daily Apr-
Sept M-F 10-4.30 except BHs.
(G6) 01326 240550
www.bonythonmanor.co.uk

Breage Church

Goonhilly Downs. High
central plateau on Lizard
Peninsula. One of the oldest
nature conservancy reserves
in the country. Thus, of great
interest to botanists, geologists
and archaeologists. A profusion
of wild flowers sets off the
summer air to be acute with
scent. Buzzards soar up high.
Green serpentine rock forms.
Croft Pascoe Nature Reserve.
(H6)

**Goonhilly Satellite Earth
Station.** Transmitting millions
of phone calls, TV pictures &
computer data via the famous
massive satellite dishes. Visitor
Centre undergoing restoration.
Hence, closed. (H5)
www.goonhilly.bt.com

Grange Fruit Farm. PYO
fruit (strawberries). Farm shop.
Nursery. Cream teas and light
lunches. Open daily May-Oct.
(F4) 01326 221718.

Kestle Barton, Manaccan.
This is a community-based arts centre with ever-changing exhibitions; painting, sculpture, ceramics, and events, all set within an ancient Cornish farmstead. Fabulous garden. Circular walk to Helford. Open late Mar to early Nov Tu-Sa 10.30-5.(J3) 01326 2318111 www.kestlebarton.co.uk

Lizard Adventure.
Fancy some exploration and wetsuit thrills? Try bushcraft, coasteering, kayaking, suping (paddle boarding), rock climbing. Open all year. (G10) 01326 290894 www.lizardadventure.co.uk
Lizard Lighthouse Heritage Centre. Large and famous building completed in 1752, with alterations in 1903. Stands amid the treacherous coast haunted by many shipwrecks. Open daily.(G10) www.lizardlighthouse.co.uk

Poltesco Nature Trail.
Three miles of wooded valley caves and cliffs. (H8)

Porthallow Arts.
Gallery and workshop specialises in birds and sculptural forms, promotes local artists' work, and runs day courses. Open East-Sept M-Th & Sa 10-6, Su 12-4. (M4) 01326 280722 www.porthallowarts.co.uk

RNAS Culdrose.
The largest helicopter base in Europe employs 3,000 persons. Much is stored underground. Viewing enclosure with café and shop. Open Day in late July; see local adverts for details. (F3) www.forcesculdrose.2day.ws

Trelowarren Gallery.
Original home of the Cornwall Crafts Association; with fellow gallery at Trelissick holds members and touring

exhibitions. Education Projects. Open daily 10.30-5.30 Mar-Nov. (G4) 01326 221567 www.cornwallcrafts.co.uk

Trelowarren. Home of the Vyvyan family since 1427. Acres of woodland and farmland surround the house. Spa Treatments, Yoga and Pool. Chateau camping, eco-buildings for sale and rent, and (dog friendly) woodland walks. New Yard Restaurant. (G4) 01326 221224 www.trelowarren.com

Wood Studio, Rosuick Farm. Sculptural woodturning by Samvado. The wonder of wood, turned into amazing shapes: bowls, spheres, obelisks. Open most days 10-6. (J5) 01326 231783 samvadosculpturecornwall.co.uk

Trebah Gardens ff

Porthleven

MULLION

A busy village, and centre for much of the Lizard Peninsula. It has a splendid church, some popular pubs, an active cricket club and a successful school. The One-Way system will draw you in and lead you out. A visit to the Cove is a must. The beaches close to, Poldhu and Polurrian, are popular with the locals and will often be empty of visitors. (E6)

WHAT TO SEE & VISIT...

Marconi Monument. The first transatlantic morse code messages were transmitted from this spot on 12 December 1901, and picked up by Gugliemo Marconi in St John's, Newfoundland. (E6)

Mullion Cove. Dramatic cove at the foot of tall cliffs, with harbour built in 1895. Lifeboat until 1901. Offshore, a bird sanctuary on Mullion Island. Fishing trips. (E7)

Mullion Church. Late medieval with fascinating bench ends. (F6)

Mullion Gallery, Nansmellyon Rd. Work of over 80 artists living on the Lizard Peninsula: paintings, ceramics, sculptures, wood carvings. Open M-Sa summer, W-Sa winter, 10-1, 3-5. (E7) 01326 241170 www. mulliongallery.supanet.com

Trecarne Pottery, Meaver Rd. Michael Roux creates colourful and functional stoneware with a touch of gallic humour, inspired by the sea and elements. (F6) 01326 241294 www.trecarnepottery.co.uk

FAMILY HOTEL...

Polurrian Hotel. Overlooks Polurrian beach guaranteeing stunning views. Restaurants. Spa with Pools. Gym. Tennis. Creche. Games Room.

Terraces. The High Point Restaurant provides fish and local produce at reasonable prices. (E7) 01326 240421 www.polurrianhotel.com

PORTHLEVEN

An attractive, large harbour with a ship building yard; C19 Harbour House and imposing Wesleyan chapel c.1890. The vulnerable harbour faces south-west, and was built for the mining industry in 1811. A south-westerly gale in 1824 washed it away, later to be rebuilt in 1855, with lock gates that were closed in 2014, which featured in the national news during the massive storms of winter 2014. Surf break for the very hardy. Fast becoming a foodie centre to rival Padstow, but without all the hype. (C3)

GALLERIES TO VISIT...

Custom House Gallery, The Harbour. Range of seascapes and landscapes paintings, ceramics, bronzes and jewellery. Open daily Apr-Oct & Xmas. (C3) 01326 569365 www.cornwall-art.co.uk

Waves Surf Art Gallery, Commercial Rd. Imagine yourself within a Barrel; in canvas and acrylic print form. 01362 368369 www.wavesgallery.co.uk

WHERE TO EAT, DRINK & BE MERRY...

Amelies at the Smokehouse. By day, café/bar with panoramic harbour views, by night, a waterfront restaurant noted for steaks, wood-fired pizzas and fresh seafood. (C3) 01326 653653 www. ameliesporthleven.co.uk

Kota, Harbourside. Foodies love this restaurant. Always something new to look forward to. Fish is the speciality in all its delicate forms with a twist of the Polynesian (Maori). Dinner

6.30-9. Rooms available. (C3) 01326 562407 www.kotarestaurant.co.uk

Kota Kai (Café), Harbourside. The stunning view across the harbour will add spice to the fab food on offer; pasta, Asian, fish, mini-kai (tapas)... Open all day, especially for lunch and dinner. Kids Room. (C3) 01326 574411 www.kotakai.co.uk

Nauti But Ice. Café serving amazing breakfasts, homemade cakes, baps, pastries and Cornish coffee. You can sit al fresco and admire the passersby, or just relax and enjoy the day. Open daily. Next door, Takeaways. (C3) 01326 573747

Rick Stein, Harbourside. More fish and chips from the Maestro, and some relish, too. Open daily. www.rickstein.com

Seadrift Kitchen Café, Fore Street. The steaks and local fish (often caught by the chef) are seriously good-value plus coffee and cakes. Open all year: W 5-9, Th-Sa from 10-10 for brunch, lunch & supper. (C3) 01326 558733 www. seadriftporthleven.co.uk. Above, and next door, a photo-gallery.

Ship Inn. A serious booser with loads of character. Offers down to earth food cooked to order, at reasonable prices. Built in the C18, it is one of the harbour's oldest buildings. Free house. Recommended. Dog friendly. (C3) 01326 564204 www.theshipinncornwall.co.uk

Mullion Gallery ss

Halzephron House II

HELFORD ESTUARY/ LIZARD PENINSULA

WHERE TO EAT, DRINK & BE MERRY...

Constantine Stores.
Established 50-years ago this little store carries over 1,000 whiskies, 150 rums, 50 cognacs and gins, and a full range of liqueurs, as well as 1st, 2nd and 3rd growth clarets and vintage champagnes. Bottoms Up! (H2) 01326 340226
www.drinkfinder.co.uk

The Cove, Maenporth Beach. Relaxed and well-priced restaurant. Offers a tasty selection of fish and meat dishes. Tapas. Open daily from 11. (L2) 01326 251136
www.thecovemaenporth.co.uk

The Greenhouse, St Keverne. Treat yourself to some modern rustic cooking at its very best. Naturally the ingredients are sourced from the finest local suppliers, many of whom are organic. Child friendly too and intimate. Something for everyone. (L5) 01326 280800 www.cornishorganiclocalrestaurant.co.uk

Fat Apples Café,
(East of) Porthallow on coast path. Sometimes you come across a place that is a godsend, especially after some hard walking. Breakfast, lunch, afternoon tea, all home made in situ by the family. Open daily East-Oct, and winter Th-Sa. Closed Nov. (M5) 01326 281559

Potager Garden & Glasshouse. This is a "Find" that emerged from a bramble-filled wilderness. Only the finest ingredients are cooked with, and it tastes so, so good. A treat. Craft studios. Open F, W/Es & BHs 10-5. (H1) 01326 341258
www.potagergarden.org

Halzephron Inn.
This C16 pub is cosy, friendly and the daily specials provide a rewarding treat, especially if you have been battling the coast path. Family room. B&B. Dog friendly. (E5) 01326 240406
www.halzephron-inn.co.uk

New Yard Restaurant, Trelowarren. Al fresco dining within an enchanting C14 estate. Simple lunches, more adventurous dinners. Open daily W-Su from 10.30, Su at 8.30 for breakfast. (G4) 01326 221595
www.newyardrestaurant.co.uk

Roskilly's. Working organic farm sells its own ice cream, fudge, clotted cream, preserves etc. Fabulous pasties. Bull Pen Gallery (furniture a speciality). Restaurant. Open daily 10-dusk (W/Es in winter). Footpaths to woods, meadows and ponds. (L6) 01326 280479
www.roskillys.co.uk

Trengilly Wartha Inn. This popular hostelry (the first gastro-pub in Cornwall) serves notable pub-grub, has an expansive wine list, an infinite selection of Malts, and yet has retained the key elements of being a pub, and all is set down a winding country lane within a wild and luscious garden. Children, cricketers and dogs are made welcome. Accommodation. (H2) 01326 340332
www.trengilly.co.uk

WHERE TO STAY...

Atlantic House, The Lizard.
A popular B&B in an ideal location from which to tackle the coastal footpath. Bright and breezy rooms of great comfort. (G10) 01326 290399
www.atlantichouselizard.co.uk

Beacon Crag, Porthleven.
Set high on the headland in 5-acres this 1887 house is in a spectacular position close to the

Nauti But Ice, Porthleven ff

coastal footpath. The bedrooms are modern and bright and open all year. (C3) 01326 573690
www.beaconcrag.com

Budock Vean. The Hotel On The (Helford) River is the traditional health spa to ease the pain of modern life, together with a 9 & 18 hole golf course, all set in a magical landscape where you can enjoy the 32-acre garden and its 350,000+ plants. Open for lunch/afternoon teas to non-residents. (K2) 01326 252100 www.budockvean.co.uk

Chyheira, Ruan Minor.
Substantial house provides 4-star B&B with all the mod cons and more; WiFi, digital tv, power showers etc. (H8) 01326 290343 www.chyheira.co.uk

Halzephron House, Gunwalloe. "The Views Are To Live And Die For." This was quite a statement by a literary visitor, and his friends (AA Milne, JM Barrie, et al). Few would argue with them. Halzephron looks over Mount's Bay, and is crossed by the coastal footpath. The rooms (sleeps 12) are described as contemporary, quirky and arty. The breakfasts are foodie-specials. There is also the Cabin, for two romantics. The rustic Cottage is spacious and sleeps 4. It is a place where dreams are made. 07899 925816
www.halzephronhouse.co.uk

Pentraeth Cove

Hen House, Tregarne.
If you seek solitude and meadows of wild flowers and wish to escape from this mad world, the Hen House may be just the place for you. B&B. Self-catering barn. No children u-12. (L5) 01326 280236 www.thehenhouse-cornwall.co.uk

Henry's Campsite, The Lizard. If you wanted to introduce your kids (or your wife, for that matter) to camping, then start here. Close to the village and coastal path. The situ is rural, and the camping is your max 4-berth tent. Everything else is exotic; from the plants, to the Easter Island décor, to the poultry. 01326 290596 www.henryscampsite.co.uk

Merthen Manor. The Vyvyans have lived in this fortified manor for 300-years. Set in 100-acres of woodland overlooking the Helford River. B&B is Country House, old-school charm, in style. Child friendly. Barns to let. Tennis Court. (H3) 01326 340664 www.merthenmanor.co.uk

Old Temperance House, St Keverne. 500-year old house full of character sits beside the church in this pretty village. Decorated with bright and colourful bedrooms and all the pre-requisites for modern life. No dogs or children u-12. (L5) 01326 280986 www.oldtemperancehouse.co.uk

Penmenner House, Penmenner Rd, The Lizard. With large beds, sea views, fresh flowers and rooms decorated to a high standard. Literary connections galore (to the Bloomsbury Group), and a stones throw from the coastal footpath. It's all arty and go, go. (G10) 01326 290370 www.penmennerhouse.com

The Round House, Church Cove. Houses the original capstan above the slipway. Available as a unique and romantic bolt-hole for two persons for around £600 per week. (G9) 01326 240333 www.cornishcottagesonline.com

BEACHES AND SURFING...

Porthleven Sands. 4-miles of sands. A steep, shelving beach with undertow. For strong swimmers only. Scene of many shipwrecks. P. Surfing - On W side of harbour channel. A much discussed reef break, produced by a big swell. LT is hollow and dangerous. HT is affected by the backwash. Strong rips when big. For the

Roskilly's

1825 Treffry Viaduct under construction. 1827 Liskeard and Looe Canal opens.

Cloudy Morning, Kynance Cove

experienced only and not for the squeamish! (C4)

Praa Sands. Mile of firm golden sands. Good family beach but HZ to bathe at LT. P/WC/LG/Café. Surfing - Bigger swell than Perranathnoe. Hence a popular beach. N end protected from W winds and may produce a fast R break. E end can create HZ rips in a big swell. (A2)

Church Cove. Pebbles and sand sided by low cliffs. Dunes cover St Winwalloe church. NT P/LG/WC/Shop. (E6)

Polurrian Cove. Access via 3/4 mile path from Mullion church to sandy beach edged by high cliffs. Strong tidal currents. Bathing HZ at LT. (E7)

Poldhu Cove. Popular family beach. Bathing HZ one hour either side of LT. P/WC/LG/ Fab Café. (E6)

Mullion Cove. Tiny beach at LT. Beautiful harbour walls. P/ WC/Café. (E7)

Kynance Cove. Large P area. 10 minute walk to steps. Good

bathing. White sand at LT. Very popular in summer. Wild-shaped serpentine rocks. At HT the roaring noise of the blow holes. Café/WC. (F9)

Pentraeth Beach. Access down slippery path to beach of grey sand and rocks. (F10)

Polpeor Cove. Steep walk down to rocky shore; the most southerly point in Britain. Old lifeboat station. P/WC/Café. (G10)

Hounsel Bay. For the agile only down a steep path to the small sandy beach. Overlooked by hotel. (G10)

Carleon Cove. Peaceful cove, 10 min walk from Poltesco.(H8)

Kennack Sands. Popular bucket and spade family beach with rock pools. Fine bathing. S-B hire/P/WC/Café. Surfing - Good waves only created after big swells. (J8)

Coverack. Tiny beach, shingle at LT. P/Café. (L7)

Lowland Point. Ice age 'Raised Beach" on which

the passenger liner Paris was shipwrecked in 1899. Access from St Keverne via Trevean or Trebarvath Farms. (M6)

Porthoustock. Pebbled shelving beach, quarries to either side. P. (M5)

Porthallow. Small pebbled beach, rocks to sides. P/Inn. (M4)

Men-Aver Beach. 20 min coastal walk from Gillan. Isolated with sandy patches and rock pools. (M4)

Gillan Harbour. Shingle and sand, rocky promontory. (L3)

Flushing. Isolated shingle beach with sand at LT. (L3)

Helford Village. Sand and shale visible at LT. P/WC. (K3)

Helford Passage. Small stony beach in front of Ferry Boat Inn. Sand at LT. P. (J3)

Durgan Beach. Small stony beach down steep hill. P. (K3)

Porthallack Beach. Shingle beach along coastal path from Durgan. (K3)

Helford River

Hendra, Praa Sands

Bream Cove. Isolated sandy beach and rock pools popular with skin-divers. (L2)

Maenporth. Popular family beach with sheltered and spacious sands. Surfing/Kayak hire/Fishing trips, P/WC/LG/ Life's A Beach Café. (L1)

COASTAL FOOTPATH...

Praa Sands to Lizard:
Approx 18 miles. Interesting coastal path: craggy cliffs and splendid sandy beaches. Start with a stiffish climb up to Trewavas Head, then a cliffside walk to Porthleven. Path follows cliff edge to Loe Bar, Gunwalloe and Church Cove, apparently buried treasure is hidden here. On to the caves, arches and black rocks of Mullion Cove. Fine walking on cliff tops around Vellan Head and past breath-taking precipices to Pigeon Ogo, a vast amphitheatre of rock. The crowning glory is Kynance Cove, a spectacle of swirling currents (at HT), whooshing blow holes and wild shaped serpentine rocks, great bathing at LT and a café. Well-trodden path to Britain's most southerly point, Lizard Point. Caves and caverns about Polpeor Cove. East is the Lion's Den, a large

collapsed sea-cave, a sudden vast hole in the cliff turf. The Chough is nesting on the cliffs.

Lizard to Falmouth: Approx 26 miles. The east side of the peninsula is less rugged, the slopes are gentler, the landscape becomes more hospitable as one travels northward. First, you pass pretty Church Cove, and along cliff top to the Devil's Frying Pan, a larger version of the Lion's Den, its blow hole roars when the easterlies blow. Through thatched Cadgwith to Kennack Sands where the path is easy going, hugging the cliff edge, and almost at sea level from Coverack to Lowland Point, scene of an Ice Age 'Raised Beach.' Offshore, at low tide 'The Manacles' are visible, a treacherous reef that has

caused the death of more than 400 sailors, many are buried in St Keverne's churchyard. The 60ft spire of the church serves as a daymark for sailors and fishermen. At Godrevy Cove, the path turns inland to Rosenithon and Porthoustock to avoid quarries, returning to the coast at Porthallow. A peaceful stretch to Gillan Harbour, possible to wade the creek at low tide, or continue to bridge crossing the head of the creek at Carne. Through tangled woods to Helford village and ferry across Helford estuary, which runs from Easter to end of October, to either Helford Passage or the beach at Durgan. From here the path passes Mawnan Church and along the cliff tops to Swanpool Beach (Falmouth).

Porthleven Sands, Gunwalloe

Ogo-dour, Predannack

Sennen Cove

Crab Pattern, Portreath

Porth Nanven

Sandy Mouth

Watergate Bay

Porthmeor, Waves Surf Gallery

Bedruthan Steps

Porthcothan

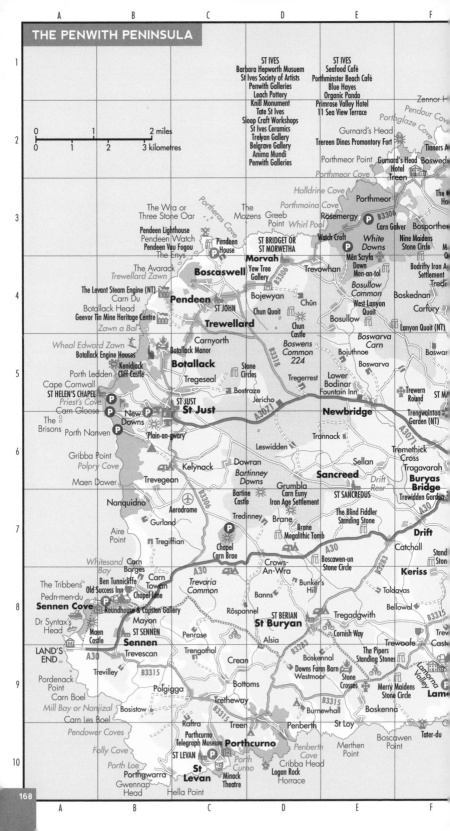

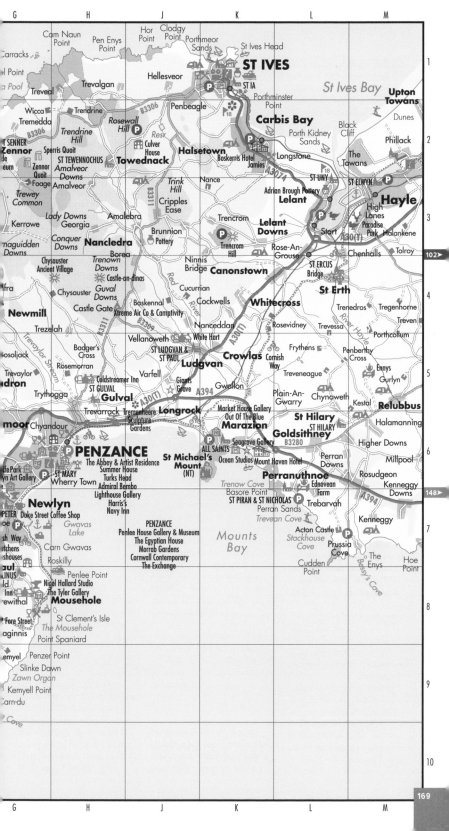

Neil Pinkett, Cornwall Contemporary

PENZANCE

For many, the last stop on the South West Line (rail service), and thus, a place of memories and nostalgic dreams. It can be a lively and busy town, well served by a gentle climate, for sub-tropical flowers grow in the Morrab Gardens, and at nearby Trengwainton. The town trail takes you to Chapel Street where there is all manner of emporia and interesting shops, pubs and hotels, and the Egyptian House opposite the Union Hotel, then onto the shops of Market Jew Street, dominated by the Ionic columns of Market House, and the Statue of Sir Humphrey Davy, inventor of the miners' Davy lamp. Look out for the Floating Harbour. Ferry to the Isles of Scilly, shark and deep sea fishing trips, swimming pools (in & outdoor - the Jubilee Pool, May-Sept. www.jubileepool. co.uk). West Cornwall Spring Show - late March. (H6) www.penzance.co.uk

WHERE TO STAY...

The Abbey, Abbey St. A sweet gem dating from the C17 lies hidden behind a walled garden and courtyard.

Luxurious with fabulous fabrics, awash with colour. Call it shabby chic, or an antique emporium, it oozes style, panache and will leave you with sweet memories. Now available to rent as one large domain (luxury holiday cottage) suitable for 6-12 guests. (H5) 07930347911 www.theabbeyonline.co.uk

Artist Residence, 20 Chapel St. A boutique-style hotel where each room is a "one-off" design by an artist. The Cornish Barn, is the in-house café/bar/grill for brunch and dinner. (H5) 01736 365664 www. artistresidencecornwall.co.uk

Chapel House, Chapel Street. A new, beautifully converted intimate, boutique hotel that marries Georgian architecture with contemporary furnishings. The 6 sizeable bedrooms have state-of-the-art bathrooms. 01736 362024 www.chapelhousepz.co.uk

Summer House, Cornwall Terrace. An enthusiasm for life and art pervades this small, boutique hotel. It all goes to amplify this

hostelry's fine qualities. They describe themselves as having chic interiors and a tropical walled garden. B&B with 5 double-rooms. (H5) 01736 363744 www.summerhouse-cornwall.com

LIGHT BITES...

The choice is large and confusing, so herewith my favourites. Ascending Market Jew Street, **The Craftbox Café**, 85 Market Jew St. For homemade cakes and coffee, and craft activities. Will keep the kids busy. Open M-Sa 10-5, Su 11-4. 01736 33364 www.thecraftboxcafe.com

Next, to the top of the street, on the rounded corner, **The Cornish Hen Delicatessen**, 27 Market Place. When in a hurry this is where I collect their tiny quiches, sausage rolls and coffees for lunch. All very gluten-free, vegan and "Cool." 01736 350223. Open daily.

But, if you have more time on hand, to idle, with a need for a table, bear R, in 50m turn R into Parade Street. **The Honey Pot**, 5 Parade St. A café has

been in this Art-Deco build for 100-years. Daily specials, exceptional soups, sarnis, panninis, coffee and cakes, all with a flourish. Open M-Sa 10-6, lunch 12-late.
01736 368686
www.thehoneypotpz.co.uk

WHERE TO EAT, DRINK & BE MERRY...

Harris's, 46 New St. Well organised establishment with a loyal clientele provides uncommonly good food. Interesting French house wines. Lunch 12-2, dinner 7-10. Tu-Sa. (H5) 01736 364408
www.harrissrestaurant.co.uk

The Navy Inn, Queen St. A traditional old pub happy for you to come in and enjoy a pint but also proud to provide first-rate food (Venison, Seabass, Guinea Fowel...) at an affordable price. Hence, its popularity and success and relaxed attitude to those just happy to read the papers with a coffee. Open 12 - late. (H6) 01736 333232
www.navyinn.co.uk

Figurehead, Penzance Docks

Artist Residence ss

Miss Ustick, Trereife Park

Simon Stooks, Cornwall Contemporary ss

CHAPEL STREET PUBS...

The Turks Head. C13 inn, claimed to be the oldest in Penzance. Selection of real ales and serves fresh fish, steaks and veggie meals. (H6) 01736 363093 www. turksheadpenzance.co.uk

The Admiral Bembo. "Shiver Me timbers....split the Main Brace!" The interior of this pub resembles the Lower Deck of a "Man o' War" galleon. Much was salvaged by the diver Rowland Morris in the 1950s from the wreck of HMS Association, 1707, off the Isles of Scilly. Good beers. (H6) 01736 363448

WHAT TO VISIT...TO SEE...

Cornwall Contemporary, 1 Parade St. One of the leading galleries in the South-West managed by Sara Brittain who has had a long and active interest in the Cornish art scene. Make sure you keep abreast of their ever-changing exhibitions. Open M-Sa 10-5. (H6) 01736 874749 www. cornwallcontemporary.com

The Egyptian House, Chapel St. Built in 1835 by John Foulton of Plymouth to be a museum and geological despository. Now houses, behind the facade, three apartments for hire. www.landmarktrust.org. uk (H6)

The Exchange, Princes St. A major art space developed in conjunction with the Newlyn Art Gallery. This showcase for national and international art holds regular educational programmes. Coffee shop. Open M-Sa 10-5, BHs 11-4 (closed M/Tu in winter). (H6) 01736 363715 www.newlynartgallery.co.uk

Glass House Gallery, 81-82 Market Jew St. A serious and attractive gallery exhibiting paintings, ceramics, sculpture and jewellery with regularly changing shows. (H6) 01736 367619 www.glasshousegallery. co.uk

Lighthouse Gallery, 25 Causeway Head. Light, fresh and friendly gallery featuring a fine selection of artists. Open M-Sa 10-5. (H6) 01736 350555 www.lighthouse-gallery.com

Madron Church. Mother-Church of Penzance; granite, and a good size with fine wagon roof. Jacobean Tower Screen, bench ends and C17 brass. (G5)

Penlee House Gallery & Museum, Morrab Rd. An elegant gallery and museum set within a Victorian house and park. Changing exhibitions mainly feature famous 'Newlyn School' artists (1880-1930). There is a fine café and well-stocked shop open daily Apr-Oct 10-5, Oct-East M-Sa 10.30-4.30. (H6) 01736 363625 www.penleehouse.org.uk

Stoneman Gallery, Madron. Run by Linda Stoneman whose late husband, Hugh Stoneman, the master printer, used a variety of techniques: etching, drypoint, woodcut and linocut to print works by Terry Frost and many masters of their art. B&B. Open by appointment. (G5) 07779099245 www. stonemangraphics.co.uk

The Union Hotel, Chapel St. No longer in its prime, but in its day it housed the Assembly Rooms, Theatre and Cockpit within the curtilage of the hotel.

1851 Madron fishwife, Mary Kelynack, walks to London to visit the Great Exhibition   1854 A forty foot Newlyn fishing boat, Mystery, sets off for Australia

Nash, Tremenheere Sculpture Garden

In 1805, the news of Nelson's death and victory at the Battle of Trafalgar was broke from the Minstrel's Gallery. (H6)

GARDENS TO VISIT...

Tremenheere Sculpture Gardens, Nr Gulval. This is a relatively new venture that opened in 2012, and all is set in a sheltered valley with stupendous views across the Bay. Within the woods, streams and sub-tropical plantings are sculptures. Café (tapas and bar) provides the food, and is, in itself a worthy destination. Open East M to early Sept M-Sa 10-5, Su 10-4. 01736 448089 (H5) www.tremenheere.co.uk

Trengwainton Gardens (NT). Large shrub garden with a vast collection of rhododendrons. Colourful in spring/early summer. Views over Mounts Bay. Open mid-Feb to 30 Oct Su-Th 10.30-5. (F6) 01736 363148

Trereife Park. Queen Anne manor house and home to the Le Grice family whose descendant, Valentine Le Grice, was a poet and friend to the Romantics, Wordsworth and Coleridge. Fine plasterwork and wood panelling. The garden is classically Cornish with parterres and terraces. Poets Café. Accommodation. Open Su-F, Apr-Oct, 2-5. (G6) 01736 362750 www.trereifepark.co.uk

Trewidden Gardens. Originally planted in the C19 by T B Bolitho, the garden comprises ten acres of paths and dells with a fine collection of camellias and magnolias. Open daily late Feb to mid-Sept 10.30-5.30 (daily in July/Aug). (F7) 01736 351979 www.trewiddengarden.co.uk

ACTION-PACKED ADVENTURES...ALTERNATE PLACE TO STAY...

Xtreme Air Co, Castle Gate. Learn to Speedsail, Blo-kart, FlyBoard, Speedkite action-packed adventures. And more. Tuition on hand. B&B. (H4) 01736 332648 and try:

Camptivity, Castle Gate. Turn up with a tooth brush and towel and step into a luxurious Bell Tent. Breakfast available, as are bikes, canoes and surfboards. (H4) 01736 332648 www.camptivity.co.uk

Penzance

MARAZION

Reputed to be the oldest town in Cornwall which lies opposite St Michael's Mount, and hence, the embarkation point for thousands who rarely venture into this village. The safe sandy beach, and children's playground are an added family attraction. Reputedly, Joseph of Arimathea traded here in tin. Classical galleried Methodist chapel built in 1862. For lunch/dinner it has to be: **Ben's Cornish Kitchen**, West End, 01736 719200. www. benscornishkitchen.com For a drink and "the" view, it has to be the: **Godolphin Arms**, West End. 01736 8885120 www.godolphinarms. co.uk (K6) A few miles to the East of the village, the **Victoria Inn** at Perranuthnoe does a splendid lunch - try the fish soup. (L6)

WHERE TO STAY...

Ednovean Farm B&B, Perranuthnoe. This is luxury B&B. Three gorgeous bedrooms decorated in designer fabrics. Immaculate bathrooms. Italian garden. A visit to their website will seduce you and lure you to Ednovean. (L6) 01736 711883 www.ednovean.co.uk

Ennys, St Hilary. Do you wish to "Get away from it all?" Seek a change of scene? Then, perhaps one of the three cottages, or luxurious suites will suit you. On hand, a heated pool, grass tennis court - all within 20-acres to roam and get lost. (M5) 01736 740262 www.ennys.co.uk

Mount Haven Hotel, Turnpike Rd. A friendly and relaxed ambience pervades this hotel whose bedrooms have been completely refurbished in contemporary designs. The owner's travels to the Far East and her interest in Buddhism are mirrored by the eclectic range of paintings and sculptures on view. The views from the terrace across to St Michael's Mount are quite superb. The restaurant boasts fresh fish caught just off the Newlyn Quay. (K6) 01736 710249 www.mounthaven.co.uk

Ocean Studios, Mounts Bay House, Turnpike Hill. Quality, self-catering, contemporarily designed accommodation. Therapies on hand to help you unwind. (K6) 01736 711040 www.theoceanstudios.com

Porth-En-Alls, Prussia Cove. A veritable collection of historic houses and coastal cottages to hire within reach of the coast path and beach. Camping and Bakery. 01736 762014 (M7) www.prussiacove.co.uk

GALLERIES IN MARAZION...

Market House Gallery, The Square. One of Cornwall's finest, and the largest gallery in the village, specialises in C20 Cornish artists and holds 6-exhibitions each year, of both one-person and group shows. Sculpture, glass and ceramics are also displayed. Open daily. (K6) 01736 710252 www. markethousegallery.co.uk

Seagrove Gallery & Coffee Shop, The Square. Wide range of textiles, jewellery, paintings, pottery and paintings. Courtyard for al fresco coffee and cakes. Self-catering. Open daily summer, winter Th-M. (K6) 01736 710732 www. marazionholidays.co.uk

Summerhouse Gallery, Market Place. The sheer enthusiasm for their artists work endears one to this gallery. Works by John Piper, Michael Praed, Amy Albright, and more. Open Tu-Sa 11-4. 01736 711400 www. summerhousegallery.co.uk

Market House Gallery, Marazion ss

St Michael's Mount Causeway

St Michael's Mount rr/nt

St Michael's Mount

(**NT**). A legendary place of romance, and pilgrimage, and a child's dream of a fairy castle. Originally, the site of a Benedictine chapel established by Edward the Confessor. In the C14, the spectacular castle was added. Later, to be used as a nunnery and military fortress before the St Aubyn family purchased it in 1659, living here ever since. Church dates from 1275. Exquisite Blue Drawing Room with Chippendale furniture. Pictures by Gainsborough and the Cornish artist, John Opie. Harbour, railway. Open Feb 1/2 term, then mid-Mar to 31 Oct M-F & Su 10.30-5, last admission 4.15. Guided tours if weather and tides permit, late Feb to mid-Mar, Tu at 11.15 & 2.15pm. Church opens on Sunday at 10.30 for 11am Service. Gardens open mid-Apr to June M-F 10.30-5, July to Oct Th & F only from 10.30. Restaurant and shop open daily Apr-Oct. Special family ticket available. Please Note: access on foot over the causeway at low tide, or during summer months only, by ferry at high tide (return ferry tickets should not be taken). Make sure the Mount is open before crossing on the ferry! (J6) (Estate Office for winter opening). 01736 710265 www.stmichaelsmount.co.uk

Blue Drawing Room, St Michael's Mount nt

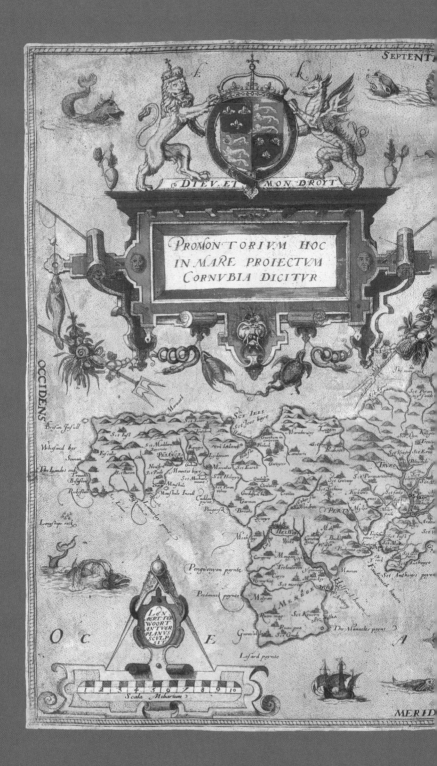

Boat Chains & Ropes, Mousehole

LAMORNA

A straggling village that became popular with artists in the early C20. The heavily wooded valley ends at the small harbour overlooking a bay of great granite boulders, many embellished with green seaweed. Summer craft exhibitions are held here. A café overlooks the cove. (F9)

WHERE TO EAT, DRINK & BE MERRY...

Lamorna Wink Inn.
Formerly in the same family for many, many years, and it told an interesting story, for all their bric-a-brac that most of us would hide away in cupboards was hanging from the ceiling. Now transformned into a contemporary inn serving pub grub. Seating area outside. Open 11.30-2.30, 6-10.30. (F9) 01736 731566 www.lamornawink.co.uk

Lamorna Cove Hotel.
In a quite exceptional location overlooking the Lamorna Valley and cove. There are 15-luxury self-catering apartments with use of the restaurant providing fab views (open to the public), swimming pool and sauna. Child friendly.(F9) 01736 732866 www.thelamornacovehotel.com

Mousehole

MOUSEHOLE

Pronounced 'Mowzle.' Arguably the most attractive of Cornish fishing villages. The stone cottages huddle around the harbour, facing east, sheltered from the prevailing winds. Originally called Port Enys, it was sacked and burnt by Spanish invaders in 1595. It is worth exploring the hidden alleyways where you will light upon tiny art galleries, tea rooms, and the odd restaurant, or if you are in need of a rest, sit on the harbour wall and watch a time capsule of fishing boats, and children at play. Famed for christmas lights and Tom Bawcock's Eve, and the children's tale, The Mousehole Cat. (G8)

WHERE TO STAY, EAT, DRINK & BE MERRY...

Old Coastguard Hotel & Restaurant, The Parade.
Panoramic sea views from this light and airy restaurant. Fish (from Newlyn Market) a speciality. Steak and Vegetarian menus, too. Stylish modern accommodation. Lunch and dinner. (G8) 01736 731222 www.oldcoastguardhotel.co.uk

Ship Inn, Harbourside.
Popular, busy pub decorated with beams and panelling. Open fires and memorabilia. Bar food and local fish dishes a speciality. St Austell ales. B&B with eight bedrooms. (G8) 01736 731234 www.shipinnmousehole.co.uk

2 Fore Street. Chic and stylish bistro/café serves coffee and cakes, and fresh fish for lunch and dinner. The design is modern and clean, and self-catering accommodation is available for 4-persons. Open daily for Brunch 10-12, lunch 12-3.30 and dinner 5.30-9.30. (G8) 01736 731164 www.2forestreet.co.uk

LIGHT BITES...

Harbour Coffee & Café.
Corner tearoom serves al fresco cream teas, cakes and light lunches. Open daily. (G8)

Hole Foods Deli & Café, North Cliffs. Freshly baked bread, cakes, vegan and gluten free produce, all with a harbour view. Open M-Sa 8-5, Su 9-4. (G8) 01736 732843 www.holefoodsdeli.co.uk

GALLERIES IN MOUSEHOLE...

The Tyler Gallery, 12 Brook St. Established by Newlyn born potter Essex Tyler who specialises in ornamental raku pottery. The gallery also displays an impressive collection of Cornish paintings and jewellery. Open daily Mar-Dec 10-6. (G8) 01736 731109 www.essextyler.com

Nigel Hallard Studios, 6-8 Keigwin Place. Nigel has crafted his art in Mousehole for 45 years, painting canvases in all styles and form, from his own Cubist style to more realistic methods. Originals and Limited Editions for sale. Open May-Oct Su-F 11-5.30. (G8) 0 8454 637607 www.nigelhallard.com

Nigel Hallard Studios, Mousehole

Newlyn

NEWLYN

Home of Cornwall's largest fishing fleet and the busiest fish market with cannery for pilchards and mackerel. The medieval quay is a delight. Like St Ives, a favourite haunt for artists - Edwardian painters formed the 'Newlyn School' artists' colony. Much of their work is on show at the Penlee House Gallery in Penzance. The Newlyn Art Gallery continues the tradition of pioneering artists. Similarly, neighbouring Mousehole, and much of old Newlyn, was destroyed by Spanish Raiders in 1595. Fresh fish and shellfish merchants, aplenty, are open for business on Fore Steet and The Coombe. Fish Festival Aug BH M. (G7) www.newlyn.info

WHERE TO EAST, DRINK & BE MERRY...

Duke Street Coffee Shop. Just the place for a cup of coffee and a pastry after wandering the galleries and delights of Newlyn. Open daily. (G7) 01736 331188

Tolcarne Inn, Newlyn. Ben Tunnicliffe has transformed the reputation of this old fisherman's pub, and is a true exponent of Cornwall's rich and varied produce; the fish comes delivered, in person, by a footman, from Newlyn's Market, a mere hundred yards distant, and the veg and meat, are all locally produced, too. Brunch and coffee are served, and the coastal footpath passes the front door. Dog friendly. Live Jazz on Sundays 1-3pm. (G7) 01736 363074 www.tolcarneinn.co.uk

The Swordfish. Pub beloved by the local trawler-men who when just back from a long trip may be a touch bellicose and unruly. So beware. B&B. Open all day. (G7) 01736 362830 www.swordfishinn.uk

WHAT TO VISIT IN NEWLYN...

Helen Feiler Gallery, 54 The Strand. Helen's a painter, print-maker and jeweller. She uses the lost-wax technique and her jewels are microcosms of the natural world. Open W Th & F 11-5. www.helenfeilergallery.com

Jelberts Ice Cream, New Road. Its Cornish, from Newlyn, and its delicious with an Olympian flavour. Worth taking your own tubs to fill. Open daily from April. (G7)

Newlyn Art Gallery, New Road. An enterprising, and at times, shocking art venue with changing exhibitions of painting, sculpture, drawing and photography. Installation and esoteric space is a concept practiced with panache, and endearment. Gallery & coffee shop. Open Tu-Sa 10-5. www.newlynartgallery.co.uk

Tolcarne Inn ss

DEEP SEA TRAWLERS

Minack Open Air Theatre ss

PORTHCURNO

Small village leads down to one of the great beaches of Cornwall (and the World) with its effervescent, turquoise sea and white sands. Best viewed from the western side of the coastal footpath, or the steps below the Minack Theatre. Museum. Café. (C10)

PLACES OF INTEREST...

Logan's Rock. A huge naturally balanced rock weighing 66 tons. It was dislodged in the early C19 by a young naval officer, a nephew of Oliver Goldsmith, and such was the outcry, that he was forced to return it almost bankrupting himself. (D10)

Minack Theatre. One of the great sights of Cornwall, indeed, an extraordinary phenomenon; an Open Air Theatre cut out of the cliff side affording stupendous views. Season of plays, musicals, operas in unique 750 seat theatre. Coffee shop. Season; End of May to mid-Sept. Exhibition Centre tells the story of Rowena Cade who built the theatre. Take a rug, hot thermos, spare jumpers and head gear. Open all year mid-

Mar to Oct 9.30-5, Nov to mid-Mar 10-4 (closed 24/25 Dec). (C10) 01736 810181 www.minack.com

Porthcurno Telegraph Museum. The site of the first undersea cable laid in 1870 that became the world's largest and busiest submarine telegraph station. Thereafter, 14 cables linked Porthcurno to the British Empire employing a binary code, the forerunner of the internet. Café. Sculpture garden and picnic areas. Open East-Oct Su-F & BH Sa 10-5, winter M 10-4. (C10) 01736 810966 porthcurno-telegraph-museum.org.uk

WHERE TO STAY...

Ardensawah Farm B&B, St Levan. Ardensawah is a busy working farm with dairy and beef cattle, wheat and barley, that extends to 700 acres. The bedrooms are tastefully decorated and afford fine seaviews. Wifi. Family room. No pets. (C10) 01736 871520 www.porthcurnofarmholidays.com

Downs Barn Farm B&B. Two luxurious double-bedrooms, lounge and dining

room are on hand for your benefit, as is, the superb location just a short distance from the spectacular coastline and Minack Theatre. (E9) 01736 810295 www.downsbarnfarm.co.uk

Driftwood Studio B&B, Porthcurno. Romantic and cosy hideaway, ideal for a couple or good friends. A mere 100 yards from the Minack. Open all year. (C10) 01736 810796 www.cornwall-online.co.uk/driftwood-studio

ST IVES

A labyrinth of narrow streets, whitewashed cottages, brightly coloured boats, sandy beaches and light, so bright, piercing and clear that you could be forgiven for thinking you were in a Mediterranean village. It was the light that drew the early artists in the C19 and C20s. The town's charm remains unaltered by the thousands who flock here. It is a special place, and worth intense exploration around the many side streets. Perhaps, a course in painting will take your fancy. The beaches are almost white, and the sea shimmers in the sunlight. To avoid the parking problem,

1928   Cornwall College opens the first College of Further Education in the country   1932   Rowena Cade and her gardener begin construction of the Minack Theatre

take the train in from Lelant. Music & Arts Festival - Sept. (K1) www.stives-cornwall.co.uk www.stives.co.uk

Alba, Wharf Rd. Great views over the harbour from this old Lifeboat Station through wide glass windows. Modern British menu. Separate kids & vegetarian menus. Open daily for lunch and dinner. (K1) 01736 797222 www.thealbarestaurant.com

The Loft Restaurant & Terrace, Norway Lane. This former sail loft is a light and airy modern restaurant with a great terrace overlooking St Ives Bay. Opens at 10 for coffee and cakes. (K1) 01736 794204 www.theloftrestaurantandterrace.co.uk

Onshore, The Wharf. A busy, bustling café ideal for the Big Breakfast, coffee, lunch and late supper...and order a pizza, pasta or fresh fish meal while you relax and people watch the thronging crowds. (K1) 01736 796000 www.onshore-stives.co.uk

Porthminster Café. This blend of café and serious restaurant overlooking magical white sands has struck a chord with many foodie aficionados who consider it their First Choice diner in the South West. Child friendly. Open all year from 10 for morning coffee, lunch and dinner. Boutique B&B. Also, runs a sister café overlooking Porthgwidden Beach. (K1) 01736 795352 www.porthminstercafe.co.uk

Seafood Café, 45 Fore St. Choose your meal from the food counter: fish, meat or fowl, and a sauce to suit you. Super fresh food, and a pleasant place to relax and dine with your cherished other half. (K1) 01736 794004 www.seafoodcafé.co.uk

LIGHT BITES...

Digey Food Room, 6 The Digey. Classy deli/café serves all-day breakfast, soups, vegan/gluten free food. Open M-Sa 10-5. 01736 799600 www.digeyfoodroom.co.uk

Mount Zion Coffee. If you get your kicks from coffee this guy will bore you with the purity and passion of his zeal. A worthwhile experience. Open daily in season. Great view over the harbour. (K1) 01736 888419 www.mountzioncoffee.co.uk

WHERE TO STAY IN ST IVES...

Organic Panda & Gallery, 1 Pednolver Terrace. A fervent passion for recycling, sustainable living and organic produce drives this house. The sheets are organic, the towels bamboo, the bedsteads reclaimed timbers in fantastic shapes. Rustic, laid-back, and a venue for their own art. Rooms are comfy too. 7-nights minimum stay. (K1) 01736 793890

Primrose Valley Hotel, Primrose Valley, Porthminster Beach. Another business passionate about sustainable living and protecting the environment. The luxurious rooms are decorated with bespoke furnishings and the latest sound systems. An eclectic wine cellar greets all devotees of the grape. Restaurant. (K1) 01736 794939 www.primroseonline.co.uk

11 Sea View Terrace. Neat, luxurious and immaculately turned out little B&B. Your host has a passion for art and it shows. The walls are festooned with bright, colourful paintings only matched by the fabulous view you get of St Ives from here. Self-catering apartment nearby. (K1) 01736 798440 www.11stives.co.uk

27 The Terrace (B&B). If you seek beach views, an elegant, luxurious bedroom (there are 9), a private walled garden, and Wifi, et al. (K1) 01736 797450 www.27theterrace.co.uk

Porthminster Cafe, St Ives

Tate St Ives, Porthmeor Beach. This is the first port-of-call for thousands who visit St Ives. They wish to walk in the shadow of Art and all its finery. Here you will discover displays of contemporary work in all variety of media. There are some very fine sculptures by Hepworth and a comprehensive show of St Ives' famous son, Alfred Wallis, fisherman and scrap merchant who didn't paint until he was 70! Worth a journey just for the view from the coffee shop and a visit to the bookshop. Open daily Mar-Oct 10-5.20, Nov-Feb Tu-Su 10-4.20, (K1) 01736 796226

Tate St Ives

Treliska, 3 Bedford Rd. A B&B with a modern, contemporary outlook; all the bedrooms have their own power shower or bathroom, the bedding is of crisp Egyptian cotton and there is access to WiFi, and not forgetting the award-winning breakfast. (K1) 01736 797678 www.treliska.com

Trevose Harbour House, 22 The Warren. A boutique guest house with 6 lovingly designed rooms in shades of blue. Wifi, Hypnos beds and much more for your every comfort. (K1) 01736 793267 www.trevosehouse.co.uk

JUST OUTSIDE ST IVES...

Boskerris Hotel, Boskerris Rd, Carbis Bay. Small, family-run hotel decorated in a bright, clever, contemporary style. The bedrooms are minimalist with up-to-the-minute bathrooms. The terrace affords superb views across the bay. (K2) 01736 795295 www.boskerrishotel.co.uk

Carbis Bay Hotel & Spa. They describe themselves as the "Hotel On The Beach." Its a mix of family, corporate and wedding venue, with its own pool, if you don't fancy saltwater, and have forgotten your wetsuit. A favourite of one, Mrs Thatcher. Self-catering cottages and apartments. 01736 795311 www.carbisbayhotel.co.uk

ALTERNATIVE PLACES TO STAY...

Ayr Holiday Park. Within walking distance of the town, and thus very convenient if you can get a pitch. Just amazing views and fab showers. Campers, caravans, tents and mobile homes. Dog friendly. 01736 795855 www.ayrholidaypark.co.uk

The Tide House, Skidden Hill. A stunning house oozing with style, comfort, contemporary design and clarity of purpose - to provide you with the best holiday. For group/family bookings. 01736 791803 www.thetidehouse.co.uk

ARTS, CRAFTS & GALLERIES TO VISIT IN ST IVES...A SELECTION

Back Road Artworks, Back Road East. 8-artists have got together to promote and sell their own works and to teach workshops. Open most days. (K1) 01736 791571 www.backroadartworks.co.uk

Barbara Hepworth Museum & Sculpture Garden, Barnoon Hill. The house, studio, sculpture garden and workshop of the late sculptress. 40 sculptures, paintings and photographs. Open all year Tu-Su 10-4.20 and daily Mar-Oct 10-5.20. (K1) 01736 796226 www.tate.org.uk/stives/hepworth

Belgrave Gallery, 22 Fore St. Specialises in the Modern Movement which centred around St Ives, 1940-1960s, plus contemporary British artists. Open M-Sa 10-6. (K1) 01736 794888 www.belgravestives.co.uk

Leach Pottery, Upper Stennack. Founded by Bernard Leach in 1920. Ceramics by Janet Leach, Trevor Corser and Joanna Wason. Open daily, all year from 10, Su from 11, Nov-Feb M-Sa 10-5. (K1) 01736 799703 www.leachpottery.com

Anima-Mundi Street-an-Pol. Considered by its Peers to be the leading, experimental and contemporary gallery, with paintings, ceramics and installations on three storeys. Regular Exhibs. Open M-Sa 11-4. (K1) 01736 793121 www.anima-mundi.co.uk

Penwith Gallery, Back Rd West. This is a fabulous work space and home of the Penwith Society of Arts who hold continuous exhibitions of paintings, sculpture and ceramics. Shop. Open M-Sa 10-5.30. (K1) 01736 795579 www.penwithgallery.com

Porthminster Gallery, Westcotts Quay. A former pilchard-press given over to modern and contemporary St Ives and British art. Open daily. (K1) 01736 795888 www.porthminstergallery.co.uk

St Ives Ceramics, Fish St. Collections of high quality ceramics. Work by John Bedding, Clive Bowen, Bernard Leach and Japanese artists from Mashiko. Open daily 10-5. (K1) 01736 794930 www.st-ives-ceramics.co.uk

St Ives School of Painting, Back Road West. Rediscover your creativity; take a course in Life Drawing, sketch and stroll, retreat into a space of inspiration. Day Courses from 10 to 4.30. Treat yourself! 01736 797180 www.schoolofpainting.co.uk

St Ives Society Of Artists, Norway Square. Founded in 1927, the Society is a well-established artists' group and holds regular exhibitions. Open daily from April, 2-5. (K1) 01736 795582 www.stisa.co.uk

The Sloop Craft Workshops, Fish St. Twelve crafts people work here: from patchworks to driftwood furniture. Open daily 10-5. (K1) 01736 796051

Penwith Gallery ss

Trelyon Gallery, Fore St. Work of over fifty contemporary leading British jewellers. Open daily 10-5 (10 summer). (K1) 01736 797955 www.trelyongallery.weebly.com

Seb West c/o Shoreline Gallery. Born in St Ives, Seb paints relief landscapes, abstracts of the Cornish sea and countryside. Open daily. (K1) 01736 740327 www.sebwestgallery.co.uk

Waterside Gallery, Street-An-Pol. Figurative pieces suitable for the home. Open daily 10.30-5.30. (K1) 01736 7988444 www.watersidestives.com

HAYLE

Formerly a small port and industrial centre. The foundries once made all the castings for every Cornish mine, and at nearby Copperhouse there were tin and copper smelting works. The Saltings is a reserve for migratory birds. 3 miles of superb sands. (A7) www.hayle.co.uk

SPECIAL PLACES TO VISIT..

Paradise Park. Wildlife conservation sanctuary with 650 birds and animals in 100 aviaries in a 7-acre garden. Australian Aviary. Eagles of Paradise flying displays. Home of the World Parrot Trust. Café/Shop. Open daily 10-6. (A7) www.paradisepark.org.uk

Trevaskis Farm. PYO fruit. Farm shop, butchery, baker, fish and deli. Open daily for breakfast, lunch and dinner. (East of M2) 01209 713931 www.trevaskisfarm.co.uk

LELANT ATTRACTIONS...

Adrian Brough Pottery, 5 Tyringham Place. Beautifully decorated pots of marine life using ceramic styles from Portugal and Korea. B&B and residential courses. Open M-F 9-5, W/Es by appoint. (L3) 01736 755515 www. adrianbroughpottery.co.uk

Scarlet Wines (Cafe, Deli, Wine Shop), **The Old Forge**. Exhausted after belting down the A30? Then stop off here for some nourishment and ogle at their wine bottles and cheeses. Perhaps, a strong cuppa to revive you. Feast Nights. Open daily from 9 for breakfast, lunch and dinner. Kids menu. 01736 753696 Opposite the entrance to the Rail Station. www.scarlet-wines.co.uk

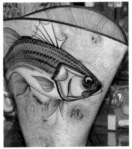

Adrian Brough Pottery

ST JUST-IN-PENWITH

A handsome little town, formerly a hectic mining centre. Imposing Doric facaded Methodist church. The area is rich in prehistoric antiquities. Home to a busy Arts and Crafts community. By Bank Square, the amphitheatre 'Plain-an-Gwary.' where medieval Cornish miracle plays were performed. Water sports festival, Priest's Cove - July. (C5) www.stjust.org www.west-penwith.org.uk/just

WHAT TO SEE, WHERE TO GO...IN AND AROUND ST JUST

Botallack Engine Houses. Remains of famous tin mine operational from 1720-1914 which employed 500 people. Tunnels and galleries were projected beneath the sea. The roaring Atlantic clearly audible above the miners' heads. In 1893 the roof collapsed drowning 29 men, 500 feet down and never recovered. NB Please keep to paths. (B5) www.trevithic-society.org.uk

Geevor Tin Mine. Mining history centre set in magnificent coastal scenery. Underground tours, museum, café & shop. Open daily from 9 except Sa. Last admission 4pm in summer, 3pm in winter. (B7) 01736 788662 www.geevor.com

Levant Mine & Beam Engine (NT), The oldest steam-powered engine in Cornwall restored after 60 years. Open mid-Mar to Oct Su-F & BHs 10.30-4. (B7) 01736 786156 www.nationaltrust.org.uk

Land's End Aerodrome, St Just. Pleasure flights and trial flying lessons over the stunning Cornish coastline. Scheduled services to the Isles of Scilly. Small café. Free parking for Pleasure Flights. Open daily 9-6. (C7) 01736 788771 www.landsendairport.co.uk

Morvah Schoolhouse & Café. 40 local designers/artists show their work here. Large upstairs gallery with sea views. Open daily. 01736 787808 (D4) www.morvah.com

Pendeen Lighthouse. Built in 1900 to protect vessels from Wra Rocks around Pendeen Watch. The lighthouse keeper's cottages are now let as holiday cottages and the automatic fog signal is controlled via a telemetry link from the Trinity House Operational Control Centre in Harwich. (C3) www.trinityhouse.co.uk

Pendeen Pottery & Gallery. Functional, beautiful and practical pots for the home. 01736 788070 www.pendeenpottery.co.uk

Steam Pottery. Distinctive work by Patrick Lester, also featuring work of other ceramicists. Open daily 10-5. (C7) 01736 788070

ART GALLERIES, CRAFT STUDIOS...REFRESHMENT IN ST JUST...

Jane Adams Ceramics, 41 Fore St. Wide range of crafts and gifts - simplistic, vivid imaginations at work. Open M-Sa 10.30-5. (B5) 01736 786695 www.janeadamceramics.co.uk

Kegan Tea Café, The Square. Home-made soup, pastries, coffee and cream teas, and freshly made baguettes. Open daily. (B5)

Stone Age Studio, 8 South Place. Sculptures inspired by the Penwith landscape in Fantastic Realism and Floral Cubism. Open most days from 1pm. Call first. (B5) 01736 787872 www.rorytetigo.co.uk

The Cookbook, 4 Cape Cornwall St. Home-made

Geevor Tin Mine ss

soup, cakes, coffee and cream teas. Supports local artists and writers. Specialist cookery bookshop. Dog and child-friendly. Open daily Tu-Su 10-5. (C6) 01736 787266 www.thecookbookstjust.co.uk

Yew Tree Gallery, Morvah.
Spacious gallery and sculpture gardens in the grounds of Keigwin Farmhouse, with contemporary fine & applied art by well-known artists within and beyond Cornwall. Open Apr-Nov Tu-Sa 10.30-5.30. (D7) 01736 786425 www.yewtreegallery.com

WHERE TO STAY...

Kelynack Caravan & Camping Park, St Just. A small, well-run and friendly site that also offers mobile homes and B&B. (C6) 01736 787633 www.kelynackholidays.co.uk

Porth Nanven Barn. For peace, seclusion and comfort just two minutes walk from the beach and coastal footpath is this converted granite barn. Sleeps 5. Book early. 01736 786104 www.brookcottages.com

PLUS...THE ONE & ONLY...

Land's End. One could argue that in this instance commercialism has hijacked the reason for one's visit; to gape in awe at the natural landscape of dramatic cliffs, rock falls and rock formations. Not forgetting the amazing sunsets. If you do manage to forget why you have actually got here then the occupants of the fun park will try and keep you amused with all manner of stuff. There is a small parking charge and toilets, too, as well as a hotel and bar. Open all year 10-dusk. (A9) 08717200044 www.landsend-landmark.co.uk

Best advised to bring stout shoes, a weatherproof jacket, camera, and or, binoculars.

Land's End

Jane Adams Ceramics

Round House & Capstan Gallery

SENNEN COVE

This most westerly village in England has developed into a centre for surfing and family beach holidays. The turquoise sea is a sight to behold. The Lifeboat Station was established in 1853, the stone pier in 1905. Whitewashed cottages and the Round House Gallery line the front. Fishing trips. Cafés. Amazing surf shop, Chapel Idne. (www.sennenbeach.com) in the car park with Celtic cross. Contorted rock faces beside coast path. (A8) www.sennen-cove.com

Round House & Capstan Gallery. Built in 1876. Houses a huge, man-powered capstan as well as work from Cornwall's finest artists and craftspeople. Open daily 11-5. (B8) 01736 871859 www.round-house.co.uk

WHERE TO EAT, DRINK & BE MERRY...

Ben Tunnicliffe at Sennen. An infinite view to die for, now under new management. Décor of wood, glass, massive artworks and retro racing cars with black slate floors. Freshly prepared local produce. Expect great seafood. Surfers Bar. Breakfast from 8.30, light lunches and supper 7-10. (B8) 01736 871191 www.benatsennen.com

Little BO Café, South End. Another spot with an unforgettable view. Breakfasts from 8 in season. Homemade cakes and pastries. Open daily. (B8)

The Old Success Inn. A popular inn with surfers and coastal walkers, and those seeking an inn for its location, rather than style. The ambience is relaxed and unpretentious. You get what you see. The rooms are simple and comfortable. The restaurant serves locally caught fish. Location, location - will that do? (B8) 01736 871232 www.oldsuccess.co.uk

TREVESCAN, Nr Sennen

Apple Tree Café & Art Studios. A sweet, cute café with a strong Cornish ambience. Coffee, cakes and sarnis. Open all year. (B9) 01736 872753 www.appletreecafe.co.uk

ZENNOR

Small village noted for the legendary 'Mermaid of Zennor' carved into an old bench end in the C15 church. A blow-hole roars below Zennor Head. Tregerthen Cottage was for a short time the home of DH Lawrence and his German wife, Frieda von Richtofen. (F2)

Wayside Folk Museum. Oldest privately owned museum in Cornwall. Over 5,000 items in 16 rooms. Cornish crafts, bookshop and riverside garden. Open Apr-Oct Su-F (Sa School & BHs). (F2) 01736 796945

WHERE TO STAY, EAT, DRINK & BE MERRY...

The Gurnard's Head. The owners describe it as a Dining Pub. It will be a welcome refuge if you have been battling against a sou'westerly head wind on the coastpath. The décor is classy and arty, the ambience is laid-back and the food will appease a mighty appetite. The staff are cool and young. The bedrooms have Vi-Spring beds and dogs are welcome in the bar. And, more important, we need more places like this in England. (F2) 01736 796928 www.gurnardshead.co.uk

Tinners Arms, Zennor. This ancient (since 1271) and friendly pub brews its own ale, Tinners Ales, and serves quality nosh. The simple décor of settles and benches, and bonhomie makes it a delight just to sit here and enjoy the scene. Dogs and children welcomed. (G2) 01736 796927 www.tinnersarms.com

Next door is **The White House**, a Grade II listed building offering quality B&B. Known as Bos Cres ('house

RNLI Lifeboat, Sennen Cove

in the middle') there are two double-rooms and two single-rooms. WiFi. Packed lunches and luggage forwarding available. Small charge for dogs. (G2) 01736 796927

Zennor Chapel Café & Guest House. Accommodation for those seeking the camaraderie of the Open Road, and a good deal. Laid back ambience with 5 newly decorated rooms. Family rooms. No pets. Wifi. Café open daily. (G2) 01736 798307 www. zennorchapelguesthouse.com

ANCIENT CORNWALL...

Boscawen-Un Stone Circle (Nine Maiden). Bronze Age circle of 19 stones. Sometimes site of Cornish Gorsedd. (D7)

Carn Euny Ancient Village. Iron Age village discovered in C19. Well preserved 65ft long fogue. (D7)

Castle An Dinas. Good viewpoint with three circular defensive walls. Two barrows. 1920 excavations unearthed arms and water supply. (H4)

Chun Castle. Impressive fort with two concentric stone ramparts of 300ft diameter. (D7)

Chysauster Ancient Village (EH). The best-preserved Iron Age village in Cornwall. Eight circular houses. Occupied

during Roman Conquest. Access via half-mile path from road. Small shop. (H4)

Chun Quoit. Mushroom shaped neolithic tomb with massive capstone, 8ft square(D7)

Gurnards Head. Cut off by ramparts and ditches. Circular stone huts. (F2)

The Giants House. 13 ft long chamber within barrow 26ft in diameter. (F3)

Lanyon Quoit (NT). Stone Age dolmen; three upright and capstone re-erected c.1824. Hidden entrance over stile beside road. (F7)

Maen Cliff. Iron Age fort with ramparts and ditches. (A8)

Men-An-Tol. A large circular slab with a hole pierced through centre set between 2 upright slabs. Famous for its legendary magical healing powers - children were passed through to cure them of rickets. Fifteen minute walk from parking area. Teas at Lanyon Farm, from Apr-Oct Tu-Su 2-5. (A7)

Nine Maidens Stone Circle. 2 circles of standing stones, 50ft and 60ft in diameter. (F3)

Merry Maidens Stone Circle. 19 stones form this perfect circle. The Legend relates that nineteen virgins

Merry Maidens Stone Circle

were turned to stone for dancing on a Sunday. You have been warned! (E9)

Pendeen Vau Fogou. Lengthy passage, stone faced and roofed with lintels. In yard of Pendeen Manor Farm. (C3)

Plain-An-Gwarry. Circular embankment (cattle pen) where old Cornish miracle plays were performed. (B6)

Trencrom Hill (NT). Well preserved fort with stone walls. (K3)

Treryn Dinas. Well fortified with five lines of ramparts and ditches. Overlooks fluorescent sea. Site of Logan Rock. (D10)

Zennor Quoit. One of England's largest dolmens. A double-chambered tomb with a massive slab. Pieces of Neolithic pottery discovered here. (G2)

Lanyon Quoit

Porthmeor Beach

BEACHES AND SURFING...

Hayle, The Towans. A vast expanse of firm golden sands ideal for families who want to spread out. Swift currents to be avoided at mouth of estuary, surfing with S-B hire/WC/ LG. (M2)

Lelant - Porth Kidney Sands. Massive expanse of sand, ideal for beach games, HZ bathing; avoid estuary. LG. (L2)

Carbis Bay. Popular family beach with firm sands and rocks. WC/Café. P is a problem. (K2)

St Ives - Porthminster Beach. Sheltered, good for children. Access from road, all facilities. (K1)

St Ives - Towan Beach (Harbour). Sand at LT, easy access and all facilities. (K1)

St Ives - Porthgwidden Beach. Sheltered, good bathing, popular with children. East of St Ives Head, all facilities. (K1)

St Ives - Porthmeor Beach. Heavy surf, strong currents, spacious at LT, most popular St Ives beach. S-B hire/LG/all facilities. Surfing - popular with locals. Fine peaks from S-SW winds. (J1)

Portheras Cove. Isolated, white sandy cove reached by foot from P at Pendeen Lighthouse. Stream and waterfall. (C3)

Pendeen Beach. Sandy cove at LT. Rock fishing below lighthouse. (C3)

Cape Cornwall. Tiny, visible at LT, strong currents around headland. WC/Café. (B5)

Porth Nanven (Cot Valley). Sand at LT. Boulders like sculptures or pieces of ceramic. (B6)

Gwenvor (Aire Point). Surfing - Guaranteed a swell in most weather. Works well at 3-6 feet. Has shifting peaks and strong rips. LG. (B7)

Whitesand Bay, Sennen Cove. Superb rolling surf and turquoise sea, bathing safest at HT. P/WC/LG/Café. Surfing - crowded in summer. Constant swell with shifting peaks and strong rips. (B7)

Nanjizal. Ever-changing sands and sea caves - not for the faint hearted. Dramatic and isolated. (B10)

Porthminster Beach

1990   Winds of 177 mph are recorded on the Lizard   1991   Delabole Wind Farm opens, the first commercial wind farm in Cornwall

Sennen Cove

Porthgwarra. Tiny beach with WC/Café. Two ancient tunnels cut out for horses and carts to transport fertilised seaweed. (B10)

Porth Chapel. Isolated sandy cove below St Levan church, steep descent from coast path. (C10)

Porthcurno. Superb white shell-sand beach and turquoise sea, surrounded by high granite cliffs. Strong undertow at HT. Tidal sands and lagoons at Pedn Vounder below Treen - access via descent of tricky path. P/WC/LG. Beach Shop/Café open daily in season. Surfing - Fine waves after a big SW swell. (C10)

Lamorna Cove. Patches of sand and huge granite boulders, harbour P/WC/Café. (F9)

Newlyn. Pebbled beach, sand at LT, access P. (G7)

Penzance. Wide expanse of shingly sand stretches from Eastern Green Beach to Marazion. Entrance under railway line at Eastern Green. Two other access points at Longrock. WC/Café at east end. (H6)

Marazion. Popular and safe family beach, firm, spacious sands. Causeway to St Michael's Mount at LT. WC/Café. (J6)

Perran Sands (Parranuthnoe). Surfing, spacious sands. P/WC. Surfing - Novices beach. Good RH breaks close to rocks at NW end of beach. Cabin Beach Café. (L7)

Prussia Cove. No real sandy/pebbly beach, but there are rocks to lie on, and natural pools to swim. Accessed via rough, private track from parking area. Camping/Shop/Holiday Lets. (M7)

Old Harbour, Newlyn

Porth Nanven

Porthcurno

Pordenack Point, Land's End

COASTAL FOOTPATH...

St Ives to Land's End Approx 22 miles. Considered by some to be the finest stretch of all: wild, rugged and besieged relentlessly by the elements. The path is lonely and remote, up and down and at times, very hard going following the cliff edge and cliff top. Seals laze on the Carracks. A blow hole roars below Zennor Head. It's worth a detour to Zennor for refreshments and to meet the mermaid in the church. On to Gurnard's Head (good pub), sphinx-like with great views, and then you are entering the heart of tin mining country, so beware of unprotected mine shafts. The cliffs between St Ives and Pendeen sometimes glitter with minerals. Hereabouts, paths criss-cross in all directions and there's much to interest the industrial archaeologist, especially at Geevor, Levant and Botallack. Following the cliff tops, Cape Cornwall appears, marked by a lonely stack, remains of a mine abandoned in the 1870s. The cliff drops to Aire Point, and ahead the thunderous breakers, and the dedicated surfers of Whitesand Bay. And now, the well worn path to Land's End.

Botallack Engine Houses

| 2002 | The Cornish Language is to be included in the European Charter for regional language | 2004 | Boscastle floods devastate the village, again |

Mine Shafts, Botallack

Land's End to Hoe Point

Approx 27 miles. Another superb stretch of coastline: precipitous cliffs, great blocks of granite, sandy coves and minute valleys with sub-tropical vegetation. Spectacular rock formations to Gwennap Head, equally as wild a headland as Land's End. Here are great gnarled granite boulders, cracked and sculpted by the elements - a popular place for climbers, and below a haunt for seals. There are two paths: the first follows every cranny and contour, the second cuts off along the headlands for a wonderfully invigorating walk. Down into tiny Porthgwarra, and on up to St Levan's Well above the little cove of Porthchapel. Then along to Porthcurno passing the famous open-air Minack Theatre; beyond an improbably turquoise sea and the outline of Logan's Rock. On around the dramatic granite columns of Treen Cliff and then Cribba Head, to the tiny fishing cove of Penberth. Along clifftops to Lamorna Cove, a favourite spot for artists.

The path continues along the clifftop until Mousehole. Then resumes east of Penzance at Eastern Green where it crosses the railway line to follow the line of the beach to Marazion, with spectacular views of St Michael's Mount just offshore. Then inland to Perranuthnoe. The going is fairly easy to Hoe Point (Praa Sands).

Cape Cornwall from Sennen Cove

Mousehole Reflections

Neil Canning, Lander Gallery ss

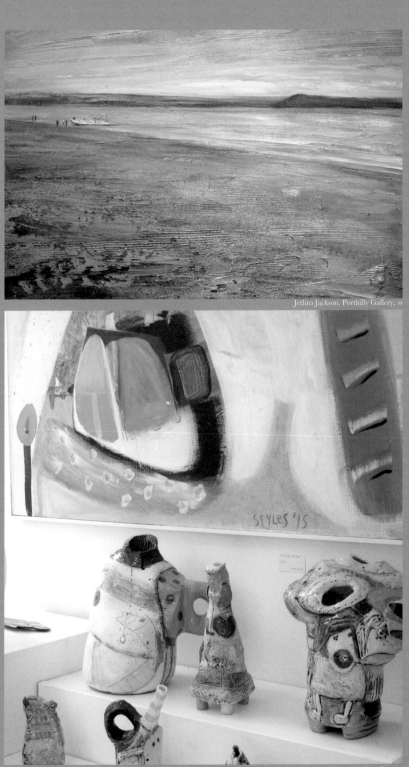

Jethro Jackson, Porthilly Gallery, ss

STYLES '15

Linda Styles, Fannie & Fox, Penryn

Alfred Wallis, Tate St Ives 33

A mere seven miles separates the two communities of St Ives and Newlyn. Visited by JMW Turner in 1811, to be followed by Whistler, Brangwyn and the English Impressionist, Walter Sickert in 1895, other famous artists to St Ives included Alfred Munnings and Augustus John but they did not settle here. An active, if migratory artist's community, based on marine and 'plein air' painting began in the late 1870s with the advent of the railway, coinciding with the downturn in the local fishing industry. Bernard Leach set up his pottery in 1920 and the writers DH Lawrence and Virginia Woolf visited, and wrote about the area.

With the arrival of Ben Nicholson and Barbara Hepworth at the outbreak of WWII, St Ives became an outpost of the abstract avant-garde movement. But its real heyday was in the 50s and 60s following the War. A new generation of artists arrived to flee the cities of dark, satanic mills and to bathe in the brilliant, Mediterranean light. The light shone on these artists who revelled in their new freedoms. Gone were the shackles of realism. A New Age was dawning. It was to become the Age of the Beatles and the Pill.

LEADING FIGURES (IN ORDER OF BIRTH)

Alfred Wallis 1855-1942
Artist, Fisherman, Marine Scrap Merchant. Born in Davenport. He took up painting at the age of 70 following the death of his wife, 'for company' according to Ben Nicholson and Christopher 'Kit' Wood who discovered him on a walk through the back streets of St Ives. He was illiterate and inarticulate; his style is Primitive, simple paintings of ships, harbours, seascapes and St Ives. Despite recognition and admiration from artistic circles, Wallis's work did not capture the public's imagination during his lifetime and he died in poverty in Madron Workhouse unaware of what his work would fetch at auction in later years.

Julius Olsson, ARA, RA, 1864-1942
Seascape Painter. Born in London. A self trained artist who exhibited at the Royal Academy in 1890, the same year he settled in St Ives (for 20 years) and founded the School of Painting in 1895. He was an energetic man of great enthusiasm. He painted Cornish coastal scenes and seascapes and during WWI he was a Lieutenant in the Royal Naval Voluntary Reserve.

Borlasse Smart 1881-1947
Painter. An enthusiastic supporter of the more experimental work of Barnes-Graham, Ben Nicholson and Barbara Hepworth.

Bernard Leach 1887-1979
Potter. Born in the Far East where his father was a Hong Kong Judge, and his maternal grandparents missionaries in Japan. Educated at the Slade School of Art and the London School of Art. He returned to Japan in 1909, learnt the craft of Raku from Kenzan VI, the great ceramicist and heir to a ceramics dynasty. Built a lasting friendship with the great Japanese potter Shoji Hamada, an inspiration for many studio potters. He returned to England in 1920 and settled in St Ives. Later, in 1927, the Elmhirsts invited him to set up a rural arts and crafts centre at Dartington, before setting up his own pottery in 1932. A struggling potter until his first book was published after WWII, he gained instant recognition with The Potter's Book, his third of thirteen books. He started a Leach dynasty of potters with his descendants, potting from Hartland to Muchelney, and beyond.

Ben Nicholson OM 1894-1982
Painter. Born in Denham, Buckinghamshire and educated at Greshams School and the Slade School of Art. The son of artists Sir William Nicholson and Mabel Pryde, his early work was influenced by his father,

post- Impressionism, synthetic Cubism and early English Art. As a young man he travelled widely through France, Italy and Spain (1912-14) and the United States (1917-19). His first marriage to artist Winifred Nicholson 1920-31 was followed by his second, to the sculptor Barbara Hepworth, 1933-51. With her he met and was influenced by Brancusi, Braque, Mondrian, Moore and Picasso. He moved to Cornwall in 1939 and resumed painting landscapes and abstracts but added more colour. He had retrospectives at the Venice Biennale, 1954 and the Tate Gallery, 1955. In 1958 he moved to Switzerland with his third wife Felicitas Vogler. He is among the most celebrated and internationally-recognised painters of the C20. His work represents the embodiment of British Modernism.

Barbara Hepworth DBE 1903-1975

Artist & Sculptor. Born in Wakefield, she was educated at Wakefield Girls High School, and won scholarships to Leeds School of Art and the Royal College of Art. Travelled to Italy with her first husband, sculptor John Skeaping and received a thorough training in carving. Her early work was quasi-naturalistic with detail submerged in simple forms. By the early 30s she was working closely with Moore and Nicholson (whom she married) and developing an abstract style. She moved to St Ives in 1939 staying there until she tragically died in a studio fire. She worked both in wood and stone exploring mass and space and the relationship between the inside and the outside of her sculptures. Her understanding of the materials she used was immense. By the 1950s she was one of the most internationally famous of sculptors and received the commission for a memorial outside the United Nations in New York. Her Trewyn Studio

is now the Barbara Hepworth Museum and Sculpture Garden.

Wilhelmina Barns-Graham, CBE, RSA, 1912-2004

Painter, Teacher. Born in St Andrews, Fife and educated at the Edinburgh College of Art. She moved to St Ives in 1940 and became a member of the Penwith Society of Artists living all her life in Cornwall, but for two short-terms teaching jobs in Leeds and London. From 1960 she spent her summers in Cornwall and winters in Scotland. One of our foremost abstract painters with an exceptional sense of colour, her images derive from acute observations of natural forms and sense of place. Exhibited at the Tate, V&A and the British Museum.

Sir Terry Frost RA 1915-2003

Abstract Painter, Prisoner of War, Teacher. Born in Leamington Spa, he began painting during his time as a Prisoner of War after the fall of Crete. He received an Ex-Serviceman's grant and moved to St Ives in 1946, before enrolling at the Camberwell School of Art in 1947. In 1950 he became a member of the Penwith Society of Arts and assistant to Barbara Hepworth. Encouraged by Ben Nicholson towards abstraction. Later as an established painter he taught at the Bath Academy of Art. An abstract painter after beginning in the realist tradition, his canvases were inspired by the Cornish light, boats and reflections and are often of geometric shapes - crescents, balls, spots, hearts, or curves in bright, joyous colours.

Peter Lanyon 1918-1964

Painter, Sculptor, Teacher. Born in St Ives. Educated at Clifton College, Penzance School of Art and the Euston Road School. Took private tuition with Ben Nicholson. Served with the RAF in the

Western Desert during WWII. Founder member of the Penwith Society of Artists and a leading figure in the St Ives group of artists. Taught at the Bath Academy of Art. Specialised in abstract landscapes, constructions and sculpture. Very taken with Rothko's work on visit to New York in 1957. Sadly died in a gliding accident, a devastating loss for the St Ives community.

Patrick Heron 1920-1999

Painter, Art Critic, Designer, Teacher, Writer. Born in Headingley, Leeds, where his father, a businessman and founder of Cresta Silks, worked. Aged 13 he was overwhelmed by Paul Cezanne's paintings at the National Gallery, and as a part-time student aged 17 he enrolled at the Slade School of Art. As a Conscientious Objector during WWII he worked as a farm labourer, then as assistant at the Leach Pottery until 1945. He travelled widely in 1953 and his early influences were Braques, Bonnard and Matisse. From 1953 – 56 he taught at the Central School of Arts & Crafts. His later influences were the American Abstract Expressionists, Pollack, Rothko and de Kooning. They prompted new themes such as more vibrant colour, and an analysis of space and form, stripes and organic shapes using oils and gouaches. He also designed textiles and the window for Tate St Ives. He lived at Eagle's Nest, Zennor from 1956 until his death in 1999.

A LIST OF OTHER ARTISTS ASSOCIATED WITH ST IVES:
Sven Berlin,
Naum Gabo,
Paul Feller,
Leonard Fuller,
Roger Hilton,
Denis Mitchell,
Adrian Stokes,
Karl Weschke,
John Wells
and Bryan Winter.

Newlyn Harbour

THE NEWLYN SCHOOL OF PAINTERS

Penlee House Gallery

Groups and individual artists descended on Newlyn and its environs, Penzance and Lamorna, in the late C19 and early C20. The opening of the Great Western Railway in 1877 made travel easier and Cornwall more accessible. The artists were drawn to Newlyn by the brilliant light, the beauty of the coastline, the drama of the sea and the cheap living. There was much to draw and paint - scenes from rural life and a fascination with the community of fishermen and their wives and children, and nature in its purest form.

The colony of artists drew much of their inspiration from the clear, natural light and can be compared to the Barbizon School in France. The leading figure, Stanhope Forbes, was greatly impressed and influenced by the Plein Air movement, or outdoor painting, as opposed to painting in the studio. Forbes wished to follow in the role undertaken by the French artist, Jules Bretton, who strove to portray society in a realistic style. Forbes, along with his great friend Lamorna Birch, encouraged all who came to live and paint in Newlyn. He set up a School of Painting to teach the Plein Air method and to study the weather in all its changing moods. Strong colours attracted them. Paint would be used straight out of the tube rather than a mixed concoction. Forbes wrote to his mother following a trip to Brittany: "Newlyn is a sort of English Concarneau, and is the haunt of many artists." Forbes was an inspiring teacher. His encouragement and genial temperament provided a warm haven of creativity for the many who had pulled up their roots and perhaps taken a risky decision to follow their creative

instincts and move west to Cornwall, and the unknown.

LEADING FIGURES (IN ORDER OF BIRTH)

Stanhope Forbes RA, ARA 1857-1947
Born in Dublin. Irish Realist Painter. Studied at the Lambeth School of Art, and in Paris under Leon Bonnat. Moved to Newlyn in 1884 and Father of the Newlyn School, influential member and great encourager to his fellow artists. Passionate about the Plein Air Movement (painting outdoors) after a visit to Brittany in 1881. He founded the Newlyn School of Painting in 1899.

Henry Scott Tuke 1858-1929
Marine Painter of controversy. Born in Yorkshire. He studied at the Slade School of Art, in Florence and Paris. His paintings depict the Cornish coast and scenes of naked boys. This caused controversy amongst Victorian society when exhibited. He lived in Newlyn and Falmouth having bought an old brig, the Julie of Nantes, and anchored it in Falmouth Harbour using it as a floating studio.

Lamorna Birch RA 1869-1955
Born in Cheshire. A self-taught artist who worked in oils and watercolours. He settled in the Lamorna Valley where he could follow his passion for nature and fishing. Very much regarded as a leading figure of the "Newlyn School." He had over 200 works exhibited at the Royal Academy. Taken under the wing of Stanhope Forbes, the father figure of the Newlyn ensemble.

A LIST OF OTHER ARTISTS ASSOCIATED WITH NEWLYN:

Albert Chevalier Taylor,
Fred Hall,
Thomas Cooper Gotch,
Norman Garstin,
Elizabeth Forbes,
Walter Langley,
Laura Knight,
Harold Knight,
Fred Bramley,
Fred Millard,
Ralph Todd,
Ernest Procter.

St Petroc, Patron Saint of Cornwall

These Celebrities are listed by order of birth. They have been selected because they have achieved greatness or notoriety in their chosen fields, sometimes posthumously, and have an attachment to Cornwall either by birth or by choosing to live in Cornwall.

St Piran (Sen Piln)

Patron Saint of Tin Miners, and the National Saint of Cornwall. His origins are steeped in mystery but he is thought to have been born in the C6 in Ireland. He studied scripture in Rome and returned to monastic life in County Ossary later to export his missionary zeal to Cornwall landing on Perrran Beach where he built a tiny oratory (chapel). St Piran's flag is the white cross on a black background, and St Piran's Day is the 5th March. Thousands flock to the dunes dressed in black, white and gold carrying the Cornish flag.

St Petroc

The Patron Saint of Cornwall. A Welsh nobleman educated in an Irish monastery in the C6 or C7. With a band of followers he landed on the Camel Estuary and set up a monastery at Lanwethnic, all according to the Domesday Survey. Built churches at Padstow (Petroc's-Stow), Little Petherick and Bodmin which was to become a religious centre in the Middle Ages. In 1177 his bodily remains were carried off to the Abbey of St Meen in Brittany but such was the outcry that the Prior of Bodmin set forth to recover his relics. In 1994 his casket was stolen from St Petroc's Bodmin, later to be found in Yorkshire.

Thomas Flamank and Michael an Gof (Michael Joseph)

Co-Leaders of the Cornish Rebellion of 1497. Two patriotic Cornishmen, one a lawyer, the other a village blacksmith. They shared passionate dreams for their beloved county. Henry VII was fighting a war against the Scots and required funds. He raised taxes and these two men believed, along with 15,000 rebels, that Cornwall and her poverty-stricken citizens could ill afford such sufferage. The rebels reached Blackheath Common but poorly armed with bows, arrow, scythes and pitchforks were no match for the King's mercenaries. These two were found guilty of high treason. Their punishment to be dragged on hurdles from the Tower to Tyburn, then hung, drawn and quartered, and their heads displayed on pike staffs on London Bridge. In 1997 a statue was unveiled in St Keverne to commemorate the 500th Anniversary of these fine Cornishmen: "a name perpetual, and a fame permanent and immortal".

Sir Humphrey Arundell 1513-1550

Conservative Catholic, Landowner, Proud Cornishman, Soldier. Born in Helland near Bodmin. Commanded a small garrison at St Michael's Mount. Took military charge of the rebels (to hold back their excesses) during the Prayer Book Rebellion against Edward VI. Found guilty of high treason and was subsequently hung, drawn and quartered at Tyburn. His estates were thus handed to Sir Gawen Carew.

Sir Richard Grenville 1542-1591

Explorer, Privateer, Soldier. He was born at Buckland Abbey in Devon. Educated at Cambridge and the Inner Temple. Immortalised in Tennyson's poem 'The Revenge.' His voyages to Virginia, the Azores and Roanoke Island were the stuff of legend. Later became Sheriff of Cornwall in 1577. Turned Bideford, Devon, into a major trading centre. Fought with Raleigh to defend Cornwall and Devon against the Spanish Armada.

Sir Bevil Grenville 1596-1643

Civil War Commander, Cornish Hero, Cornish Landowner, MP, Royalist. Born near Withiel, educated at Exeter College, Oxford. Knighted in 1639 having served in the King's bodyguard. He raised an army in Cornwall to fight for the King. Won battles at Braddock Down, Stratton Hill (Bude) and Lansdown outside Bath where he was mortally wounded. Buried in Kilkhampton Church. Monument erected in a field above Bath to commemorate his heroism and those of his Cornish Pikemen.

Jonathan Trelawney 1650-1721

Bishop, Catholic Zealot, Royalist, Scholar. Born in Pelynt. Educated at Westminster

School and Christ Church, Oxford. He became Bishop of Bristol, Exeter and finally, Winchester. Famous as one of the seven bishops who took umbrage at James II for his "Declaration of Indulgence" in 1682 which declared religious freedom in England. The bishops were temporarily committed to the Tower. This invited the ballad "The Song of the Western Man" by Stephen Hawker, "And shall Trelawney die" etc.

Admiral Edward Boscawen 1711-1761

Sailor, MP, Privy Councillor. Joined the Navy at twelve, appointed midshipman at fourteen. Known as "Old Dreadnought" or "Wry-necked Dick" due to his courage and resilience. Reputation grew during the War of the Austrian Succession, 1740-48. Appointed Admiral in 1758 and led expedition to Cape Breton. Later, in 1759, his greatest victory over the French in the Battle of Lagos prevented their invasion plans. Died of a fever and is buried at St Michaels Penkivel.

Samuel Wallis 1728-1795

Naval Officer, Navigator, Pacific Explorer. Born in Lanteglos-By-Camelford, he rose through the ranks under the patronage of Admiral Boscawen. In 1766 he was given command of HMS Dolphin to explore the Southern Hemisphere. He discovered Tahiti, Easter Island and Wallis Island in 1767, to eventually reach Batavia (Jakarta) where most of his crew perished from dysentery.

John Arnold 1736-1779

Inventor, Watchmaker. The son of a Bodmin watchmaker who learnt much of his trade in Holland. Returning to London he set up a chronometer factory in Essex. His most innovative design was to solve the problems of friction in a balance spring and to use a bi-

metallic strip to aid temperature compensation. His watches were used by King George III and his chronometers by Captain James Cook on his South Sea voyages. The great quest of the day was to calculate Longitude aboard ships. His travails were documented in Dava Sobel's book, Longitude.

Captain William Bligh 1754-1817

Cartographer, Naval Officer, Navigator, Governor of New South Wales. Born in Plymouth to Cornish parents. Joined the Royal Navy at the age of seven. Accompanied Captain James Cook in Resolution on his third, fatal voyage to the Pacific where he learned much of his navigational skill. Appointed Commander of the Bounty in 1787, a merchant vessel sent to Tahiti to collect breadfruit trees for cultivation in the Caribbean slave trade. The Mutiny on the Bounty, 28 April 1789, saw him and eighteen of his loyal

St Piran

Sir Richard Grenville, Kilkhampton Church

crew placed in a 23-foot launch. They sailed an incredible 3,619 nautical miles in 47 days before reaching Timor, an unheard of piece of navigation. One crewman lost his life in the ordeal. He was acquitted at his Court Martial. All records show him to be a just man not given to ruthless punishment. He believed in exercise, regular bathing, clean laundry and a healthy diet learnt in the company of Captain Cook. In Australia, he experienced the Rum Rebellion in 1810.

Henry Bone RA 1755-1834
Enamel Painter. Born in Truro. He became the enamel painter to George III and painted portraits on watches, brooches and fans.

William Gregor 1761-1817
Chemist, Geologist, Inventor, Rector. Born at Trewarthenick near Tregony. Educated at Bristol Grammar School and St John's College, Cambridge where he excelled in Classics and Mathematics. Known as the 'Scientific Parson' of Creed and through his interests in minerals and the discovery of black powder on the Lizard, he was to discover 'Menachite,' later to be

called Titanium.

John Carter 1770-1807
Fisherman, Pirate, Rogue, Smuggler. Born in Breage near Helston, Carter became known as the 'King of Prussia' for his admiration of Frederick the Great and because his smuggling activities centred around Piskey's Cove, Prussia Cove and Bessies Cove. Always at odds with the Customs, his running of contraband around the English and French coasts was the stuff of legend. Despite this he was known as an upright, honest and god-fearing man who forbade drink on Sundays. He disappeared off the coast of Cornwall in 1807, never to be heard of again.

John Opie, FRA 1770-1807
Portrait Painter. Born near St Agnes. Apprenticed as a carpenter then discovered by Dr John Walcot who recognised his enormous potential and so taught him mathematics and science. Walcot introduced him to Sir Joshua Reynolds, President of the Royal Academy. Opie's style was considered similar to Rembrandt's and for twenty years he was London Society's

most sort after portrait painter. He was appointed Professor of Painting at the Royal Academy. He died, sadly very young, and lies buried in St Paul's Cathedral. The Newlyn Gallery was founded in 1895, in his honour.

Richard Trevithick 1771-1833
Cornish Giant, Inventor, Mining Engineer, Pioneer. Born at Tregajorran near Camborne where his father was a mine 'Captain.' His early life was spent tinkering with the machinery. He became one of the leading figures and a pioneer of the Industrial revolution. A man of vision, ahead of his times, who lacked business acumen, and who sadly failed to capitalise on his success as an inventor. His inventions included the High Pressure Steam Engine, Floating Docks, London Steam Carriage, Ship's Propeller, Iron Tanks, Water-Jet Propulsion, Thames Dredger, Portable Stoves, Threshing Machine and Railway Locomotives, and whilst in Peru, he built a gun for the Rebels. He died of pneumonia in Dartford, in extreme poverty.

Henry Trengrouse 1772-1854
Cabinet Maker, Cornish Hero, Inventor, Saver of Lives. Born and educated in Helston. He invented the rocket line apparatus which fired a rope to stricken ships. This invention went on to save at least 20,000 lives. The idea originated in having witnessed the shipwrecked HMS Anson off Loe Bar with her loss of 120 drowned sailors, and a firework display honouring George III's birthday. The government bought a dozen off him, then manufactured their own giving him £50 in compensation. The Czar of Russia awarded him a diamond ring in recognition of lives saved in the Baltic. The Life Jacket was another of his inventions. He died a pauper.

William Bickford
1774-1834

Currier, Leather-maker, Inventor of the Safety Fuse. Born in Ashburton, Devon, he was to move to Truro, then Tuckingmill where he was to establish a factory making safety fuses. This invention was inspired by his early days working in the mining industry where loss of life from explosions was common. Prompted after visiting a friend who owned a rope factory. He never saw the fruits of his labours having suffered a stroke but in its first year his factory made 45 miles of fuse, and one hundred years later had made 104,545 miles of fuse. The general design has changed little and has saved hundreds of lives.

Sir Bevil Grenville, Hartland Abbey

Sir Humphry Davy
1778-1829

Chemist, Inventor, Lecturer, Physicist, Surgeon. Born in Penzance, he was apprenticed to an apothecary-surgeon. He moved up to London, became a Professor of Chemistry in 1801 and a popular and entertaining lecturer of chemical experiments at the Royal Institution, often experimenting with gases by inhaling them and causing himself near fatal injuries. His most famous invention, the Miner's Safety (Davy) Lamp, saved thousands of lives. Electrolysis was another favourite subject. He was appointed President of the Royal Society, and gave employment to Michael Faraday who was to eclipse all his deeds.

Joseph Austen (Thomas) Treffry 1782-1850

Engineer, Mining Industrialist, Landowner. Born in Plymouth, later to inherit the family estate in Fowey. As a partner in various mines he instigated the construction of harbours at Fowey and Par, as well as canals, railways, trams and the Treffry Viaduct.

Edward John Trelawney
1792-1881

Adventurer, Biographer, Novelist, Pirate, Romantic, Sailor, Soldier. A friend of Byron and Shelley, he was at Livorno (Leghorn) when Shelley was drowned in 1822 (he plucked Shelley's heart from the funeral pyre on the beach) and later served with Byron in the Greek War of Independence. His biographical accounts of the lives of Byron and Shelley are considered a little rich and fanciful. He was buried beside Shelley in Rome's Protestant Cemetery.

Sir Goldsworthy Gurney
1793-1875

Architect, Builder, Chemist, Inventor, Pianist, Scientist, Surgeon. Born near Padstow and educated at Truro Grammar School, he was apprenticed to a Doctor of Medicine then became a GP in Wadebridge. He later moved to London, and in 1832 devised the Oxy-Hydrogen Blowpipe. His other inventions included the Steam Carriage in 1825, or Horseless Carriage known as the 'Gurney Drag', and the Gurney Stove, used in various abbeys and cathedrals. The Bude Light

was another invention designed for lighthouses. He built The Castle in Bude as his home causing much controversy. Not justly recognised in his own lifetime, he is today considered one of the leading scientific minds of his day. Buried in Launcells churchyard.

Richard Lander 1804-1834

Adventurer, Explorer, Mariner, Servant. Born in Truro at the Fighting Cock Inn (now Dolphin). Aged 9 he walked to London, aged 11 he sailed to the West Indies on a merchant ship and later joined explorations to West Africa seeking the course of the Niger River. He was awarded the first Gold Medal of the Royal Geographical Society in 1832. On his third trip to West Africa he was attacked by natives and died of his wounds. A statue celebrates his life at the top of Lemon Street in Truro.

Neville Northey Burnard
1818-1878

Sculptor. Born in Alarnum, the son of a stonemason. He became a celebrated society sculptor and exhibited at the Royal Academy. His sculpture of Richard Lander stands at the top of Lemon Street, Truro.

Sir Humphry Davy, Penzance

The death of his daughter turned him to drink. Thrown out of house and home he took to the road and lived as a tramp to eventually die in a Redruth Workhouse.

Sir Arthur Quiller-Couch 1863-1944

Editor, Journalist, Lecturer, Novelist, Professor, Yachtsman. Born in Bodmin, educated at Clifton College and Trinity College, Oxford. A prolific writer of Cornish tales under the pseudonym 'Q,' many of his stories tackled the supernatural. He became a Professor of Literature at Cambridge and edited The Oxford Books of English Verse and English Prose. He also edited anthologies of ghost stories. His novels often featured Troy (or Fowey) where he lived from 1892. Commodore of the Royal Fowey Yacht Club and Gorseth Bard.

Selina Cooper 1864-1946

Anti-Fascist, Pacifist, Suffragette, Trade Unionist. Born in Callington but moved to Lancashire as a child. Started work in a textile mill aged 12. Became a trade unionist activist seeking equal rights. Chosen by her local NUWSS to represent Nelson as an independent Parliamentary candidate but was turned down by the male dominated Labour Party.

Anne Treneer 1891-1966

Author, Biographer, Poet, Schoolteacher. Born in Gorran, the daughter of the local schoolmaster. She is best known for her autobiographical trilogy of a Cornish childhood, Schoolhouse in the Wind, recently brought back into print, and her biography of Humphrey Davy.

Rowena Cade 1893-1983

Founder of the Minack Theatre. Born in Derbyshire and brought up in Cheltenham. During the First World War she broke in horses for use on the Front Line. Then moved to Lamorna with her mother, bought the Minack (a rocky place) for £100 and built a house on it with granite from St Levan Quarry. Her interest in theatrical productions grew out of her experience as a wardrobe mistress for local productions. She started cutting out the rock in the winter of 1931-32, and continued to work well into her eighties. Many of today's stars began their careers here - Michael York, Sarah Brightman, John Nettles, Charlotte Church, to name a few.

Sir John Betjeman 1906-1984

Essayist, Poet, Satirist, Travel Writer. Born in Highgate, North London the son of a Cabinet Maker who owned many properties in North Cornwall around the Trebetherick/ Polzeath area. Family holidays were spent here and his love of Cornwall developed from

an early age. Educated at Marlborough and Magdalen College, Oxford. He had a life-long passion for architecture and English churches. His poetry reflected the vicissitudes and enigmas of the Home Counties. He is buried at St Enodoc near Rock.

Daphne du Maurier (Lady Browning), DBE 1907-1989

Biographer, Novelist, Playwright. Born in London where her father was the actor-manager Sir Gerald du Maurier. Most of her life was spent living at Menabilly, west of Fowey. She married Lieutenant-General Sir Frederick "Boy" Browning and bore him three children. Commander of the 1st Airborne Division, he was the chief architect of the disastrous Operation Market Garden filmed as A Bridge Too Far which incensed du Maurier and led her to write letters to the press decrying the film producers unforgivable treatment of her husband's memory. Her novels have sold millions of copies in many languages and have been filmed many times. Who can forget Rebecca, Jamaica Inn, The Birds, or Frenchman's Creek, an unforgettable blend of romanticism, suspense and escapism?

Winston Graham 1910-2003

Coastguard, Novelist, Writer. Born in Manchester, he settled in Perranporth aged 17 where he was to write the first four Poldark novels between 1945 and 1953. These had a cult following, as did the TV series starring Robin Ellis and Angharad Rees. The bungalow overlooking the beach has disappeared but a plaque has been planned. His book, Marnie, was filmed by Alfred Hitchcock and starred the relatively unknown Sean Connery. A private and modest man, he lived to write 40 novels living to the grand age of 93.

Fellow of the Royal Society of Literature.

Sir William Golding 1911-1993

Essayist, Nobel Laureate (1983), Novelist, Pianist, Playwright, Poet, Seaman, Teacher. Born in Newquay, he was educated at Marlborough Grammar School where his father Alec was the Science Master, later Brasenose College, Oxford. He saw active service aboard HMS Galatea in the North Atlantic, later to take part in the D-Day landings and the invasion of Walcheren. Taught at the Bishop Wordworth's School, Salisbury. Lord of the Flies accepted for publication by Faber and Faber in 1953. Became full-time writer in 1962. Knighted in 1988. He was awarded the Booker Prize in 1980 for Rites of Passage; in all he wrote twelve novels.

George Lloyd 1913-1998

Composer, Market Gardener, Naval Gunner, Romantic. Heralded as a musical genius at an early age. His first symphony was premiered by the Bournemouth Symphony Orchestra whilst he was only 19 years old. His second symphony was performed in Eastbourne in 1935. He expressed his music through the C19 traditions of melody and harmony. Inspired by the Late Romantics and the Italian Operatic Masters Verdi, Puccini, Donizetti, Bellini, and our own Elgar. His development as a musician was halted by his traumatic experiences in the arctic convoys. His ship was torpedoed by a German U-Boat and his fellow gunners were drowned in oil. His creativity dried up for twenty years. He enjoyed an Indian Summer to his career when the BBC eventually agreed to play his work in 1969 and at the 1981 Proms.

Charles Causley 1917-2003

Cornish Poet, Naval Coder, Playwright, Primary School Teacher. Born in Launceston, he lived much of his life in Cornwall. His verse was simple and straightforward and much admired by Larkin and Betjeman. Ted Hughes was his closest friend who said of him, "One of our best loved and most needed poets." Very much influenced by William Blake and John Clare, his poems grew out of folk songs, hymns and ballads. Awarded the Queen's Gold Medal for Poetry in 1967.

John Le Carré (David John Moore Cornwell) Born 1931, Poole

Novelist, Political Commentator, Schoolteacher, Spy. Resident of St Buryan for 40 years. Educated at Sherborne School, University of Berne and Lincoln College Oxford. Taught at Eton for two years, five years in the British Foreign Service, then recruited into MI6. Cover blown by Kim Philby. Took to writing spy novels. His later work has involved more social and political comment; see "The Constant Gardner" and "The Mission Song", as opposed to his earlier work such as "The Spy Who Came In From The Cold", "The Russia House", "Tinker Sailor, Soldier Spy"

etc., many of which have been turned into films. More recently he has written critiques of the Iraq War and the NHS. Arguably, our finest living novelist. Turned down a knighthood. Latest novel "A Delicate Truth." More recently, the subject of Adam Sisman's brilliant biography. This year a TV adaption of "The Night Manager" and film of "Our Kind of Traitor" will popularise his work.

Benjamin Luxon, CBE Born 1937, Redruth

Baritone, Concert, Lieder & Opera Singer. He studied with Walter Grunner at the Guildhall School of Music and has performed major roles in Eugene Onegin (1972), Owen Wingrave (1971), Don Giovanni, Papageno, Wolfran and Eisenstein.

John Nettles Born 1943, St Austell.

Actor, Historian, Philosopher. Adopted at birth, he never knew his father. His mother was an Irish nurse. Studied history and philosophy at

Southampton University. Starred in 87 episodes of Bergerac, and numerous Midsomer Murders. Member of the Royal Shakespeare Company for five seasons.

Tim Rice KBE Born 1944, Amersham.
Cricket Fanatic, Lyricist. Cornish resident who has won countless awards (Tony, Grammy, Academy) for his lyrics to world-famous musicals. Best known for his collaboration with Andrew Lloyd Webber on Joseph, Jesus Christ Superstar, Evita, Chess, and with Elton John in The Lion King and Aida. Past President of the MCC, and stalwart of the Heartaches Cricket Club who make an annual tour to South-West Cornwall.

Mick Fleetwood - Born Redruth 1947.
Actor, Drummer, Musician. Brought up by an RAF father

in Egypt and Norway. The drummer with the rock band, Fleetwood Mac, the name combined with John Mcvie, and led by Peter Green. In 1974 he invited Stevie Nicks and Lindsey Buckingham to join. They went on to produce the LP, Rumours, selling in excess of 30,000,000 copies. Now resident in Los Angeles, California where he has a second career as an actor.

Christopher Richard (Rick) Stein, OBE - Born Churchill, Oxfordshire 1947.
Chef, Entrepreneur, Restaurateur, Traveller, TV Personality, Writer. Resident of Padstow since 1972. Educated at Uppingham School and New College, Oxford. Acorns to oak trees; from a mobile disco to a harbour-side bistro, to the Seafood Restaurant, fame and fortune. The business employs 450 people in Padstow, and beyond.

Jethro - Born St Buryan 1948.
Carpenter, Comic, Timberman, Tin Miner. A born entertainer who has appeared in over 170 theatres. A keen bass singer, horseman and golfer, he is an active charity fundraiser. Lives at Lewdown on the Devon-Cornwall border.

Dawn French - Born 1957 Holyhead.
Actress, Comedian, Novelist. A resident of Fowey. An English comedienne noted for her roles in French and Saunders, The Vicar of Dibley, Jam & Jerusalem, Wild West and winner of countless awards. The first, Chancellor of Falmouth University.

Timothy Bartel Smit KBE - Born 1954 in Holland.
Entrepreneur, Environmentalist, Gardener, Music Impresario. Educated at Cranbrook School and Durham University

John Le Carré - The Night Manager - Photo Credit Ink Factory Films/BBC

where he read Archaeology and Anthropology. Tiring of archaeology he moved into the music business for ten years and produced records for Barry Manilow and the Nolan Sisters. In 1987 he moved to Cornwall, met John Nelson and together they discovered, then restored the "Lost Gardens of Heligan", recently voted the Nation's Favourite Garden. With £40m of Lottery Money he had a vision to convert the massive clay dumps into what has become the Eden Project. Designed by Nicholas Gimshaw Architects with assistance from the structural engineering firm of Anthony Hunt and Associates. He has plans to develop an inter-active visitor centre called "The Ark" near Tiverton, Devon to showcase Devon's plant life.

Kristin Scott-Thomas, DBE - Born Redruth 1960.
Actress, Francophile. Educated at Cheltenham Ladies College and London's Central School of Speech and Drama. Her father was an RAF pilot killed in a flying accident. The same fate fell to her step-father six years later. Her sister, Serena, has appeared as a Bond girl opposite Pierce Brosnan. She has collected numerous awards including BAFTA and the Légion d'honneur from the French government. Appeared in numerous films such as The English Patient, Four Weddings & A Funeral, Mission Impossible, Gosford Park and Nowhere Boy, and on the London stage in Chekov's Three Sisters. Last film "The Kitchen Boy."

Patrick Gale Born in 1962. Book Reviewer, British Writer, Pianist, Quirister (Cathedral Chorister). Educated at Winchester College and New College, Oxford. Resident of West Penwith and highly acclaimed contemporary novelist with 13 novels and numerous short stories in print. Father Prison Governor of Wandsworth and Camp Hill Prison, Isle of Wight. Latest book: 'A Place Called Winter.' Very much a patron of the Cornish literary scene.

Tori (Myra Ellen) Amos - Born 1963 in North Carolina, USA. Award-Winning Singer-Songwriter. Now resident in Bude, North Cornwall and married to an English sound engineer. Her songs are emotionally intense, idiosyncratic and about love, sensuality and joy. Classically trained, she plays the piano, harpsichord and harmonium and has won numerous Grammy Awards having sold in excess of 12,000,000 discs. Last album "Unrepentant Geraldines." More recently, a musical with Samuel Adamson, The Light Princess.

John Le Carre's Our Kind of Traitor Photo Credit: Studio Canal

TOURIST INFORMATION CENTRES

Bodmin
Shire Hall, Mount Folly,
PL31 2DQ
01208 76616
www.bodminmoor.co.uk
www.bodminlive.com

Boscastle
Boscastle Visitor Centre, The
Harbour, PL35 OHD
01840 250010
boscastlevc@btconnect.com
www.visitboscastleandtintagel.
com

Bude
The Crescent Car Park,
EX23 8LE
01288 354240
bude-tic@visitbude.info
www.budelive.com

Falmouth
11 Market Strand, Prince of
Wales Pier, TR11 3DF
01326 312300
info@falmouthtic.co.uk
www.discoverfalmouth.co.uk

Fowey
Daphne Du Maurier Literary
Centre, 5 South St., PL23 1AR
01726 833616
info@fowey.co.uk
www.fowey.co.uk

Hayle
Hayle Library, Commercial
Rd., TR27 4DE
Tel: 01736 754399
hayle.library@cornwall.gov.uk

Isles of Scilly
01720 424031

Launceston
Market House, The Arcade,
PL15 8EP
01566 772321
Launcestontica@btconnect.com
www.visitlaunceston.com

Liskeard
Foresters Hall, Pike St., PL14
3JE
01579 349148
tourism@liskeard.gov.uk
www.liskeard.gov.uk

Looe
The Guildhall, Fore St., East

Looe, PL13 1AA
01503 262072
looetic@btconnect.com
www.visit-southeastcornwall.
co.uk

Lostwithiel
Lostwithiel Community Centre,
Liddicoat Rd., PL22 0HE
01208 872207
tourism@lostwithieltic.
wanadoo.co.uk
www.lostwithieltic.org.uk

Mevagissey
St Georges Square, PL26 6UB
01726 844440
info@mevagissey-cornwall.co.uk
www.mevagissey-cornwall.co.uk

Newquay
Municipal Offices, Marcus Hill,
TR7 1BD
01637 854020
newquay.tic@cornwall.gov.uk
www.visitnewquay.org

Padstow
Red Brick Building, North
Quay, PL28 8AF
01841 533449
padstowtic@btconnect.com
www.padstowlive.com

Penzance
Station Approach, TR18 2NF.
01736 362207
penzancetic@cornwall.gov.uk
www.visit-westcornwall.com

Perranporth
8 Tywarnhayle Square
TR6 0ER
01872 575254
info@perranporthinfo.co.uk
www.perranporthinfo.co.uk

Redruth
The Cornwall Centre, Alma
Place, TR15 2AT
01209 219048
cornishstudies.library@
cornwall.gov.uk
www.cornwall.gov.uk

St Agnes
18 Vicarage Rd., TR5 0TL
01872 554150
ticstagnes@yahoo.co.uk
www.st-agnes.com

St Austell
By Pass Service Station,
Southbourne Rd., PL25 4RS
01726 879500
tic@cornish-riviera.co.uk
www.visitthecornishriviera.co.uk

St Ives
The Guildhall, Street an Pol,
TR26 2DS
01736 796297
stivestic@cornwall.gov.uk
www.visit-westcornwall.com

Tintagel
Tintagel Visitor Centre,
Bossiney Rd., PL34 0NJ
01840 779084
tintagelvc@btconnect.com
www.visitboscastleandtintagel.
com

Truro
Municipal Building, Boscawen
St., TR1 2NE
01872 274555
tic@truro.gov.uk
www.truro.gov.uk

St Just
The Library, Market St.,
TR19 7HX
01736 788165
stjusttourist@cornwall.gov.uk
www.visitcornwall.com

St Mawes
Roseland Visitor Centre, The
Millennium Rooms, The
Square, TR2 5AG
01326 270440
manager@roselandinfo.com
stmawesandtheroseland.co.uk

May Day, Padstow

January
Wadebridge. North Cornwall Point to Point

February
St Columb. Cornish Hurling
St Ives Hurling the Silver Ball

March
Cotehele Daffodils Festival
Eden Bulb Mania
Liskeard Annual Art Exhibition
Mount Edgcumbe Camelia Collection
St Piran's Day

April
Boscastle Walking Week
Camborne Trevithick Day
Porthleven Food & Music Festival
St Endellion Music Festival

May
Cornish International Male Voice Choir Festival
Falmouth Asparagus Festival
Fowey Daphne Du Maurier Festival of Arts & Literature
Helston Furry/Flora Dance
Launceston Steam & Vintage Rally
Newquay Longboard Championships
Padstow 'Obby Oss' Celebrations

June
Falmouth. Fal River Festival
Kernow Midsummer Bonfires
Liskeard Festival
Mevagissey Festival Week
Penzance. Golowan Festival
Polperro Festival
Saltash Town Regatta
St Keverne. An Gov Day
St Merryn Steam Rally
Wadebridge· Royal Cornwall Show

July
Boconnoc Steam Fair
Bodmin Riding & Heritage Day
InterCeltic Watersports Festival
Liskeard & District Agricultural Show
Looe Lions Carnival Week
Padstow Vintage Rally
Pendeen Band Week
Perranporth Carnival
Porthleven Lifeboat Day
Ruan Minor Vintage Car Rally
Rock Sailing Club. Shrimper Week
St Endellion Music

July (continued)
St Germans. Port Eliot Literary Festival
St Mawes Regatta
Stithians Show
Tremough. Celtic Congress
Wadebridge Wheels

August
Bude Carnival
Bude Horticultural Show
Camel Sailing Week
Camelford Agricultural Show
Cornwall Folk Festival
Crying the Neck
Delabole Wind Fair
Falmouth Week
Fowey Royal Regatta & Carnival Week
Hayle Festival
Henri-Lloyd Falmouth Week
Mount Edgcumbe. Classic Car Rally & Fayre
Morvah Pasty Day Festival
Morval Vintage Steam Rally
Newlyn Fish Festival
Newquay. Rip Curl Boardmasters
Padstow Carnival
Padstow Lifeboat Day
Polruan Regatta
St Agnes Festival
St Keverne Ox St Just Feast
Wadebridge Carnival

September
Bude Jazz Festival
Truro. Cornish Food & Drink Festival
Looe Valley Walking Festival
Penzance. Open Gorseth
St Ives Festival

October
Boscastle. Food, Arts & Crafts Festival
Falmouth Oyster Festival
Perranporth. Lowender Peran

November
Falmouth & Penryn. Cornwall Film Festival
Looe Food Festival
Roseland Festival
Wadebridge Prime Stock Show

December
Padstow Christmas Festival
Mousehole. Tom Bawcock's Eve

For specific dates please contact the local Tourist Information Centre

Working Boat and Tender, Penryn

ACKNOWLEDGMENTS

I would like to thank my wife Caroline for her love, encouragement and patience. And, to my children Flora and Harry for their knowledge of the café culture, and the surfing scene. And, thank you Izy, too, for your editorial and research skills, as well as your impeccable taste for the best places to eat and drink.

A big thank you to Arwen Fitch at Tate St Ives for checking my chapter on the Modernist Artists of St Ives and for her advice. The same goes to Alison Bevan at the Penlee House Gallery for her help.

Not to be forgotten, all the kind persons at the many attractions, places to stay and eat, for showing me around their establishments and for putting up with my endless questions.

Finally, I must thank my daughter Flora for her typographic and graphic design skills, who has refreshed and improved the clarity of the pages despite my constant desire to have yet another (to her chagrin) image of a boat, and or, harbour.

Goldeneye would like to thank the following photographers for providing us with their images:

Ab   Andrew Besley
ac   Al Churcher
ff   Flora Fricker   hf Harry Fricker
jh   Jon Hicks
ml   Mike Lacey, Waves Surf Gallery
nt   National Trust's Cornwall Regional Library
ss   Supplied By Subject

Loan of Images
Goldeneye would like to thank the following for allowing us to photograph their properties, or for providing us with an image to illustrate their properties: Mark Harold & Liz Luck of the National Trust (Cornwall Regional Office), Lady Stucley of Hartland Abbey, Cornwall Contemporary, Penzance, Hotel Tresanton, St Mawes, The British Library, The Rector, St Germans Church, Wesley Cottage, Altarnum, Paul Jackson of Helland Bridge Pottery, Poughill Church, Kilkhampton Church, The Castle Museum, Bude, Curgurrell Farm, Portscatho, Outdoor Adventure, Bude, Launcells Church, Tamar Otter & Wildlife Trust, Prideaux Place, Padstow, Rick Stein, Padstow, St Kew Church, St Enodoc Bar, RNLI Trevose Head, Newquay, Extreme Academy, Watergate Bay, China Clay Country Park, Pengellys Fishmongers, Looe, St Winnow Church, St Neot's Church, Lanreath Church, The Rum Store, St Neots, Tate St Ives, Truro Cathedral, Heligan Gardens, Caerhays Castle, The Harbour Master, Newlyn, Breage Church, Trebah Gardens, Mullion Gallery, Lucy Thorp of Halzephron House, Roskilly's, Penlee House Gallery, Penzance, Jane Adams Ceramics, St Just, Nigel Hallard Studios, Mousehole, J H Turner, Newlyn, Minack Theatre, Barbara Hepworth Museum, St Ives, Adrian Brough Pottery, Hayle, Geevor Tin Mines, Cornish Tipi Holidays, And, for this 5th Edition: Mammoth Screen/BBC, The Idle Rocks Hotel, St Mawes, Rick Stein's, The Gurnard's Head Hotel, Henry's Campsite, The Lizard, Strong Adolfos Cafe, Hawksfield, Devonport Inn, Kingsand, Rod and Line, Tideford, Lord and Lady St Germans, Port Eliot, St Nonna Parish Church, Altarnun, South Penquite Farm, Pencarrow House, Jethro Jackson, Porthilly Gallery, Harry Fricker (Cold Water Surfer), The Seafood Restaurant, Padstow, Eden Project, St Austell, Stones Bakery, Falmouth, David Page, Nauti But Ice, Porthleven, Tremenheere Sculpture Garden, Gulval, Market House Gallery, Marazion, Porthminster Beach Cafe, St Ives, Penwith Gallery, St Ives, Jane Adams Ceramics, St Just, Roger Thorp, Millennium Gallery, St Ives. Linda Styles and Mike Dobie of Fannie & Fox Gallery, Penryn, Sail Agnes, Penryn, Neil Canning of Lander Gallery, Truro, Mike Lacey of Waves Surf Gallery, Porthleven, Ink Factory Films, the BBC and Studio Canal, Penwith Gallery, St Ives, Ben Tunnicliffe of Tolcarne Inn, Artist Residence, Penzance, The Tregothnan Estate, English Heritage, Hotel Scarlet, Driftwood Hotel, The Beach Bude, Hotel Endsleigh, Hubbox, Arts Cafe, Cornmish Food Box Co., Lemon Street Gallery, Lanteglos-By-Fowey Church, Wood Cafe, Bodmin and Jamie Oliver's Fifteen.

INDEX

A

Abbey, The 170
Admiral Bembo, The 172
Admiral Edward Boscawen 207
Adrian Brough Pottery 191
Advent Church 48
Alba 189
Alfred Wallis 202
Altarnun 46
Althea House 74
Alvorada, The 133
Amelies at the Smokehouse 157
Amity 90
An Chy Coth B&B 132
Angelato 134
Anne Treneer 210
Antony House & Garden 32
Antony Woodland Garden 32
Apple Tree Café & Art Studios 194
Archie Browns 134
Ardensawah Farm B&B 188
Artist Residence 170
Arthurian Centre 49
Atlantic Highway 64
Atlantic House 159
Austell's 124
Ayr Holiday Park 190

B

Back Road Artists 190
Banjo Pier 125
Barbara Hepworth 203
Barbara Hepworth Museum 190
Bay View Inn, The 64
Beach Hut, The 93
Beach Restaurant, The 194
Beachmodern 64
Beacon Crag 159
Bedknobs at Polgwyn 113
Bedruthan Steps 85
Bedruthan Steps Hotel 91
Beerwolf 131
Belgrave Gallery 190
Ben Nicholson 203
Ben Tunnicliffe at Sennen 194
Benjamin Luxon 212
Ben's Cornish Kitchen 177
Ben's Crib Box Café 73
Bernard Leach 262
Beside The Wave 130
Beyond The Sea 72
Big Blue Surf School 67
Bin Two 73
Blisland 46
Blue Anchor, The 150
Blue Bar 106
Blue Hayes Hotel 189
Blue Hills Tin Streams 100
Blue Peter Inn 120
Blue Plate 33
Blue Reef Aquarium 91
Boat House Inn, Falmouth 131
Boat House, Fowey 117
Boathouse, The 90
Bodhi's Café 100
Bodmin & Wenford Railway 112
Bodmin 112
Bodmin Moor 46
Bodmin Museum 112
Bodrugan's Leap 133

Bone China 134
Bonython Estate Gardens 155
Booby's Bay 85
Books & Beer 134
Borlasse Smart 202
Bosanneth Guest House 132
Boscastle 67
Boscastle's Farm Shop & Café 68
Boscastle's NT Visitor Centre 68
Boscawen-Un-Stone Circle 195
Boscundle Manor 121
Boskerris Hotel 190
Bossiney Haven 69
Bosvigo 140
Botallack Engine Houses 192
Bow Or Vault Beach 145
Breage Church 154
Breakers Surf School Café 99
Bream Cove 163
Brown Sugar 115
Bude 64
Budock Vean Hotel 159
Burncoose Nurseries & Garden 105
Burger & Fish Charcoal Grill 73
Bush Inn 56
Bush Peppers 90
Buttervilla Farm 32

C

Cadgwith 150
Cadgwith Cove Inn 150
Caerhays Castle & Gardens 140
Café Chandlers & Deli 140
Café Cinnamon 131
Café Fleur 117
Café Uneeka 134
Calogero's 119
Calstock 43
Calstock Church 43
Calstock Viaduct 43
Camborne & Redruth 104
Camel Trail 84
Camel Valley Vineyards 92
Camelford 48
Camptivity 173
Cape Cornwall Beach 196
Captain William Bligh 208
Carbis Bay 196
Carbis Bay Hotel & Spa 190
Cardinham Church 48
Cardinham Woods 112
Carleon Cove 161
Carlyon Bay 124
Carn Brea 106
Carn Euny Ancient Village 195
Carnglaze Slate Caverns 124
Caroline Fricker Bridal Wear & Makery 133
Carrick Roads 144
Carwynen Quoit 106
Castle an Dinas 195
Castle an Dinas 93
Castle Beach 144
Castle Bude, The 64
Castle Dore 142
Cawsand & Kingsand 30
Cawsand & Kingsand Beaches 37
Chapel House 171
Chapel Porth 106
Charles Causley 211

Charlestown 113
Charlestown Beach 124
Charlie's, Tintagel 76
Charlotte's Tea House 135
Cheesewring, The 46
China Clay Country Park 93
Christopher Richard "Rick" Stein 212
Chun Castle 195
Chun Quoit 195
Church Cove 161
Church of St Columba 93
Church of St John the Baptist 56
Church of the Holy Trinity, St Austell 121
Chyheira 159
Chysauster Ancient Village 195
Ciuri Ciuri Italian Gelato 134
Clapper Yard Gallery 77
Cliff House 32
Clifftop Café 33
Clipper House 119
Coast to Coast Trail 104
Coastal Footpath...
...Looe to Cremyll Point 35
...Marsland Mouth to Northcott Mouth 58
...Bude to Boscastle 69
...Boscastle to Park Head 84
...Park Head to Newquay 95
...Newquay To Chapel Porth 101
...Trevaunance Cove to Hayle 109
...From Chapel Porth to Porthtowan 109
...From Portreath to Godrevy Point 109
...Porthpean to Looe 127
...Falmouth To Porthpean 145
...Praa Sands to Lizard 163
...Lizard to Falmouth 163
...St Ives to Land's End 198
...Land's End to Hoe Point 199
Cofro 133
Coldstreamer Inn, The 170
Collon Barton 119
Combe Valley Nature Trail 56
Constantine Bay 85
Constantine Stores 159
Cookbook, The 193
Cormorant Hotel & Riverview Restaurant 113
Cornish Arms 74
Cornish Birds of Prey Centre 92
Cornish Cyder Farm 105
Cornish Food Box Co 135
Cornish Hen Deli 171
Cornish Mines & Engines 104
Cornish Orchards 124
Cornish Tipi Holidays 77
Cornubian Arts & Science Trust, The 150
Cornwall Contemporary 172
Cornwall Pearl 92
Coswarth House 74
Cotehele 36
Cotehele Gallery 36
Cotehele House 36
Cotehele Quay 36
Couch's Restaurant 120
County Flowers Coffee Shop 119
Courtyard Deli 131
Coverack 150

Coverack Beach 161
Crackington Haven 69
Crackington Haven Church 67
Craft Box Café, Helston 150
Craft Box Café, Penzance 171
Crantock 100
Crantock Beach 100
Crantock Church 100
Crealy Adventure Park 92
Creed Church 143
Creed House Gardens 140
Creftow Gallery 150
Crooklets Beach 69
Crumpets Tea Shop 121
Cubert Church 100
Culloden Farmhouse 48
Custom House Gallery 157
Curgurrell Farm 137
D
Dairyland Farmworld 92
Dancing Taipan, The 77
Daphne Du Maurier 210
Daphne Du Maurier Literary Centre 113
Dawn French 212
Daymer Bay 85
Delabole Slate Quarry 76
Devonport Inn 33
Digey Food Room 189
Doc Martin's Surgery 74
Dolcoath Mine 104
Dolly's Tea Room 131
Downderry Beach 37
Downs Barn Farm B&B 188
Dozmary Pool 46
Drang Gallery 73
Driftwood Brewery 99
Driftwood Hotel 137
Driftwood Spars Hotel 99
Driftwood Studio B&B 188
Duchy Coffee Shop 119
Duckpool 58
Duke of Cornwall's Light Infantry Museum 112
Duke Street Coffee Shop 185
Duke Street Sandwich Deli 134
Durgan Beach 161
Dwelling House 115
E
Earth & Water Deli 133
East & West Portholland 145
Ebenezer Gallery 120
Eden Project 121
Ednovean Farm B&B 177
Edward John Trelawney 209
Egloshayle Bells & Clocks 77
Egyptian House, 172
Elements 64
11 Sea View Terrace 189
Ennys 177
Enys Gardens 133
Era Adventures 75
Exchange, The 172
Extreme Academy 93
F
Fal River Links 130
Falmouth 130
Falmouth Art Gallery 130
Falmouth School of Sailing 130

Fannie & Fox Gallery 133
Fat Apples Café 159
Fernacre Stone Circle 46
Fifteen Cornwall 93
Fistral Beach 95
Fistral Beach Bar 90
Fistral Beach Complex 91
Flambards Experience 150
Floe Creek 144
Flushing 132
Flushing Beach 161
Food For Thought 117
Fowey 117
Fowey Aquarium 113
Fowey Church 143
Fowey Hall Hotel & Restaurant 115
Fowey River 113
Fowey River Expeditions 113
Fowey River Gallery 113
Fowey Town Museum 113
Fraddon Gallery 93
Freathy & Tregonhawke Beach 37
Freathy Colony of Huts 32
FSC Surf Diner 90
G
Galleon Café 79
Gardens Cottage 126
Geevor Tin Mine 192
George Lloyd 211
Giants House, The 195
Gillan Harbour 161
Gilmore's 91
Glasney College 133
Glass House Gallery 172
Glasshouse 77
Glendurgan Gardens 154
Globe Inn 119
Godolphin Arms 177
Godolphin House 105
Godrevy Beach Café 106
Godrevy Towans 106
Golant Church 143
Golden Lion Inn 74
Golitha Falls 119
Good Vibes 131
Goonhilly Downs 155
Goonhilly Satellite Earth Station 155
Gorran Haven Beach 145
Grange Fruit Farm 155
Gravy Boesti 135
Great Western Beach 95
Greenbank Hotel, The 132
Greenhouse, The 159
Guild of Ten 134
Gunwalloe Church 154
Gurnard's Head Hotel 194
Gurnards Head 195
Gusto Deli Bar 91
Gweek 152
Gwennap 105
Gwennap Pit 105
Gwenvor 196
Gwithian Towans 106
Gylly Beach Café 133
Gyllynvase Beach 144
H
Halliggye Fogou 154
Halzephron House 159
Halzephron Inn 159

Hannifore Beach 125
Harbour Cafe, Looe 117
Harbour Coffee & Café 184
Harbour Cove 85
Harbour Gallery, The 137
Harbour Lights 134
Harlyn Bay 85
Harlyn Bay Ancient Burial Ground 78
Harris's 170
Hartswell Farm 119
Hawksfield 77
Hay Barton 142
Haye Farm Cider 124
Hayle 191
Hayle Bay 85
Helen Feiler Gallery 185
Helford Passage Beach 161
Helford & Helford River 152
Helford Village Beach 161
Heligan Gardens 140
Helland Bridge Pottery 49
Helston 150
Helston Folk Museum 150
Hemmick Beach 145
Hen House 160
Heritage Museum of Smuggling 120
Henry Bone 208
Henry Scott Tuke 205
Henry Trengrouse 209
Henry's Campsite 159
Herodsfoot Forest 124
Heron Inn 132
Hewitt's 77
Hidden Hut 137
Hidden Valley 42
Highcliffe Guest House 132
Higher Lank Farm 49
Hole Foods Deli & Café 184
Holywell Bay 101
Holywell Bay Fun Park 99
Honey Pot, The 171
Hooked On The Rocks 131
Hornacott 43
Hotel Endsleigh 43
Hotel Tresanton 141
Hounsel Bay 161
House in the Sea, The 91
Hubbox 135
Huel Vor 150
Hunkdory 130
Hurlers Stone Circle 46
I
Island View Café 117
J
Jamaica Inn 49
Jam Jar Café 91
Jane Adams Ceramics, The 192
Jane Reeves Gallery 73
Janosik 134
Japanese Garden & Bonsai Nursery 78
Jelberts Ice Cream 185
Jethro 212
John Arnold 208
John Carter 208
John Le Carré 212
John Nettles 212
John Opie 208
Jolly Sailor 117
Jonathan Trelawney 207

INDEX

Joseph Austen Treffry 209
Jubilee Wharf 133
Julius Olsson 202

K

Kacho 131
Kegan Tea Café 192
Kelynack Caravan & Camping Park 193
Ken-Caro Gardens 42
Kennack Sands 161
Kennal Vale Nature Reserve 104
Kestle Barton 152
Kiberick Cove 145
Kidzworld 121
Kilkhampton Church 56
King Arthur's Great Hall & Hall of Chivalry 76
King Arthur's Hall 46
King Doniert's Stone 46
King of Prussia, The 115
King's Head 137
Kitchen, The 120
Kittows of Fowey 115
Kota 157
Kota Kai (café) 157
Kristin Scott-Thomas 213
Kynance Cove 161

L

Lakeside Gallery 42
Lambriggan Court 100
Lamorna 183
Lamorna Birch 205
Lamorna Cove 197
Lamorna Wink Inn 183
Lamorran House Gardens 140
Land of Legend & Model Village 120
Land's End 193
Land's End Aerodrome 192
Lander Gallery 134
Landewednack Church 154
Landulph Church 32
Laneast Church 48
Lanhydrock House 114
Lanreath Church 124
Lantallack Farm 32
Lanteglos-By-Camelford Church 48
Lanteglos-By-Fowey Church 124
Lantic Bay 125
Lantivet Bay 125
Lanyon Quoit 195
Lappa Valley Railway & Leisure Park 92
Launcells Church 67
Launceston 42
Launceston Castle 42
Launceston Steam Railway 42
Lavethan 49
Lawrence House Museum 42
Leach Pottery 190
Lemon Street Gallery 134
Lenny Henry 213
Levant Mine & Beam Engine 192
Lewinnick Lodge 91
Lewis's Deli 75
Lewsey Lou's Fish Bar 99
Life Buoy Café 115
Life's A Beach 64
Lighthouse Gallery 172
Linkinhorne Church 43

Liskeard 117
Liskeard Church 124
Little BO Café 194
Little Feathers Gallery 100
Little Petherick Church 78
Little Roseland B&B 137
Lizard Lighthouse Heritage Centre 155
Loe Beach 144
Loe Pool & Penrose Estate 150
Loft Restaurant & Terrace, The 189
Logan's Rock 188
Longcross Hotel & Victorian Garden 77
Looe 117
Lostwithiel 119
Lostwithiel Church 119
Lower Barn B&B 142
Lowland Point 161
Lugger Hotel, The 137
Lusty Glaze 95
Luxulyan Valley 113

M

Madron Church 170
Maen Cliff 195
Maenporth Beach 163
Maker Heights 32
Malcolm Barnecutt's 75
Malcolm Sutcliffe Glass 133
Maltsters Arms 79
Mannings 135
Marazion 177
Marazion Beach 197
Marconi Monument 157
Market House Gallery 177
Mary Newman's Cottage 35
Mawgan In Meneage Church 154
Mawgan Porth 95
Meat Counter, The 134
Men-An-Tol 195
Men-Aver Beach 161
Merry Maidens Stone Circle 195
Merthen Manor 160
Mesmear 79
Mevagissey 133
Mevagissey Folk Museum 133
Michael an Gof 207
Michaelstow Church 48
Mick Fleetwood 212
Mid Town Deli & Café 135
Mid-Cornwall Galleries 121
Middle Beach 69
Millendreath Beach 37
Millennium Gallery 190
Mill House Inn 76
Millook Haven 69
Minack Theatre 188
Mineral Tramways Discovery Centre 104
Miner's Arms 100
Minions Heritage Centre 49
Minster Church 78
Molesworth Manor 79
Monkey Sanctuary (Trust) 32
Morans Café & Deli 33
Morvah Schoolhouse & Café 192
Morwenstow 56
Mother Ivey Cottage 74
Mother Ivey's Bay 85

Mount Edgcumbe House & Park 32
Mount Haven Hotel 177
Mount Hawke – Sk8 105
Mount Zion Coffee 189
Mousehole 184
Mowhay Café & Restaurant 79
Mullion 157
Mullion Church 157
Mullion Cove 157
Mullion Cove Beach 161
Mullion Gallery 157
Museum of Witchcraft 68
Mylor Church 143
Mylor Churchtown 144

N

Nancherrow Studio 192
Napoleon Inn 68
National Lobster Hatchery 72
National Maritime Museum 130
National Seal Sanctuary 152
Nauti But Ice 157
Navy Inn, The 171
Neville Northey Burnard 210
New Gallery, The 137
New Yard Restaurant 159
Newlyn 185
Newlyn Art Gallery 185
Newlyn Beach 197
Newquay 90
Newquay Fun Factory 92
Newquay Zoo 92
Nigel Hallard Studios 184
Nine Maidens Stone Circle 195
No 4, Peterville 99
No 11 Fore Street 193
No 6 Restaurant & Rooms 73
North Hill Church 43
North Shore Bude 64
Northcott Mouth 58
Number 20 133

O

Ocean Studios 177
Offshore Bar & Bistro 100
Old Ale House 134
Old Canal 64
Old Coastguard Hotel 184
Old Ferry Inn 115
Old Macdonalds Farm 78
Old Parsonage, The 68
Old Post Office, The 76
Old Quay House Hotel, The 115
Old Rectory, The 68
Old School Hotel & Restaurant, The 74
Old Success Inn, The 194
Old Temperance House 160
Old Vicarage, The 56
Olde Plough House 117
Olive Garden, The 76
Olivers 133
Onshore 189
Orca Sea Safaris 130
Organic Panda 189
Out Of The Blue 177
Outdoor Adventure 67
Outlaws Fish Kitchen 74
Oystercatcher Bar 78

P

Padstow 72

Padstow Farm Shop 73
Padstow Museum 73
Padstow Seafood School 73
Pandora Inn 132
Par Sands 125
Paradise Park 191
Park Farmhouse 49
Park Yurt Village 91
Patrick Gale 213
Patrick Heron 203
Pawton Quoit 78
Pencalenick House 115
Pencarrow House 49
Pendeen Beach 196
Pendeen Lighthouse 192
Pendeen Pottery & Gallery 192
Pendeen Vau Fogou 195
Pendennis Castle 142
Pendower & Carne Beach 145
Pengellys 117
Pengersick Castle 150
Penhale & Perran Beach 101
Penjerrick Gardens 105
Penlee House Gallery 172
Penmenner House 160
Penryn 132
Penryn Museum 133
Pentewan 145
Pentraeth Beach 161
Penwith Galleries 190
Penzance 170
Penzance Beach 197
Perran Sands 197
Perranporth 99
Perranporth Beach 101
Peter Lanyon 203
Pirate's Quest 92
Pityme Arms 75
Plaidy Beach 125
Plain-An-Gwarry 195
Plume of Feathers 93
Pier House Hotel 113
Pinky Murphy's Café 115
Poldark Mine 104
Poldhu Cove 161
Poldridmouth Cove 125
Polgaver Bay 125
Polkerris 121
Polkerris Beach 125
Polpeor Cove 161
Polperro 120
Polperro Arts 120
Polruan 121
Poltesco Nature Trail 155
Polurrian Cove 161
Polurrian Hotel 157
Porfell Animal Land 124
Port Eliot 34
Port Isaac 74
Port Isaac Pottery 74
Port Quin 74
Port William Inn 76
Porteath Bee Centre 78
Portgaverne 74
Portgaverne Restaurant & Hotel 74
Porth-En-Alls 177
Porth Beach 95
Porth Chapel Beach197
Porth Joke 101

Porth Kidney Sands 196
Porth Nanven 196
Porth Nanven Barn 193
Porthallack Beach 161
Porthallow Arts 155
Porthallow Beach 161
Porthcothan 85
Porthcurnick Beach 145
Porthcurno 188
Porthcurno Beach197
Porthcurno Telegraph Museum 188
Portheras Cove 196
Porthgwarra 197
Porthgwidden Beach 196
Porthilly Cove 85
Porthilly Gallery 75
Porthleven 157
Porthleven Sands 160
Porthluney Beach 145
Porthmeor Beach 196
Porthminster Beach 196
Porthminster Café 189
Porthminster Gallery 190
Porthoustock Beach 161
Porthpean 145
Porthtowan 106
Portloe 137
Portloe Beach 145
Portmellon Beach 145
Portnadler Bay 125
Portreath 106
Portreath Beach 109
Portscatho 137
Portwrinkle Beach 37
Potter Morgan Glass Studio 46
Poughill Church 56
Praa Sands 161
Prawn On The Lawn 73
Prideaux Place 73
Primrose Valley Hotel 189
Prindl Pottery 112
Probus Church 143
Provedore 133
Prussia Cove 197

R
Raj Bar & Restaurant 77
Rame Barton B&B 32
Rame Church 33
Rashleigh Arms 113
Rashleigh Inn, The 121
Raven Surf School 67
Readymoney Cove 125
Rectory Tea Rooms 56
Red Lion, The 159
Reddivallen 68
Relish 77
Restaurant Nathan Outlaw, Port
Isaac 74
Restaurant Nathan Outlaw, St Enodoc
Hotel 79
Restormel Castle 119
Retorrick Mill 91
Richard Lander 209
Richard Trevithick 208
Rick Stein, Fistral 90
Rick Stein, Porthleven 157
Rick Stein's Café 73
Rick Stein's Fish & Chips 133
Rick Steins 74

Rillaton Round Barrow 46
Rising Sun Inn 46
Rising Sun, The 140
Riverview Restaurant 117
RNAS Culdrose 155
Roche Rock 93
Rock 75
Rod and Line 33
Rojano's, Padstow 73
Roseland Inn 137
Roseland Peninsula 137
Rosemary B&B, The 132
Roses Kitchen 64
Rosevine Hotel 137
Roskilly's 159
Round House & Capstan Gallery 194
Round House, The 160
Round Houses, Veryan 144
Roundhouse Barn B&B 137
Rowena Cade 210
Royal Albert Bridge 35
Royal Cornwall Museum 134
Rum Store 126
Ruby Tuesday 74
Rumps Point 78
Ruthern Valley Holidays 93

S
Sail Agnes 133
Saltash 35
Saltwater 79
Samuel Wallis 208
Sam's, Fowey 115
Sam's On The Beach 121
Sandbar Café/Deli 78
Sands Resort Hotel 91
Sandy Mouth 58
Sarah's Pasty Shop 117
Scarlet, The 90
Schooners Bistro 99
Screech Owl Sanctuary 92
Scrummies Café 64
Secret Gartden Café 134
Seadrift Kitchen Café 157
Seafood Bar 133
Seafood Café 189
Seafood Restaurant, The 73
Seagrove Gallery 177
Seaton Beach 37
Seb West @ Shoreline Gallery 191
Selina Cooper 210
Sennen Cove 194
Shamrock Cabin 32
Sheviock Barton 32
Ship Inn, Fowey 115
Ship Inn, Mousehole 184
Ship Inn, Porthleven 157
Shipwreck & Heritage Centre 113
Shire Horse Farm & Carriage
Museum 105
Simply Fish 117
Sir Arthur Quiller-Couch 210
Sir Bevil Grenville 207
Sir Goldsworthy Gurney 209
Sir Humphrey Arundell 207
Sir Humphrey Davy 209
Sir John Betjeman 210
Sir Richard Grenville 207
Sir Terry Frost 203
Sir Tim Rice 212

INDEX

Sir William Golding 211
Sixteen Falmouth 134
Skinner's Brewery 135
Slaughter Bridge 49
Slipway Hotel & Restaurant, The 74
Sloop Craft Workshops, The 191
Soup & Juice 134
South Penquite Farm 49
Spindrift Gallery 137
Springer Spaniel, The 43
Springfields Fun Park & Pony Centre 92
Square Gallery, The 144
St Agnes 99
St Agnes Bakery 99
St Agnes Hotel 99
St Agnes Museum 100
St Agnes Pottery 90
St Austell 121
St Austell Brewery Visitor Centre 121
St Charles The Martyr, Falmouth 143
St Clement Church 143
St Columb Major 93
St Endellion Church 78
St Enodoc Church 78
St Enodoc Hotel 79
St Georges Cove 85
St Germans 35
St Germanus Church 35
St Ives 188
St Ives Ceramics 190
St Ives School of Painting 190
St Ives Society of Artists 191
St Just in Penwith 192
St Just in Roseland Church 143
St Keverne Church 154
St Kew Church 78
St Kew Inn 79
St Martin-By-Looe Church 124
St Mary Magdalene 42
St Mawes 140
St Mawes Bakery 140
St Mawes Castle 142
St Mawes Hotel 140
St Mawgan-in-Pydar Church 78
St Michael Penkevil Church 143
St Michael's Hotel & Spa 132
St Michael's Mount 179
St Moritz Hotel 79
St Neot's Church 124
St Nonna Church 46
St Petroc 207
St Petroc's Bistro 73
St Petroc's Church, Bodmin 112
St Piran 207
St Piran's Oratory 100
St Piran's Round 99
St Protus & St Hyacinth 48
St Tudy Inn 79
St Winnow 124
Stanbury Mouth 58
Stanhope Forbes 205
Star & Garter 130
Steam Pottery 192
Stein's Deli 73
Stein's Fish & Chips 73
Stein's Fisheries 73
Sterts Theatre 42
Stone Age Studio 192

Stone's Bakery 131
Stoneman Gallery 172
Studio Tea Room Gallery 99
Stratton 64
Summer House 170
Summerleaze Beach 69
Sunset Surf Café 106
Swanpool Beach 144
Swordfish, The 185
T
Tabb's Restaurant 137
Talland Bay 125
Talland Bay Hotel 121
Tamar Lake Country Lakes 56
Tamar Otter & Wildlife Centre 68
Taste Restaurant 99
Tate St Ives 190
Tatum Stonebaked 137
The Basement, Padstow 73
The Beach 65
The Cove, Lamorna 183
The Cove, Maenporth Beach 159
The Cribber 95
The Dining Room 75
The Fish House 91
The Hotel, Watergate Bay 91
The Idle Rocks 140
The Lizard Peninsula 155
The Lugger 121
The Mariners 75
The Poly 130
The Potager 159
The Rock Inn 75
The Rockpool 106
The Shed, Shack & Ranch 131
The Stables Pizza, Pie, Fistral 90
The Stables Pizza, Pie 134
The Strangles 69
The Taphouse 99
The Thirsty Scholar 133
The Towans, Hayle 196
The Wheelhouse 122
The Wheelhouse Crab & Oyster Bar 131
Thomas Daniell 134
Thomas Flamank 207
Tide House, The 190
Tim Lake Ceramics 108
Tim Smit 213
Tinners Arms 194
Tintagel 76
Tintagel Castle 76
Tintagel Church 76
Tintagel Visitors Centre 76
Tolcarne Inn 185
Tolcarne Sands 95
Toll Bar 117
Tolmen Centre 152
Tori Amos 213
Towan Beach, Falmouth 145
Towan Beach, Newquay 95
Towan Beach, St Ives 196
Trebah Gardens 154
Trebarwith Strand 85
Trevibban Mill Vineyard & Orchards 93
Trecarne Pottery 157
Tregantle Beach 37
Tregantle Fort 33

Tregantle Longsands Beach 37
Treglisson 105
Tregoose B&B 143
Tregrehan Garden Cottages & Nursery 121
Treliska 190
Trelissick Gallery 144
Trelissick Garden 141
Trelowarren 155
Trelowarren Gallery 155
Trelyon Gallery 191
Tremenheere Sculpture Gardens 173
Trenance Leisure Park & Gardens 92
Trencrom Hill 195
Trenderway Farm 121
Trengilly Wartha Inn 159
Trengwainton Gardens 173
Trereife Park 173
Trerice 92
Treryn Dinas 195
Tresco Abbey Gardens 173
Trethias, Pepper Cove & Fox Cove 85
Trethorne Leisure Farm 43
Trevadlock Manor 49
Trevalsa Court Hotel 143
Trevaskis Farm 108
Trevathan Farm 74
Trevaunance Cove 106
Trevaunance Cove Workshops 100
Trevethy Quoit 46
Trevilla House 143
Trevithick's Cottage 104
Trevone Bay 85
Trevose Harbour House 190
Trewidden Gardens 173
Trewithen Gardens 142
Trewithen Restaurant 119
Trewothan Farm B&B 74
Treyarnon Bay 85
Truro 134
Truro Cathedral 134
Turks Head, The 172
2 Fore Street 184
27 The Terrace 189
Tyler Gallery, The 184
U
Union Hotel 172
Upton 69
V
Vean, The 142
Victory Inn 140
View Restaurant 33
W
Wadebridge 76
Waterfront, The 79
Watergate Bay 95
Watering Hole, The 99
Waterside Gallery 191
Wave 7 Studio Gallery 77
Waves Surf Art Gallery 157
Wayside Folk Museum 194
Welcombe Mouth 58
Wellington, The 68
Wesley Cottage 48
Westcroft Gallery 33
Whitehouse, The 194
Whitesand Bay 197
Whitewater Gallery 78
Whitsand Bay 37

MAP SYMBOLS EXPLAINED

♔	Abbey/Cathedral		Pub/Inn		Leisure/Sports Centre
✕	Battle Site		Railway Interest		Lifeboat
	Bed & Breakfast Accomodation	✕	Restaurant	Ⓟ	Parking
	Café		Self Catering Accommodation		Picnic Site
	Castle		Standing Stone/Barrow		Tents & Caravans
	Church/Chapel of Interest		Theatre/Concert Hall		Sailing
	Cinema		Tourist Information		Surfing
	Craft Interest	☼	Tumulus/Tumuli		Tourist Information
	Cross		Viewpoint		Windsurfing
	Cycleway		Windmill/Wind Farm	▲	Youth Hostel
	Fun Park/Leisure Park	⊕	Airfield		Agricultural Interest
✳	Hill Fort/Ancient Settlement		Aquarium		Arboretum
	Historic Building		Boat Trips		Bird Reserve
	Hotel		Camping Site (Tents)		Garden of Interest
	Industrial Interest		Caravan Site		Vineyard
	Karting		Ferry (Pedestrians)		Walks/Nature Trails
	Lighthouse		Ferry (Vehicles)		Wildlife Park
	Mining Interest/Engine Houses		Fishing Trips		Zoo
☆	Miscellaneous/Natural Attraction		9/18 Hole Golf Course	Ⓟ	National Trust Car Park
	Museum/Art Gallery		Harbour		
	Pottery		Inshore Rescue Boat		

▬▬▬	A Road
▬▬▬	B Road
═══	Minor Road
┄┄┄	Other Road or Track (not necessarily with public or vehicular access)
●━	Railway
⋯⋯⋯	Cycleway

Open Space owned by the National Trust

Built-up Area

Scale 1:100,000

0 — 1 (miles) — 2
0 — 1 — 2 (km)

381m.
305m.
229m.
152m
76m.

Poughill Church

Widemouth Sand 69
Wild Escapes 142
Wilhelmina Barns-Graham 203
William Bickford 209
William Cookworthy 92
William Gregor 208
Winston Graham 211
Wood Design 77

Wood Studio 155
Woods Café 112
World of Model Railways 133
Wreckers 113
X
Xtreme Air Co 191
Y

Yew Tree Gallery 193
Yvonne Arlott Studio 77
Z
Zennor 194
Zennor Chapel Café & Guest House 195
Zennor Quoit 195

William Fricker, photographed by his son Harry, checking out an off-road route.

William Fricker was born in Somerset and educated at Stonyhurst College, Lancashire, and in various places of learning in Austria and Germany. He has worked in publishing for over forty years.

William first worked for William Collins (now Harper Collins) in London, where he became a Creative Director in their paperback division before taking a sabbatical, to make a 4,000 mile trek across Europe (France-The Alps-Italy, to Greece) along the old mule tracks, footpaths and pilgrim's routes. Inspired by Patrick Leigh Fermor's A Time of Gifts, and Laurie Lee's As I Walked Out One Midsummer Morning. On reaching Greece, his original plan was to then head south and walk up the Nile, but he believes his better judgement prevailed, and returned on a bicycle via North Africa, Spain and France. For the past thirty years he has built up Goldeneye compiling the research, editorial and photography, for more than two hundred UK travel guides and books; on cycling, touring and walking. More recently, he plans to revise his Guidebook series, and expand his books of photography titled: "The Landscape of Britain". Last year he moved with his wife Caroline, and their children, to Penryn, Cornwall.